MURDER ON MONTANA'S HI-LINE

CLEM C. PELLETT

Edited by Suzanne G. Fox

Published by The History Press
An imprint of Arcadia Publishing
Charleston, SC
www.historypress.com

First published 2025

Manufactured in the United States

ISBN 9781467158381

Library of Congress Control Number: 2025931949

Notice: The information in this book is true and complete to the best of our knowledge. It is offered without guarantee on the part of the author or The History Press. The author and The History Press disclaim all liability in connection with the use of this book.

This book is based on true events. Depictions herein are based on multiple historical sources. Some dialogue has been recreated.

To Cynde, my partner, my confidante and my best friend…
I'm so lucky you said yes five decades ago.

To Reed, the best daughter a father could ever have.

To my extended family, the Pelletts, who have given me a sense of belonging.

CONTENTS

ACKNOWLEDGEMENTS

This book is a passion project. It exists only because of the patience and reinforcement of many people—and all the obstacles that served as stepping stones to finding justice.

Thank you to the Montana Historical Society, especially Molly Kruckenberg, who never tired of my requests.

Thank you to the Montana State University Library Special Collections.

And a big thank-you to my editor, Suzanne Fox; without her patience, reinforcement and belief that this story must be told, it would never have happened.

It wasn't until my fifty-sixth year that I learned that I'm a son of the Hi-Line—and I'm proud of it!

"You never fail until you stop trying." —Albert Einstein

CAST OF CHARACTERS

The Pellett Family

Clarence Chester Pellett (C.C.P.): the author's grandfather and the murder victim, known as C.C. and Shorty

Nellie Sharpe Pellett: C.C.P.'s second wife

Marion Franklin Pellett: the author's father and the only child of C.C.P. and Nellie

Joan M. Pellett: the author's mother, Marion's wife

Theron Pellett: eldest son of C.C.P. and his first wife

Vernon "Curly" Pellett: second son of C.C.P. and his first wife

Law Enforcement

Charles O. Dunstall: Toole County sheriff

Rinaldo F. Denision, "Smokey": Shelby police chief

The People's Voice Newspaper

Gretchen G. Billings: coeditor of the weekly newspaper with her husband, Harry Billings

Attorneys

John C. Hoyt: Toole County attorney, first prosecutor of Frank Dryman, from 1951 to1952

William Black: Frank Dryman's public defender from 1951 to 1952

Jerry J. O'Connell: co-defense counsel with Black from 1951 to 1952, solo defense counsel from 1953 to 1955

Lewis P. Donovan: Toole County special prosecutor and second prosecutor of Frank Dryman, 1953

John "Luke" McKeon: third and final prosecutor of Frank Dryman, from 1954 to 1955

Judges

R.M. Hattersley: presided over bench trial in Shelby in 1951 and first jury trial in Shelby in 1953

C.B. Ewell: presided over second jury trial in Havre in 1955

INTRODUCTION

The sky was clear. The desert air smelled sweet. The temperature was ninety degrees, a far cry from springtime in Montana, where my wife, Cynde, and I were raised. It was the best of days, the wedding day of our one and only child, our daughter, Reed.

When I rounded the corner at the top of the stairs, I froze, transfixed by the vision of our daughter in her wedding dress. Against the adobe walls of the courtyard, her white satin dress gleamed. She looked radiant, angelic. I didn't try to hold back my tears.

As sunset turned the western sky from cobalt blue to a cascade of fiery colors, the wedding party lined up for the ceremony. My mind was flooded with memories of my little girl half asleep on my shoulder as I carried her up the stairs, reading her bedtime stories, playing "I spy," Christmas Eves at the Space Needle, chasing her up and down grocery store aisles, butterfly kisses.

For most of those years, I was the man in her life. But now my little girl and I were about to walk down a different aisle, where she would take the hand of the new man in her life.

As we waited, I couldn't help reflecting on my sixty-nine years. My name is Clem C. Pellett. Clem is not short for Clement, nor is it a nickname—it's my mother's maiden name. I'm named after my father's father, but not in the traditional sense. I'm not the second or the third. I wasn't given a middle name, just a *C.* My initials, C.C.P., match those of my paternal grandfather, Clarence Chester Pellett.

Growing up in 1950s Montana named Clem was akin to living Johnny Cash's song "A Boy Named Sue." I'm an only child, with no extended family to speak of on either my mother Jo's side or my father Marion's side. Murder

From left to right: Clem, Reed and Cynde Pellett on Reed's wedding day, March 26, 2022. *Author's collection.*

had torn Dad's large family apart two years before I was a twinkle in his eye. The loss of his father and what led to his estrangement from his family were never mentioned. It was always just the three of us. My father would say, "The more family, the more problems." I didn't miss what I never had.

My childhood was wonderful—until my father's sudden passing when I was fourteen. That awful day rocked my foundation. As the years progressed, I especially missed him at milestones: graduations, my wedding to Cynde forty-six years ago, the birth of his granddaughter and now her wedding day.

The string quartet struck up, heralding the arrival of the bride, with the silhouettes of Pinnacle Peak and saguaro cacti as a backdrop. Arm in arm, we started our walk down the rose petal–covered aisle.

Before us was a sea of smiling faces. Many had traveled from all corners of the United States: the East Coast, the West Coast, even Montana. The effort people had made to share this special day was the embodiment of friendship, a tribute to the power of family. After six decades of separation, among the guests were my "new" family members. To most, sharing one of life's milestones with relatives would be a given: ordinary, perhaps mundane. But for me, this was a first.

Not so long ago, none of the Pellett family would have been there. But that was before I tracked down my grandfather's murderer.

Chapter 1

THE MURDER

Nineteen-year-old Frank Dryman pulled out two quarters, a dime and the scraps of a five-dollar bill he'd been tearing to shreds since he started hitching from Reno to Shelby, Montana, a few days before. But there wasn't enough of Uncle Sam's tender left to pass off as a whole bill. Still, he put the scraps back into his pocket.

Instead, he slapped two quarters on the countertop for the two hamburgers he'd just inhaled, spun around on the stool and sauntered to the jukebox. As he slipped his last dime into the slot, he checked out the reflection of his duck's-ass haircut in the glass and then pushed the buttons for Fats Domino's latest hit, "Don't You Lie to Me."

It was dusk. He'd already burned daylight hitching a ride in the wrong direction. The moment he made the driver stop and let him out, he knew he'd made a big mistake. He was on the northern plains of Montana—there was only prairie as far as the eye could see. A spring storm was blowing down from Canada. Clad only in a split-tail sport coat, he was frozen to the bone in no time. Fortunately, the driver took pity on him, turned around and took him back to Shelby.

The song having ended, Dryman braced himself for the weather. When he stepped outside the 49er Drive In, his long hair and coattails whipped in the wind.

With his back to the gale, he stood by the roadside, holding out his thumb. He was already numb when a car with a pregnant girl about his age behind the wheel slowed down. He broke into a trot, but just as he was about to open the passenger door, the driver sped off.

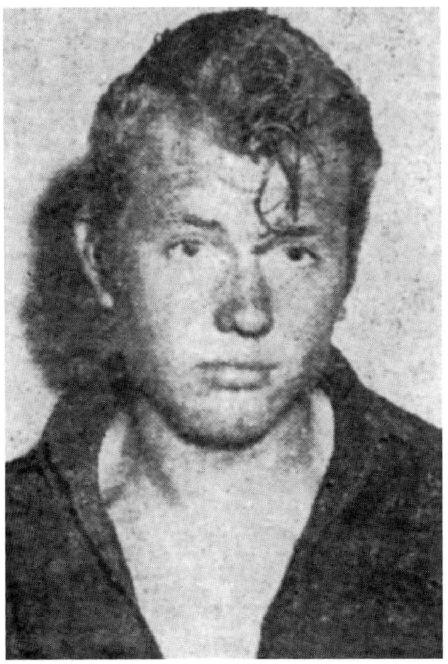

Left: Frank Dryman, a.k.a. Frank Valentine, age nineteen. *From the* Shelby Promoter and Tribune of Shelby, *April 5, 1951.*

Right: Clarence Chester Pellett. *Author's collection.*

"Come on, you goddamned bitch!" Rage surged through him.

In her rearview mirror, the driver saw a new, light green 1951 Plymouth pull up next to the shaggy-haired hitchhiker. Clarence Pellett, an overweight, elderly man, rolled down the passenger-side window.

"Looks like you need a ride."

Dryman put his hand on the roof and leaned into the car. "Yeah, anything to get out of this wind." He tumbled into the passenger seat.

Immediately, the old fellow peppered his rider with questions. Dryman, still fuming, was in no mood for chitchat. Motionless, he stared straight ahead. Daylight was fading. Oncoming cars dimmed their headlights, and one was driving with only parking lights.

Pellett was relentless. With each question, Dryman grew more furious. "The old fellow just wouldn't shut up," he later recalled.

For fifteen minutes, the hitchhiker never answered one question or even made a sound. Pellett sensed that he had made a mistake. After eighteen miles, they reached Four Corners. Pellett informed the youth that this was the turnoff to his house and that was as far as he was going.

Site of Clarence Chester Pellett's murder, near Four Corners, eighteen miles north of Shelby. *Author's collection.*

"The old man was going to let me out in the dark on a road in the middle of nowhere in the cold," Dryman remembered. "I wasn't going to be left out to freeze again."

Dryman pulled a M1911 Colt .45 pistol from the shoulder holster under his jacket. He ordered Pellett to keep going and turn off onto the first side road.

Pellett kept pleading, "Don't do this and don't do that," Dryman recounted.

> *We just kept driving until we were out a ways. I thought we were far enough off the main road not to be seen. He asked me what I was going to do, and I told him I had to kill him. There wasn't anything I could do about it. If I let him go, he'd call the cops, and way out here in the sticks, I wouldn't have a chance to get away.*
>
> *I ordered him to get out of the car. He was begging for mercy, practically down on his knees. All that blubbering made me mad. When I raised the gun, he started running and I started shooting. I fired once but missed. I took off after him and let him have a second one.*

This slug entered the nape of Pellett's neck and exited his left eye.

> *He stopped, but he didn't fall. I gave him another one while I was coming at him, and he went down. After that, I just stood over and let him have the rest: I emptied the gun into him.*
>
> *I knelt beside him to see if he could be helped, but it was easy to see he was dead. "You just asked too many fucking questions." I went through his pockets and took his wallet.*
>
> *The next thing I knew, I'm standing above him with a smoking gun in my hand. I realize again that it's awfully cold and snowing. My ears were still ringing as I turned around and ran to the car, holding the gun next to me, taking comfort in its warmth against the bitter cold.*

Adrenalin coursed through Dryman's body. He took a fresh clip from his leather ammunition pouch, ejected the empty one and slammed the full one into his pistol. He took thirty dollars out of Pellett's wallet and threw the wallet into the back seat.

Dryman fired up the engine and stomped on the gas. The car fishtailed. The spinning tires threw mud and rocks into the air as he pulled out of the open field onto the road he and Pellett had come in on. He found his way back to the main highway and drove north about twenty miles to Sweetgrass, on the Canadian border.

Chapter 2

THE INVESTIGATION

The Hi-Line is vast, stretching across northcentral Montana along the Canadian border. Shelby, 50 miles south of Canada, is its unofficial hub. Great Falls, then Montana's largest city, is 90 miles south. The farming and railroad town of Havre is 106 miles east, while Browning, on the Blackfoot Indian Reservation and adjacent to Glacier National Park, is 50 miles west.

Clarence Pellett, fifty-nine, had lived for nearly twenty-five years on Montana's Hi-Line. Born in Saint Paul, Minnesota, in 1892, he lost his first wife to the 1918 Spanish flu epidemic, leaving him with five children, ages two to eleven. In 1922, oil was discovered in northcentral Montana. Hearing jobs were plentiful there, in his mid-thirties, Pellett moved his brood; his new teenaged wife, the former Nellie Sharpe, who was two months older than her eldest stepson; and their infant son, Marion, to Four Corners, Montana, eighteen miles north of Shelby.

By 1951, Clarence and Nellie were the proud grandparents of sixteen. Clarence, nicknamed C.C. or Shorty, was known in the community of 3,100 as a thoughtful family man with a big laugh,

That Wednesday night, a spring blizzard was raging across the Hi-Line, making driving dicey. Pellett called Nellie around six o'clock, saying he was on his way home. Meticulously punctual, Clarence had never been even ten minutes late. But by eight thirty, he still hadn't shown up. Frantic, Nellie called Toole County Sheriff Charles O. Dunstall, a good friend of the Pellett clan.

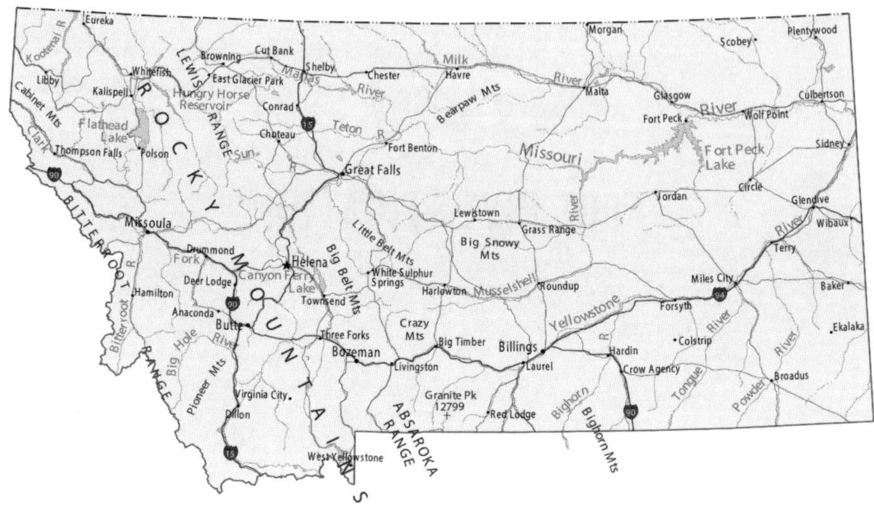

Ten years earlier, Charlie Dunstall, who had no background in law enforcement, decided to run for county sheriff for no other reason than that he needed a job. A typical politician, he'd been able to hold onto the position of Toole County sheriff ever since.

"Charlie, I'm afraid something has happened," Nellie said. "He's never been so late before."

Hearing the panic in Nellie's voice, Charlie replied, "We haven't had any accidents reported. Maybe he was held up on business. Do you know where he called from?"

Nellie couldn't help. However, she knew he'd been in Shelby during the day, seeing some men about oil leases.

"I'll look around town for him and his car," Dunstall assured her. Small towns being what they were, the sheriff was familiar with Clarence's car, a light green 1951 Plymouth sedan.

Dunstall put on his heavy coat and steeled himself. When he opened the door, the freezing wind stung his hands and face. His breath steamed as he plodded from the Toole County Courthouse toward Main Street. In no time, his face was numb. He reached up and checked his glass eye to be sure it was secure. He had lost his left eye in an accident years before.

Short and a bit portly, Dunstall ambled up the three blocks of Main Street, checking the Montana Bar, the Roxy Movie House and the general store, but there was no sign of Pellett or his car. He turned off Main Street and walked into the Toole County jailhouse. Sitting at his desk was Shelby Police

Opposite: The Hi-Line's name came from the BNSF Railway Company's northernmost line between Havre and Whitefish. Today, "Montana's Hi-Line" generally refers to the areas parallel to the Canadian border and US Highway 2, stretching the length of the state. *GISGeography.com.*

Above: Hi-Line oil rigs near Kevin, Ferdig, Sunburst and Oilmont. *PAc2006-10A1p19g MTHS Photo Archives.*

Left: Clarence and Nellie (Sharpe) Pellett, circa 1925. *Author's collection.*

Following: Shelby township, circa 1950. *Courtesy of* Shelby, Montana: The First Hundred Years.

Chief Rinaldo "Smokey" F. Denison. Born and raised on the Hi-Line, he had known the Pellett family for twenty years.

Athletic and manly, Smokey stood over six feet tall. Most agreed that during his formative years, it was a toss-up which side of the law he would end up on. But for three decades, he had been a fixture of Hi-Line law enforcement as a patrolman, a deputy sheriff and, for the last seven years, Shelby's chief of police.

Dunstall briefed Smokey on Mrs. Pellett's call and his walk down Main Street. He asked if the chief had heard of any stranded motorists or accidents over the State Highway Patrol radio. Smokey shook his head.

Together, Dunstall and Smokey made another sweep. In a town as small as Shelby, there were few places a man could go unnoticed, but in a storm like this, most were hunkered down. The town was deserted.

However, on this pass, a few folks told the officers they'd seen C.C. talking with two strangers at the Capital Café that afternoon. Established in 1929, the café was Shelby's gathering place. Said one witness, "I reckon they had some kind of oil deal going. They were talking a blue streak and doing a lot of figuring on paper."

That matched what Nellie had told Charlie. C.C. was an oil rig operator for puffer pumps and a field representative for the Texas Pacific Oil and Coal Company, which operated several ground leases in the Shelby, Kevin and Sweetgrass areas.

Dunstall phoned Mrs. Pellett at ten o'clock and told her there was still no sign of Clarence. "Smokey and I will drive north; maybe he had car trouble," Charlie reassured her.

The officers climbed into the sheriff's car. Driving north, using the spotlights mounted on both sides of the squad car, the pair scanned the road and the barrow pits on either side. The howling wind blew up a ground blizzard that limited their vision and quickly erased any tire tracks.

Finding no sign of the missing man on the road to Four Corners, they decided to go to the Pellett home. They managed to navigate the snow-covered field road leading to the square tar-paper house not far off the main highway. Leaning into the wind, they struggled to the front porch.

Mrs. Pellett opened the front door. She could see by the officers' expressions that they hadn't found her husband.

Nellie cried, "I just can't understand it!" Her eyes filled, and a tear spilled down her cheek. "Clarence has never been even an hour late without calling me—he knows how I worry."

Dunstall, shifting from concerned friend to sheriff, attempted to reconstruct Pellett's day. "Do you know who he was with today?"

"He had a long-distance call this morning," Nellie said. "Two men calling from Great Falls, I think it was something about oil leases. He made an appointment to meet in Shelby. He had to go to town for supplies anyway."

Money was always tight on the Hi-Line. Every member of the family contributed. Occasionally, the Pellett boys made a run to Canada to bring down bootleg whisky. Years before, Nellie, along with her oldest stepson Theron's wife, Sis, had set up a long table in the front room to feed the oil crews working the nearby rigs. From one small stove, they managed to feed dozens of workers.

Both Nellie and Sis were taller than their husbands. They were in-charge women who were comfortable with oil crews. Rarely seen without their aprons, they were always cooking or cleaning. Clarence pitched in, delivering groceries and supplies and doing general maintenance around the place. Business was good. The year before last, they'd moved the café out of their house to a small building their sons constructed just off the main highway at Four Corners.

Dunstall asked, "Did you hear any names?"

Nellie sighed. "No, I was busy. This morning, after he shoveled a load of pea gravel for the parking lot of the café, he said he'd be back early." Her face was taut with anguish. "What could have happened to him? Why hasn't he come home?"

Smokey tried to reassure Nellie. "Maybe he drove south to Great Falls on business."

Nellie shot back, "That's ninety miles! If he had changed his mind, he would have called me again."

The officers promised to keep looking. They struggled back to their car and drove back to Shelby. From the sheriff's office in the Toole County Courthouse, Charlie called the highway patrol on the radio. Hopefully, he asked, "Any sightings of a light green Plymouth, license plate number 21-1740? Or a report of an accident?"

"None reported," replied the dispatcher.

As the night gave way to the wee hours of the morning, Smokey called Great Falls Police Chief Harold Mady. A well-seasoned law officer, Mady was a cop's cop. A World War I marine vet, he was awarded a Purple Heart and the Croix de Guerre for bravery fighting the kaiser in France. Chief Mady was also Pellett's friend. He promised Smokey that he would get his men right on it. "If one of them finds the Plymouth or C.C., I'll notify you immediately."

"Harold, there's something else," said Smokey. "Nellie told us that she overheard a phone call Clarence had with two men about meeting in Shelby yesterday morning. We know these two men drove up from Great Falls and met Clarence here. Any chance you can get their names by tracing through the telephone company?"

Mady replied, "I'll try, but it will take time to go over the telephone company files."

By dawn, word was spreading that Pellett was missing. In large cities like Chicago or New York, a report of a missing man might not raise much concern, but on the Hi-Line, even though neighbors could be separated by as many as one hundred miles, people were tight-knit. Pellett was one of their own. This was personal. Offers of help poured in.

Throughout the morning, the officers continued to interview Shelby's business owners. Capital Café operator Lyle Flech told them that the day before, C.C. had lunch with two strangers. "They sat in a booth talking business for several hours after they had finished their meal."

Elmer Pedersen, who was eavesdropping, interrupted. "I saw Pellett after he left the restaurant. He was with two fellows in a new black Buick sedan. I talked to Shorty for a few minutes."

"What time?" Smokey asked.

"I reckon about four o'clock. He was going over to Wilson's Wholesale House."

Smokey drove to the wholesale grocery. Wilson recalled that Pellett had indeed been in around four and placed an order.

"You know C.C., how he can talk; he didn't seem to be in a hurry. I guess he left about five."

The storm had passed, and people had emerged from their homes. Several neighbors came up, offering help. Sam Fleming reported he had talked with Pellett around five thirty.

"He said he was going to head on home. I walked up the street with him, and I saw him get in his car."

"Alone?" asked Dunstall.

"Yep, leastways when I left him, he was. I saw him get in his car and pull out. He was headed north toward the 49er Drive In."

There were a few reports that Pellett had been seen offering a ride to a young man with bushy hair in front of the 49er Drive In. These sightings were especially troubling. A few months prior, starting in December 1950, sensationalized headlines had chronicled twenty-one-year-old hitchhiker Bill Cook's crime spree. Roaming the Southwest along Route 66, Cook kidnapped and murdered six innocent people who made the mistake of offering him a ride. Among Cook's acts of savagery, he gunned down a family of five, including three children ages seven, five and three, along with their dog, and callously dropped their bodies down a mine shaft. Captured on January 15, 1951, in Mexico, "Badman Bill Cook" or "Cockeyed Cook" instantly became a criminal celebrity.

Dunstall went to Shelby's radio station, KIWI, and broadcast that Clarence Pellett was missing: "Foul play is a very definite possibility. We'll stay on the search until we find out what happened to him." In no time, a general alarm spread across the whole of the Hi-Line. Smokey called nearby

The 49er Drive In. *Courtesy of* Shelby, Montana, The First Hundred Years.

towns: Cut Bank, Browning, Glacier, Kevin, Sweetgrass, Oilmont, Havre. Still, there was no sign of Pellett or his car.

By ten o'clock that morning, Dunstall and Smokey had run out of options. They feared for their friend.

At ten thirty, a radio call came in from a highway patrol officer. Pellett's Plymouth had been found on the edge of Highway 91 just south of Sweetgrass, close to the Canadian border.

"Any sign of C.C.?" Dunstall asked.

"No, just the car," the patrolman replied.

"We'll be right up," Dunstall said.

The patrolman added, "You've got to know, the car is parked close to where bartender George H. Monroe was found dead yesterday. We could have two murders on our hands."

Smokey replied, "We're on our way."

The sky had cleared, but the temperature remained well below freezing, and the wind was unrelenting. The water in the barrow pits on either side of the road was frozen. The sunshine reflecting off the fresh snow looked like a blanket of shimmering crystals stretching out over the prairie.

By the time they had driven the fifty miles to Sweetgrass, a small crowd was already standing around Pellett's car. The officers motioned for them to step back and inspected the scene closely. The roadbed was intact, and there were no scuff marks in the gravel. The tall grass near the road wasn't trampled. The car was unlocked, and the key was in the ignition. Dunstall turned it, and the car started right up. The gas gauge showed the tank was half full, and the parking brake was on. On the front seat was a box of Kleenex. Several wadded-up tissues were scattered on the floorboards. Lying on the back seat was an empty wallet, a watch and a pair of leather gloves with "FV" embroidered on the cuffs.

Finding the car only raised more questions. Why leave a perfectly running car in the middle of a storm?

"It couldn't have been Clarence," declared Dunstall. "He knows these parts. He would never have driven up here in that storm and parked so randomly on the side of the highway." More ominously, Dunstall recognized the watch and wallet as Pellett's.

Sweetgrass gas station owner Fred Price reported, "I closed at eight last night. On my way home, I drove right by where that car is now, but I don't remember seeing it."

The drive to Sweetgrass from Shelby takes an hour, longer in a storm. Dunstall stated, "He phoned Nellie at six saying he was on his way home. That puts it around seven, seven thirty at the most for him to get up here." According to Price, the car wasn't there at eight. What happened between six and past eight?

Who were the two men Clarence was with in the Capital Café? Was it just a strange coincidence that the car and Monroe's body were found so close together, a day apart? Where did those gloves with the initials "FV" come from? And what about the shaggy-haired hitchhiker who was seen getting into Pellett's car in front of the 49er? Nothing was adding up.

The officers decided to drive the half mile to the border. Both U.S. and Canadian customs officials said no persons or cars had crossed the border after six o'clock the previous evening. It was another dead end.

Chapter 3

THE HI-LINE POSSE AND THE HUNT FOR THE HOLLYWOOD HAIRCUT

KIWI announcer Jerry Black broadcast the location of Pellett's Plymouth. By the time the officers returned to the abandoned car, a few dozen Hi-Line folk had descended on it. The sheriff got out of the squad car, walked over to those gathered and divided them into search parties, telling them to fan out into the surrounding fields about half a mile in all directions. An hour later, they were back. There was no sign of C.C.

Three of the Pellett boys, Theron, Vernon ("Curly") and Riley, arrived. Like Smokey and Dunstall, they couldn't understand why their father would have driven past their home, only to leave his car alongside the road thirty miles away.

Dunstall told the Pellett boys, "About the only answer to all of this is that your dad got out of his car and into another one. The lack of blood or signs of violence is a good sign. Maybe later he was let out in a remote area and wasn't able to find a phone."

Curly pointed out that his dad was almost sixty: if he was out in the open, he wouldn't have survived the storm.

To cover more ground, Smokey and Dunstall decided to split up. Dunstall would follow up on the hitchhiker, and Smokey would concentrate on the two strangers.

Before he headed back to Shelby, Smokey pulled out his fingerprint equipment. Seeing the wadded-up Kleenex scattered around the interior, Smokey suspected the car had been wiped down. To his relief, he found that whoever did it hadn't done much of a job. He lifted fifteen prints. Most were smudged, but one on the steering wheel was clear.

Local Man Object Of Wide Search

Clarence E. Pellett, about 6?, of Four Corners, was the object of a widespread search by the sheriff's office, individuals, and the U. S. Immigration Service at Sweetgrass this morning.

Pellett's new automobile was found at Sweetgrass early today, after his family had become alarmed at his non-appearance at home last night.

A check showed that Pellett had been seen picking up a hitchhiker at the Shelby 49'er Drive-in about 7:30 Wednesday. According to the Toole County Sheriff's office, his coat and watch were found in the back seat of the auto, and his empty wallet in the front seat.

Description of the hitchhiker, as given to police, was that he was 30 to 40 years old, about 165 pounds, light curly hair, wearing a light gray sport coat. He was carrying a small grip at the time he was observed getting into Pellett's car.

From the Shelby Promoter, *April 5, 1951.*

As he was packing up his equipment, Smokey turned to Dunstall. "Charlie, I don't like the looks of it. He must have picked up somebody in Shelby who forced him to drive out here. That hitchhiker!"

The sheriff nodded. Smokey got into his squad car and headed south to Shelby.

Dunstall motioned the Pellett boys over. "Theron, we're done with your dad's car. You can take it back home."

Theron said, "Charlie, I think you should know: Dad was getting ready to sell his car. He had recorded the mileage yesterday. Curly noticed the odometer had no more than ten extra miles on it than it would have taken to drive straight from Shelby to where it was abandoned."

Charlie replied, "Thanks, Theron. We'll take it from here. Take care of your mom."

Finally, the lawman had something concrete with which to narrow the search area. As cars loaded with friends and neighbors arrived, the sheriff assigned each an area to search, concentrating on a few miles on either side of Highway 91 from Sweetgrass to Four Corners. On foot and on horseback, they searched abandoned buildings in case C.C. had taken shelter in one.

Back in Shelby, Smokey called Chief Mady again. Mady didn't have any news, but he asked, "How about I contact the Civil Aeronautics Board on Gore Hill? Maybe they can help."

"Good idea," Smokey said. "Thanks, Harold."

In no time, three small planes were airborne, flying low over the rolling hills of the Hi-Line. Students from Sunburst High School and elementary schools in Oilmont, Sweetgrass and Sunburst joined in the search. Local clergy rallied, too.

By noon, the whole Hi-Line was being searched by land and air. The *Cut Bank Pioneer Press* later reported "it was as if by magic" how quickly the farmers and townsfolk of northcentral Montana came to the aid of a local family. Still, there was no sign of Pellett.

By midafternoon, Main Street in Sweetgrass was crowded with cars. While Sheriff Dunstall was canvassing businesses, he noticed a man standing in front of a hotel/café, taking in all the activity. As they shook hands, the man identified himself as U.S. Customs Inspector T.J. Weatherly. He told Dunstall that he and his wife owned the hotel. He said that at about nine o'clock the previous night, he noticed a long-haired young man in his early twenties standing in the vestibule of their place. Weatherly opened the inside door and asked if he needed help, to which the young man said he was looking for something to eat.

Weatherly advised him that the café was closed, and the hotel was full. The young man thanked him and went across the street to the Border Inn.

Charlie thanked the inspector and crossed the street. When he opened the front door of the inn, the smell of stale beer and cigarettes assaulted his nose. Once his eye adjusted to the dark, he could see two men sitting at the bar, owner George Smith and bar regular Earl Ferries.

The sheriff identified himself and told the pair he was looking for a young transient who may have hitched a ride up from Shelby the night before. Ferris told him he crossed the border from Canada at nine o'clock the previous night and saw a man by the old bank building across the street. Ferris parked and went into the bar, where ten minutes later, that same young man walked in and sat down in the first booth.

Smith said he had served the bushy-haired youth a couple shots of whiskey. After finishing his drinks, the young man pulled a chair over the floor heat register and seemed to doze off. Four or five times, he got up, walked to the window and looked out. At one thirty in the morning, Smith tapped the man on the shoulder and told him he was closing the bar. He asked the man if he had a place to stay. The man shook his head no. Smith told him he couldn't get a room on this side of the border that night and he might have better luck on the other side, in Coutts, at the Sunshine Motel.

The sheriff thanked the men, left the bar and walked to the gas station. Using a pay phone, he sent a dispatch to the Royal Canadian Mounted

Police (RCMP) in Coutts: "Be on the lookout for a transient, approximately twenty years old, slightly built with long hair, to be held for questioning in connection with Pellett's hitchhiker."

Back in Shelby, Smokey, Officers Wilfred Johnson and Del Rwadon and Deputy Stromme canvassed the town. They talked to a waitress at the Capital Café who had served Pellett and the two strangers lunch. She confirmed, "They stayed long after they had finished eating, going over maps and figures."

The waitress described the strangers. One was tall and dark with thinning hair, wearing a gray suit with a gabardine topcoat. The other was shorter, mostly bald, dressed in a brown tweed overcoat and a brown hat. Both were dark and weather-beaten, like they worked outside. "They were really nice and left a big tip."

Sam Fleming saw Pellett get in his car at five thirty and drive off alone. Maybe, Smokey reasoned, Pellett drove to an oil lease and met those two men in that black Buick and things went sideways. But why hurt Clarence? He was five feet, two inches tall, rotund and kindly—he was no threat. Over the teletype, Smokey sent out a BOLO for a dark Buick sedan with the descriptions of the two strangers.

A young waitress about to start her lunch shift at the 49er Drive In had heard the reports of the missing man on the radio. Using the diner's pay

The Capital Café. *Courtesy of* Shelby, Montana, The First Hundred Years.

phone, she called Chief Denison. "I don't know Mr. Pellett, but from the description on the radio, I'm pretty sure he's the man who used the telephone here yesterday."

Smokey drove straight over and sat at the counter. "It was about quarter to six," the waitress recalled. "He used the pay phone on the wall by the front door. He sat at the counter, took his hat off, set it on the stool next to him and had a cup of coffee. I asked him if he wanted anything more and he said no because he was on his way home; his supper was waiting for him."

"He was alone?" Smokey asked.

"Yes, quite alone, I'm sure."

"Was anyone else in here at the time?"

She thought for a moment and then remembered there was a young man eating a couple of hamburgers at the counter. "This kid did put a dime in the jukebox."

Smokey asked her to describe the young man. Without hesitation, the waitress said, "In his early twenties, wearing a light gray sport coat with split tails and tan trousers. He didn't have a hat, and his hair was cut long at the back like they wear it in Hollywood. Not many guys wear their hair like that around here."

"Do you think he was a stranger to these parts?" Smokey asked.

"I sort of gathered he was a stranger, 'cause I know most of the fellas around here, or maybe it was because of his haircut."

Early that afternoon, local Canadian radio stations broadcast the description of the hitchhiker with the Hollywood haircut wanted in connection with the missing Montana man across southern Alberta. Around one o'clock, an elderly couple, the Dunns, had just finished lunch. Glancing out the window of their Lethbridge home, they noticed a man standing on the north side of First Avenue, thumbing a ride. The couple had heard the radio broadcasts.

Mr. Dunn phoned the RCMP, reporting, "The man answering the wanted hitchhiker's description has just thumbed a ride in a new model car headed west." Mrs. Dunn took the phone: "It had one of those new yellow Alberta license plates—number 57-334 or 37-334."

The RCMP dispatched their brand-new patrol cars equipped with two-way radios. Using this latest tool in crime fighting, Mounties were able to coordinate road blocks as they worked toward each other, west from Lethbridge and east from Macleod, checking everything on wheels.

Corporal John L. Wilson and another RCMP officer set up a roadblock east of Macleod on Highway 3. At 2:40 p.m., they stopped a car bearing the reported Alberta license plate and arrested the young man with a Hollywood hairstyle inside it.

En route to the Lethbridge station, Wilson asked the suspect where he had come from. The youth told the officer he hitchhiked from Montana the previous day and crossed the line into Canada at two o'clock in the morning. Wilson told him he was going to be deported for illegally entering Canada and that a sheriff in Montana wanted to talk with him.

Meanwhile, on the U.S. side of the border, near Sweetgrass, rancher Ray Hoister was riding fences on the U.S.-Canadian border. Back at his ranch house, he was unsaddling his horse when he heard the radio broadcasts about the missing man. He jumped into his pickup and drove to Sweetgrass, looking for Dunstall. He caught up with the sheriff around three o'clock.

"Sheriff," Ray said, "I'm pretty sure I saw Pellett's car along the road last night."

"What time?" Dunstall asked.

"About ten o'clock. My wife and I were over to Al Logan's place. We came by here and I saw a car, a light green Plymouth, and figured maybe somebody was in trouble, but nobody was around." That meant Clarence's car must have been abandoned sometime after eight o'clock and before ten o'clock.

At the Lethbridge RCMP office, the suspect offered to make a statement, which Mountie Wilson recorded in longhand. The suspect explained that Dryman was the name on his birth certificate, but he went by Valentine and that he served in the U.S. Navy as Frank Valentine and in the U.S. Air Force as Frank Dryman.

"A man picked me up last night north of Shelby," he explained. He described Pellett's car right down to the 1951 Montana license plate, 21-1740. "The old fellow dropped me off in Sweetgrass, just inside the American border, by a hotel," he claimed. "I walked away from the car. It was cold, so I went into a bar. I fell asleep; the manager woke me up when the bar closed. I walked over the line to Coutts, stayed in a motel lobby overnight. I caught the seven o'clock Greyhound bus to Lethbridge this morning."

He signed the document "Frank R. Dryman (alias) Frank R. Valentine."

Chapter 4

THE BODY FOUND

Just north of Shelby, a mile west of Four Corners, sheepherder George "Scotty" Jenkins was walking up a little hill to the pasture where he was looking after a herd of sheep for rancher Barney Hurley. Scotty noticed a number of birds circling overhead. Having lived in the area since 1909, he knew that a large flock of birds was a sure sign something had recently died on the prairie. His first concern was that a coyote had killed a lamb, but a flock this huge meant it could be something as large as a horse.

Scotty picked up his pace. In no time, he was at the edge of the pasture. At the far corner, he noticed what looked like a pile of rocks. As he walked east, diagonally across the pasture, the sheep separated ahead of him. Closer now, he saw not rocks or a lamb but a body, sprawled face down on blood-soaked dirt. He recognized Clarence Pellett.

At four o'clock in the afternoon, the call everyone on the Hi-Line was dreading came into Dunstall's office: Clarence Pellett had been found dead. Coincidentally, Toole County Attorney John C. Hoyt was in the sheriff's office. Raised in Shelby, Hoyt, twenty-nine, was a World War II hero, a local celebrity. The 1948 graduate of the University of Montana law school had been the county's prosecutor for two years.

Immediately, Dunstall and Hoyt jumped into a car driven by Highway Patrolman Yost. On the way, Dunstall radioed Toole County Coroner William F. Burns the location to meet them.

At Four Corners, the trio turned off the main highway and followed field roads till they reached a little knoll on the wind-blown prairie, where the

Pellett Obituary

Final homage was paid to Clarence C. Pellett in last rites held at the Community Methodist church in Shelby under the direction of Rev. George Sanders. Members of the Loyal Order of Moose had charge of the graveside service. Burial was in the Shelby cemetery.

Clarence Pellett was born at St. Paul, Minnesota, on January 10, 1892. He received most of his education at McKinney, North Dakota. He first came to Montana in 1910 and homesteaded for two years north of Joplin. He sold his homestead and moved to Tolley, North Dakota where he lived until 1927 when he moved to Ferdig. At Ferdig he went to work for the Texas Pacific Coal and Oil Company. He was still employed by them at the time of his death.

He was married to Jessie Rounds at Minot, North Dakota on August 19, 1907. She died in 1918. He was married to Nellie Sharp at Tolley, North Dakota, August 20, 1924.

Survivors in addition to his wife include five sons, Theron, Ferdig; Vernon, Kevin; Riley, Hawthorne, Nevada; Lyle, Great Falls; Marion, Bozeman; one daughter, Mrs. Earl Thompson, Kevin; six sisters and one brother and 16 grandchildren.

Pellett was an Odd Fellow lodge members for many years and at the time of his death was a member of the Moose lodge.

Attending the funeral services were Mr. and Mrs. Ira Pellett, Mr. and Mrs. Harvey Ray, Mrs. Harrison Kholes, Mrs. Gene Mosher and Mr. and Mrs. C. J. Sharp, all of Babbitt, Nevada, Mrs. Inez Breevoort, Hawthorne, Nevada, and Mrs. John Bird, Kenmare North Dakota. Ira Pellett is a brother of the deceased, while the ladies are his sisters.

Acting pallbearers were John Fauque, Ed Doby, Earl Rambo, W. R. Britt, Harry Flynn and Frank Welch. Honorary pallbearers were L. Cooper, Cecil Shue, Earl Addy, Fred Pfannsmith, A. G. Swenson, George Welch, Ray German, Eddie Vanderpas and Dewey Sandell.

Clarence Chester Pellett's obituary. *From the* Shelby Promoter, *April 12, 1951.*

body of their friend C.C. lay spread-eagle, face down in the blood-soaked mud. His feet pointed north. His head was tilted to the right, his left hand resting beside his face. A slug protruded from his right palm. His coat was riddled with bullet holes. Within two feet of the body were his hat and six .45-caliber brass casings.

Hoyt paced off about forty-five feet from the body to a pair of fresh tire tracks. Close to the tracks were two additional casings.

Not far from the scene, Mr. and Mrs. Galloway were driving their family car south from Kevin to Shelby to take in a movie. Seated in the back was their eldest, ten-year-old Edwin; next to him was his younger sister. All four were excited for the family outing to the Roxy Theater. Entertainment on the Hi-Line was hard to come by, and a movie was a rare treat.

As they neared Shelby on Highway 91, a speeding ambulance with lights flashing and siren blaring zipped past, going the opposite direction. The Galloways, along with the rest of the Hi-Line, had kept up with the radio reports of the missing man all day. Mr. Galloway said, "That must be for Mr. Pellett!"

Mr. Galloway made a quick U-turn, and the kids were flung against the back seat passenger-side door. Brother and sister looked at each other, eyes wide, as their car sped up. Following the flashing lights, Mr. Galloway turned off the paved road onto the prairie. They caught up to the ambulance, now parked, lights still flashing.

Little Ed grabbed the back of the front seat and pulled himself forward. Looking out the windshield, he saw, directly in front of the car, what looked like a pile of dark rocks. His father opened the driver's side door.

Ed scrambled over the seat back and joined his dad. His mother and sister stayed in the car.

As father and son cautiously walked forward, the boy reached up and grabbed one of his father's belt loops. Spotting four men absorbed in conversation, they recognized one as Sheriff C.O. Dunstall. Without a word, the sheriff raised his hand, gesturing for them to stop.

The pair was only ten feet from what was obviously a man lying prone, face down in the dirt. Blood stained the ground around the corpse. Shocked to see his first dead body, little Ed let go of his father's belt loop and hugged his dad's leg with both arms. The boy looked away from all the blood, focusing on the heels of the victim's shoes. The toes were dug into the dirt.

Father and son heard Sheriff Dunstall say, "It looks like he was in the act of praying when he was shot."

With his son Bob assisting, Bill Burnes lifted Pellett's stiff body into the ambulance. The body had been lying face down for twenty-four hours; Pellett's facial features were smashed flat, almost unrecognizable.

Hoyt collected the eight brass casings and etched his initials, "JCH," into them.

Addressing Hoyt, Stromme and Yost, Dunstall said, "Boys, the pattern of the casings tells a story. There are eight empty .45-caliber shells between the tire tracks and the body." Pointing at the edge of the tire tracks, he continued, "The shooter must have come up behind him and fired the first shot from here." Walking to a spot halfway between the tire tracks and where Clarence was found, he said, "He let him have it again from here, then stood over him and emptied the magazine."

"Why such a vicious attack?" Deputy Stromme asked. "Why pump the whole magazine into his back?"

"This can't be robbery," Dunstall said. "Too much overkill. We're losing daylight. You all head back to town; I'll finish up here. We'll come back in the morning."

Charlie needed time to process the loss of his friend. "Stromme, I'm going to walk over to the Pelletts' at the Texas Petroleum camp. Pick me up there."

It was only half a mile from where Clarence was found to the Pellett house. Why hadn't Nellie mentioned hearing gunshots? All day, KIWI had updated the entire Hi-Line on the search. Now they broadcast that Pellett had been found dead, face down out on the prairie, shot in the back.

By the time Dunstall reached the Pelletts' house, a crowd of mourners had gathered in front of the home. Standing in the front room were Theron, Curly, Riley and Lyle. Marion, Nellie's only child, named after her grandfather, was working in Idaho. The news of her husband's death had so shocked Nellie that she was incapacitated in the bedroom with the door closed.

Dunstall asked the Pellett boys if their mother had mentioned hearing gunfire. She hadn't. Theron said, "Maybe she was listening to the radio."

The Pellett boys asked the sheriff if he had any news about the shooter. Dunstall shook his head. "Where your dad was found, there were actively working oil pumps," he said. "Any chance he came out to meet with the two men he'd been seen talking with in town?"

Sensing where the sheriff was going, Curly said, "Charlie, you know Dad didn't have any enemies. He was always fair in all his business dealings. I can't think of a reason for a thing like this."

At the Toole County jail, Smokey answered a call from Chief Mady. "One of my patrolmen, Jack Anderson, traced that telephone call made to Pellett. It was made from a phone booth here in the lobby of the Rainbow Hotel. No one saw who made the call, but I have a strong suspicion it was one of two fellows registered under the names of Royal Cordes and Arthur Frisbin, both of Spokane, Washington. The two of them had been around a few days, talking oil leases. They checked out last night around nine. The clerk said they seemed to be in a hurry."

Smokey was growing less interested in the two strangers, and finding C.C.'s car close to where Monroe was murdered was looking more and more like a simple coincidence to him. He focused instead on the shaggy-haired hitchhiker.

Hoyt drove Smokey out to the murder scene. By the time they arrived, it was dark. Stars filled the clear sky. The sheep were gone, and it was quiet. For once, the wind was calm. Smokey turned to Hoyt. "John, you say the brass you picked up was .45 caliber."

"Yeah, semi-auto pistol, I think."

"Well, that rules out a connection with the Monroe murder, where a .22 was used. I see the tire tracks the sheriff was talking about. I'll come out in the morning to make plaster casts."

At seven o'clock that evening, Dunstall radioed Deputy Stromme and Matthew Lohmiller of the U.S. Border Patrol. "That hitchhiking suspect has been picked up in Canada. Report to the RCMP barracks at Coutts, take him into custody, bring him over the line and return to the Shelby station. He goes by Frank R. Dryman, alias Frank R. Valentine."

Earlier that afternoon, Dryman was escorted from Lethbridge south to Coutts, Alberta, where he was interrogated by the officer in charge of

Canadian immigration, Bert Hills, at the jail in the RCMP barracks, near Coutts and only yards from the U.S. border.

Hills explained to the suspect that when he walked across the line the previous morning, he entered Canada illegally, and thus he was subject to immediate deportation. However, as a suspect in the case of a missing Montana man, he couldn't simply be released back into the United States. Hills decided to grant Dryman a voluntary departure, skipping extradition procedures.

The previous night's storm had made dirt roads impassable. It took Stromme and Lohmiller an hour to travel the twenty-five miles to Sweetgrass. When they arrived at the border station, Stromme met John A. Phillips of U.S. Immigration and Naturalization, who handed Stromme the documents he had to present to the Canadian authorities to take custody of the suspect.

Stromme and Lohmiller drove over the border and on to the Mounties' barracks. At a little past eight o'clock in the evening, they took custody of the suspect. With Dryman handcuffed in the back seat, they started back.

Meantime, immediately south of Sweetgrass, cars were parked on both sides of Highway 91. Chants of "That dirty rat shot him in the back!" and "Hang 'um!" rippled through the angry mob. A couple of hangman's nooses appeared in the crowd.

As they approached the U.S. border, the officers could hear the chants. They opted to skip the U.S. border station and skirt the mob. Unnoticed, they crossed the border. The officers delivered Dryman to the Toole County jail at nine o'clock. Curious onlookers, mostly women, were standing outside the jail. They kept their distance, standing quietly across the alley, partway up the courthouse hill: no chanting, no shouting, no nooses.

A little more than twenty-four hours after the kid with the Hollywood haircut hitched a ride in the green Plymouth, both Pellett and Dryman were back in Shelby, one in the Toole County jail, the other in the city morgue.

Chapter 5

THE INTERROGATION

The young transient gave his name as Frank R. Dryman, a.k.a. Frank R. Valentine. Stromme ordered him to empty his pockets.

Along with U.S. Navy discharge papers, he was carrying a gripsack, a paper clip, a rubber band and a fragment of a five-dollar bill. The suspect's belongings were placed in a metal box and put on a shelf in the tall cabinet next to Denison's desk. After Dryman was fingerprinted, Dunstall walked the prisoner down the narrow hallway to the back room on the main floor of the Toole County jailhouse. In the room was a small jail cell, a table and a few metal chairs. The only light came from a single bare light bulb hanging from the ceiling.

Dunstall sat Dryman down, still handcuffed. Crowded into the room with the sheriff were Hoyt, Curly Pellett, Highway Patrolman Kelly and Art Anderson. Smokey towered over the group.

Dunstall wasted no time, shouting, "I want to know all about it!" Dryman sat silent, mutinous. With the image of his friend's stiff, mutilated body still vivid in his mind, Charlie exploded. He pulled a sap from his coat pocket and struck Dryman three times on the back of his left wrist and leg.

"Stop!" Hoyt yelled.

Disgusted, Smokey turned and walked back down the hall. He didn't approve of Dunstall using a sap, even though the blows hadn't broken the skin.

Dunstall asked no more questions. He opened the cell door and motioned Dryman inside. As Dryman stepped into the cell, the sheriff gave him a shove and locked the door behind him. The entourage filed silently out of the jailhouse.

That Thursday evening, at around ten thirty, Toole County Coroner Dr. Stephen Adaskavich reported to the city morgue. An hour later, he began the autopsy of Clarence Chester Pellett. He finished it at two thirty the next morning.

On Friday, April 6, at nine o'clock in the morning, twenty-year-old Cut Bank resident Dorothy Holeman heard the radio reports that Pellett had been murdered. She immediately phoned Cut Bank Police Chief Toay and told him that a couple of days before, she and two friends were driving home from Great Falls when they picked up a young hitchhiker with long hair near Vaughn. They dropped him off in Shelby near the Snack Shack.

"Anything you remember about him? Anything unusual?" Toay asked.

"Well, he was telling stories about hitching all around the country," Dorothy said. "Then it got strange. He told us, 'When cars slow down to look at me and I run up to them and they speed away, I could blow their heads off!' I think that's the guy that shot Mr. Pellett."

After hearing Dorothy's story, Toay drove her to the Toole County jail and took her to the backroom cell. Dryman stood up and, in a snotty tone, said, "So we meet again."

Earlier that same morning, Smokey, Hoyt and a photographer drove back to the murder site. Using a jackknife, Smokey probed the bloodstained ground. He found four slugs embedded in the dirt directly under where the body was found. Fired at such close range, they had passed through Pellett intact.

With his knife, Smokey etched a large *D* with the letter *R* inside it into the soft lead at the blunt end of each slug. Hoyt took charge of the slugs, putting them into a manila envelope.

While the photographer took pictures, the other two knelt to take a close look at a section of the tire tracks where the dirt and large rocks were dislodged. A car had obviously made a tight turn at great acceleration.

Looking at all the tire tracks, they could see where the car had come to a stop. The tread pattern was clear. The soft prairie ground was ideal for making plaster of Paris casts. Smokey made seven of them.

Back in Shelby by eleven o'clock that morning, Smokey and Hoyt went to the Toole County jail, where they found Dunstall, Toay and Stromme at the office. As Smokey put the plaster casts in a tall cabinet by his desk, they discussed their interrogation strategy.

All agreed that building a rapport with Dryman was their best chance to get him to give up what he knew. Smokey remarked, "Yeah, Charlie, you know that you catch more flies with honey than vinegar."

"We won't get anything by hitting him," Hoyt said.

Dunstall responded, "I don't agree, but if you don't get anywhere with him, I'm here."

Deputy Stromme walked to the back room, unlocked the cell door and sat Dryman in the same chair as the previous night. Smokey and Hoyt each took a chair across the desk from Dryman. Toay and Stromme looked on.

Hoyt instructed, "Frank, start from the beginning. Tell us how you got up to Canada." Sticking to the statement he made to the Mounties, Dryman admitted to hitching a ride by the drive-in but claimed that the "old fellow" let him out at Sweetgrass. Over the next hour, he steadfastly denied having anything to do with the killing.

Seeing that they weren't making progress, Smokey said, "Let's take a little ride." Stromme handcuffed Dryman and loaded him into the back seat of one of Toole County's squad cars, a 1950 Hudson sedan. The deputy and Smokey drove Dryman to the city morgue. Burns opened the alley door. Smokey grabbed Dryman's left bicep tightly. Dryman's feet were barely touching the floor as they walked down the hall to a room filled with stainless steel embalming equipment. The scent of formaldehyde filled the air.

In the middle of the room was a metal gurney. On the gurney lay a body covered by a white sheet. Still gripping Dryman's arm, Smokey pulled him close to the gurney, then left the room. Burns removed the sheet. From behind, Burns and his son pushed Dryman's face into what had been Pellett's chest. Red-tinged fluid oozed from the body onto the gurney. "See what you did!" shouted Burns.

In a shot, Dryman pulled himself upright. Body fluids dripped from his face onto his shirt. "I never seen him before! I don't have any feeling for him. Just an ordinary corpse to me—I did not do this!"

Smokey and Stromme gathered Dryman up and drove him back to the jailhouse, where lunch was waiting for him. Three times a day, the Capital Café's owner, Lyle Flesh, delivered meals to the prisoners—not just three squares but steak, eggs, ham with all the fix'ns, the best in town.

At nine o'clock that night, after the suspect had a steak dinner, Hoyt, Denison and Stromme started a casual conversation. Hoyt said, "Frank, tell us about yourself."

Dryman snarled, "Why? You writin' a book?"

Denison said, "Ease up, Frank. Start with your birthday."

"OK. I was born June 4, 1931, in Napa, California." With a smirk, he added, "Yeah, my mom fucked around. She got knocked up by Frank

Valentine while she was still married to Dryman, so my birth certificate says I'm Frank Dryman, but I go by Frank Valentine."

Hoyt asked, "You grew up there?"

"Yeah, I was baptized there at St. John the Baptist Catholic Church: Frank Joseph Valentine. Dryman was out of the picture. When I was six, we pulled up stakes and went to the Boulder Dam to look for work. We lived in a tent camp, Ragtown, near Boulder City. My dad, Valentine, was a security guard."

"You have brothers and sisters?" Hoyt asked.

"Just one sister, Ginger; she's the youngest. There's my half-brother, Hank (he's a Dryman), then me, Jack and Jim. My dad was always drunk, beat us kids. When work at the dam dried up, the family moved thirty miles down the road to Las Vegas. My dad found work with the city, driving a truck. It was steady work, things were good—until he caught my mom in bed with another man. There was a big fight, and Valentine left.

"We kids heard a loud gunshot in the house. I was the first to find her lying on the bed. There was blood, tissue and fat covering the walls and ceiling. She had blown off her left tit and part of her left shoulder with a vintage Greener 10-gauge shotgun."

Smokey exclaimed, "A Greener? You know your guns!"

"Yeah, growing up there were always a lot of guns around. After a couple of months, Valentine returned. We pulled up stakes again and moved to Hawthorne, Nevada. He was a security guard, wore a uniform complete with a gun belt holster and a Colt M1911 .45."

Smokey said, "I see you have discharge papers. I wanna hear about your time in the service."

Frank regurgitated the statement he had signed in Canada. "I got a medical discharge."

Deputy Stromme looked on as the suspect methodically described leaving Hawthorne, Nevada, in mid-March and taking a bus to Reno, where he stayed with a friend, Siegfried Sunbee, for a week or so. Then he boarded a bus to Las Vegas. Finally, on March 31, he set out hitchhiking north.

Dryman clearly recalled thumbing his way through Utah and catching a ride with three youngsters out of Great Falls five days later, on Wednesday, April 4. "They dropped me off by the bridge, near the Snack Shack here in Shelby."

Dryman recalled that in the early afternoon, he caught a ride out of Shelby with a man in a pickup truck going in the wrong direction. Later, he got a ride in another car, a light green sedan, headed north. He claimed

The Snack Shack. *Courtesy of* Shelby, Montana: The First Hundred Years.

he didn't look at the driver. Dryman described how oncoming cars dimmed their headlights. One fellow was driving with only parking lights, he said. His questioners were amazed by how clear, detailed and vivid his memories were. But then, ten miles out of Shelby, his memory failed him. "I blacked out until I got to Sweetgrass. I had a spell like I had in the navy." He snickered.

Hoyt said, "Tell me about your navy discharge."

Dryman replied, "I was discharged after being sent to the mental hospital at Bremerton, Washington."

At midnight on Saturday, April 7, 1951, Smokey said, "Let's take a break. You hungry, Frank?"

"Yeah, I could use a bite."

Smokey sent out for ham and eggs for everyone. The team talked casually while they watched Dryman eat, drink coffee and smoke a few cigarettes. An hour later, the questioning resumed.

Impatiently, Smokey said, "You were in Shelby the night before last. You stopped at a drive-in." Dryman nodded yes.

"And you hitchhiked a ride with a man named Clarence Pellett."

"Like I said before, I don't know his name. We barely talked. But I know it was a light green Plymouth sedan."

Smokey said in a powerful voice, "Pellett was killed that night, gunned down!"

Defiantly, Dryman replied, "I didn't kill him!"

"You were with him!" Smokey shot back.

"Sure, I was. I got a ride, but like I said, I didn't shoot him! I haven't handled a gun since the service!"

Finally, at three o'clock in the morning, the team threw in the towel.

The next day, April 7, Dryman sat in his cell alone until nine o'clock at night. Hoyt, Smokey, Deputy Stromme and Don Toay assembled in the back room of the jail, just outside Dryman's cell. The blinds were drawn, and Dryman sat in the same metal chair at the desk. Again, Hoyt asked where he had been before he came to Shelby. Dryman recited the same story about hitching rides from Nevada up through Utah and so on.

Dryman, a braggart, enjoyed telling the team about his adventures hitching around the country. The team knew that as long as he kept talking, it was just a matter of time until he tripped himself up. But Dryman was proving to be a surprisingly tough nut to crack. After a few hours, the session ended.

On April 8, after his usual Sunday morning sermon, Father Wagner stopped by the jail and introduced himself. "I'm Father Wagner. I understand you are Catholic."

"Yeah," Dryman said, "I was an altar boy."

The priest offered him a blessing and asked if he wanted to confess his sins.

Dryman replied, "It's too late for that, Father."

After less than ten minutes, Father Wagner left.

In Hawthorne, Nevada, after learning of her brother's murder, Mrs. Phyllis Sharp packed as many Pelletts into two cars as they would hold and drove the twenty hours to Montana. Once in Shelby, she learned the suspect was a youth named Frank Valentine. The name rang a bell.

Phyllis informed Sheriff Dunstall that a few years prior, in Hawthorne, the Sharps had neighbors named Valentine. A son, Frank, sixteen, was arrested for drunkenness and armed robbery of a liquor store. He was about to be sent to a reformatory when Phyllis and others in the community appeared in court and asked the judge to clear Frank of the charges on the condition that he joined the marines when he turned seventeen. Phyllis volunteered to be his foster parent in the interim.

Dunstall granted Phyllis permission to visit the suspect in his cell. She recognized him immediately. At first, Frank denied knowing her, but eventually, he remembered, calling her two sons by name. The accused teen recalled how she was his friend on many "troublesome" occasions.

"I ate a lot of turkey dinners at your house," he said. He was shocked to learn Clarence was her brother.

At eight o'clock in the evening on April 8, Hoyt and Denison resumed the interrogation. Dryman remained cocky, confident he was besting his questioners and unmoved that the victim was the brother of the kind woman who had taken him in.

Having served in the armed forces, each interrogator was well acquainted with the ways of the military and how its bureaucrats washed their hands of slackers. This young punk wasn't fooling them. They had him pegged not as insane but as a clever young man who didn't like the rigors of the service.

"In the navy, you said you blacked out?" Smokey asked.

"I was down in the hold of the ship on a paint detail," Dryman explained. "It was hard work. Those blackouts were a put-on deal. I outsmarted them doctors. Hee-hee!" he giggled. "My ship was an aircraft carrier, the USS *Princeton*. When we were off the coast of China, from the flight deck, we'd shoot at the chinks in fishing boats—it was fun watching them fall into the water! Hee-hee!"

Smokey asked, "What about your discharge from the air force?"

Dryman said, "I didn't like the way I was treated, so I went AWOL." He told Smokey he stayed with relatives in California until he turned himself in two months later in Los Angeles. "I claimed I was looking for my parents, that I was confused about which name to use—Dryman or Valentine. They threw me in the brig. I was going to get a hitch in the stockade, but I talked my way out of it and got a fraudulent discharge."

Smokey remarked, "You're pretty good at talking your way out of things."

With a glib smile, Dryman replied, "I am."

Smokey produced a fingerprint card from his shirt pocket, handed the suspect a magnifying glass and said, "Take a look. This is a print I lifted from the steering wheel of Pellett's car." Dryman peered through the glass.

Smokey said, "It's your left index finger. There you are! You might just as well have left your name! If Pellett let you out at Sweetgrass, why would your print be on the steering wheel? Did you drive the car?"

Frustrated, Smokey went on, "Come on, Frank. Tell us about this murder. What happened?" Dryman sat silent. Sensing an impasse, the team ended the session after two hours. After all, it was Sunday.

For four days, Dryman had steadfastly denied he knew about any murder or owned a gun. Still, Hoyt never resorted to hard-nosed grilling. Instead, he bought Dryman ham, eggs and steak at $1.25 a pop. Dryman was a voracious eater; his tab with the Capital Café was upward of $16.

Hoyt developed a rapport with Dryman by using persuasive conversation. Rather than trying to make Dryman admit he was a liar, Hoyt suggested he'd had a dream about a weapon. That way, Dryman could salve his conscience, which might lead to a confession. Using an indirect method of questioning, by the end of the morning on Monday, April 9, Hoyt had Dryman thinking he had indeed dreamed about where the gun might be found.

Around three o'clock in the afternoon on Monday, Smokey was at the wheel of the Hudson. Hoyt was in the passenger seat, and Chief Toay was in the back seat with Dryman, who was not handcuffed. Smokey glanced over his shoulder. "This is your show, Frank. Where are we going?"

Dryman replied, "North."

They were almost out of town when Dryman demanded, "I'm hungry. Pull in here." It was the 49er Drive In. Under his breath, Smokey muttered, "This kid has balls."

Hoyt walked in and ordered. Ten minutes later, he emerged carrying a couple bags of food. The officers watched as Dryman ate three burgers, fries and a strawberry milkshake.

Dryman was buoyant as he directed Smokey north on Highway 91 to Sweetgrass and across the border to Coutts. There, he led the group through the front door of the Sunshine Motel. The small lobby had just enough room for a couple of chairs, a small coffee table and a phone booth. There was a sun seat in the front window with a newspaper lying on it. Dryman picked up the paper and placed it on the seat of the same chair where he'd fallen asleep four nights before. He shoved the chair over to the phone booth in the northeast corner of the lobby and jumped up onto it. Reaching above the phone booth, he pulled down an empty .45 clip, a leather shoulder holster and a sunglasses case with a smudge of red paint on it and handed the items to Hoyt.

"I hid these last Thursday morning," Dryman explained. "I'm not sure why I put the sunglasses up there. Hee-hee, hee-hee!" That cackle was getting on Smokey's nerves.

"OK, so where is the gun?" he asked.

"Follow me," Dryman said.

He led the entourage through the back door of the motel. On the north side of the building, someone had attempted to make a garden with flags around the border. There was a large stone in the middle.

Dryman said, "You need to move that rock!"

Toay and Smokey pushed it a couple of feet. Beneath was a sizable collection of loose .45-caliber ammunition.

My father, Marion (*left*), and his oldest half-brother, Theron, worked in the oil fields on the Hi-Line. *Author's collection.*

"This is a lot of bullets," Hoyt said. "We're going to need some way to carry these."

Hoyt returned to the lobby and rang the front desk bell. He explained to the hotel clerk that he needed a container. The clerk stepped behind a curtain and came back moments later with three empty one-pint ice cream containers. Back outside, Hoyt scooped up a mix of military-issue brass and copper-colored commercial shells. He taped down the top of each container and scribbled his initials on the tape.

Dryman motioned toward a row of bricks. Smiling, he said, "I bet you'll find that gun under here."

Smokey and Toay removed half a dozen bricks and then brushed a thin layer of soil away to reveal the components of an M1911 Colt .45 pistol. Smokey spit on the frame and rubbed it with his finger. A serial number appeared: 250666. The officers gathered up the items and put them in the trunk of the Hudson.

The four drove back to Shelby in silence. No one asked the obvious question: "Is this the gun you used to shoot Mr. Pellett?" Everyone knew the answer.

At the Toole County Courthouse, Hoyt watched Charlie pour the bullets from the ice cream containers into a burlap bag. He walked up the stairs to the office of Toole County clerk of the court, Bernice Lutz, and plopped the heavy sack on her desk.

"All this is evidence."

At two o'clock in the afternoon on Tuesday, April 10, funeral services were held for Clarence Chester Pellett at Shelby's Methodist church. The Reverend George Sanders officiated. The church was overflowing. Joining the family was Clarence and Nellie's only son, Marion F. Pellett, twenty-seven. Employed as a representative for Stauffer Chemical Company, he had flown from Idaho Falls to Great Falls and then motored up to Shelby with his wife, Joan. As the Pellett family filed in, the six-foot, two-inch Marion towered over his five half-siblings.

The wailing of the grief-stricken widow drowned out much of the reverend's sermon. A long funeral procession followed the hearse up the hill to Shelby's cemetery. The day was clear, the wind whipping across the prairie. Amid the graveside grief, a palpable anger filled the air. Clarence Chester Pellett was laid to rest at five o'clock in the afternoon.

Chapter 6

THE CONFESSION

After another hearty breakfast, Dryman was questioned throughout that next day. Despite having guided the officers to the pistol cache, he denied knowing about the murder or owning a gun.

Hoyt decided to play his ace in the hole. "So your story is that you were in Reno before you hitched up here."

Dryman nodded.

"Yesterday I put in a long-distance call to Mr. Siegfried Sunbee of Reno, Nevada. You know, your friend, the guy you stayed with. Mr. Sunbee told me you purchased a .45 Colt pistol with ammunition and a shoulder holster at a hockshop in Reno. He confirmed you left town with that .45-caliber pistol. We know you own a gun."

Dryman wouldn't budge. He continued to say he hadn't owned or handled a gun for years.

Hoyt suspected that after five days of questioning, Dryman was getting too familiar with the team. At the dinner break, he phoned his law partner, Cedor B. Aronow. A Hi-Line elder statesman, Aronow had been practicing law since 1933. He was the Toole County attorney from 1937 to 1943, a member of the Montana State House of Representatives, counsel to the Blackfoot Indian Tribe and involved in the oil production business.

Hoyt said, "Cedor, we have this guy Dryman cold. But he's sticking to his story; we can't get a confession. Would you come down and give it a try?"

"I'm in the middle of dinner," Aronow said. "I'll drop over and talk with the guy and give what help I can."

At eight o'clock, Smokey, Hoyt, Toay and Aronow huddled at the jail. "I think we should get him comfortable talking," Aronow said.

Smokey replied, "Oh, he's a talker alright."

Hoyt introduced Aronow as his law partner. "He's here to help us sort this thing out—just here to listen in."

Aronow had the look of an old school-gentleman. "Mr. Dryman—or do you prefer Valentine?"

Bored, the teen answered, "Dryman will do for now."

Aronow asked, "Would you mind sketching out for me how you got up here to Shelby?"

Irked, Dryman again recited the story of how he hitched from Nevada to Lethbridge.

Aronow interrupted: "I attended Mr. Pellett's funeral today. I've never been at such a service, so many people—I daresay it was the biggest in Shelby history. I've never seen such weeping, such sadness."

Dryman didn't skip a beat. He continued regurgitating the story of his time in the navy and the air force.

Aronow remarked, "I'm a major in the Marine Corps Reserve."

Clarence Chester Pellett's grave. *Author's collection.*

This intimidated Dryman—it triggered memories of scrapes he and his brothers had gotten into with jarheads in Hawthorne. Dryman's teenage insolence faded before their eyes. He took out a handkerchief to wipe the beads of sweat off his forehead. Smokey snatched the handkerchief from his hand and held it to his nose, sniffed it once and then again. Gun oil!

"Wait a minute," Smokey said. "You've been telling us you don't have a gun."

"I don't. Don't own one."

Smokey demanded, "When was the last time you handled a gun?"

"Like I've been telling you, not since I was discharged from the navy in '49."

"Are you sure about that?"

"I'm positive!"

Smokey pounced: "Are you as positive of that as you are of all the things you've told us?"

"Yes! I'm positive! What are you getting at?" Dryman replied. The two of them were practically nose to nose.

"OK, how did gun oil get on your handkerchief?" Smokey asked.

Smokey handed it to Chief Toay, who sniffed the cloth. "That's gun oil, all right," he confirmed. Immediately, Dryman clammed up.

"Let me tell you what I think happened," Smokey said. "Mr. Pellett picked you up in his car, and you started to talk. You told him that you were headed for Canada. He told you he was only going as far as Four Corners. That's when you pulled out your gun and told him to drive off the road. Pellett started pleading. You told him to stop and get out. He got out and started to run. You shot him, and then you ran up to him and emptied the gun."

Aronow added, "You shot him and shot him dead."

"Then you got back in the car and drove to Sweetgrass at a high rate of speed," Smokey went on. "Is that about right?"

Dryman admitted, "Yep, that's about right."

"You'll get the rope for this!" Smokey said.

"Yes, I know that."

"You're entitled to a lawyer," Aronow said. "The state will pay."

"I don't want one."

"We know that gun is yours! Why don't you just tell us what happened?" Smokey said.

"I'll make a statement."

Hoyt hooked up a microphone to his office dictation recorder, an Ediphone, on the table in front of Dryman. Before he turned it on, Hoyt and his law partner informed Dryman he was under no obligation to make any statement.

Aronow said, "Don't say anything you don't want to. If you were to make a statement, any statement you make will be used against you."

Hoyt said, "You could be hung for this."

Resigned to his fate, in a voice barely above a whisper, Dryman spoke slowly into the microphone. Occasionally pausing and saying, "I guess," he told the story of how Pellett picked him up on the north side of Shelby. After they'd gone up the road by Four Corners, Pellett told him that was as far as he was going.

Dryman said, "If I let him go, he'd call the cops, and way out here in the sticks, I wouldn't have a chance to get away." He said he drew a .45 pistol from his shoulder holster and forced Pellett to drive off the road.

Dryman haltingly described how Pellett started begging and pleading to be let loose. "He was saying, 'Don't do this, don't do that.' It kept getting worse and worse." Coldly, Dryman recounted how all that blubbering irritated him. "I told him I was going to kill him. Once we were well off the main highway, I told him to stop the car and get out. I guess he had figured out I was going to go through with it, so he started to run. I missed with the first shot and dropped him with the second." He gave his account of running up to Pellett, standing over him and emptying the gun.

As though he was reliving the moment, Dryman described how he ran back to the car, holding the gun close for its warmth. In the car, he loaded another clip; then he drove to Sweetgrass. "I parked on the side of the road off the main street of Sweetgrass because I thought something was wrong with the car. It was lugging down; I could smell something burning. I got out and looked under the car; I saw flames. I ran away from the car and went to a bar to get out of the cold weather. Had a drink and fell asleep. I kept looking out the window to see if the car was on fire, 'cause that would have brought the cops. But it never did.

"The bartender woke me up at closing. I walked across the border and spent the night in a hotel lobby and then caught a bus to Lethbridge and was later picked up by the Mounties. That's the end of it."

When Hoyt clicked off the Ediphone, everyone was still, silent. Finally, Smokey stood up and grabbed Dryman. As he pushed the confessed killer back into his cell, he said: "God damn you! You'll get the rope for this!"

Before they went their separate ways, Smokey said to Hoyt, "When Charlie and I inspected C.C.'s car, we both thought it was strange the parking brake was set. C.C. must have set it when Dryman ordered him out of the car.

PLAINTIFF'S EXHIBIT

STATE OF MONTANA)
: ss.
County of Toole)

FRANK R. DRYMAN, also known as Frank R. Valentine, being first duly sworn, on oath deposes and says:

That the statements hereafter made by me are made of my own free will and are my voluntary statements. They are not made through any threats, promises or duress of any kind or nature made to me by any person whomsoever. I fully realize and it is my intention that the following statements may be used against me in any court having jurisdiction in the matter of the death of Clarence E. Pellett. The statements hereafter made by me relate to events occurring on the 4th day of April, A.D., 1951 and the early morning hours of April 5, 1951.

My statements concerning the death of Clarence E. Pellett are as follows:

I guess I got in the car at Shelby. He started asking me questions, he didn't tell me where he was going. I guess neither one of us told where we was going until we got out to Four-Corners, I guess, and he says this is where I stop, and I guess I pulled the gun, told him to keep on going, turn off on the first side road out a ways, so he turned off the side road, first he was saying this and then he was saying that, don't do this, don't do that, I guess and we just driving until I guess we thought we were far enough off the road and I told him to get out of the car and he was begging for mercy, I guess. A man would be in that condition and I guess I was talking to him about killing him or something, telling him I was going to kill him and he kept getting worse and worse, practically down on his knees, I guess, and when I raised the gun he started running and I started shooting and then I guess I was going after him when I was shooting at him. When he finally fell over, I probably went up and emptied the gun into him. Went back to the car, put in another magazine, slammed it shut, pulled out of there back up the same road - I tried to find the same road, went into Sweetgrass parked it up there by the garage, got out, tried to catch a ride, got back in - or couldn't catch a ride, was freezing to death, got back in the car, decided to take it on down to Cut Bank and not across the border, I was going to go down that road to Cut Bank. Something wrong with the car, it wouldn't run, something, I don't know what it was on the brake, or something, anyhow it's lugging the back wheels down and I could smell something burning so I managed to turn it back up and to about the same place anyhow, I got it on the first side road there and something was really burning. I jumped out of the car and looked under and there was flames or sparks from underneath and so I thought the car was going to burn and I took off out of there back down in front of the hotel. I got back down in front of the hotel, waited around awhile and the car never caught afire or anything so I headed into the bar, had a drink, fell asleep, bartender woke me up, told me to go across the border to the hotel beings this one was closed. I went out and didn't want to go over there, the car seemed to be in one piece, I went over there and started the engine up, no heat because the car wasn't moving, I guess, or something, so I guess I wiped the car off and went over to the hotel then decided to go to sleep in the chair when I couldn't get a room and then decided that I'd better get rid of the gun - I was going to stay there overnight, anybody could come in and grab me - didn't want to have the gun on me, that's for sure so I just went outside and I couldn't see anything but crawled around some rocks there and lifted up a rock, oh, I wiped all the bullets off first, one by one, and took them all out of the bag and wiped them off one by one, poured all the bullets under the rock and took the gun apart and wiped it all down and everything with a handkerchief, in fact I guess you could take the handkerchief you could find the grease and oil or something black on it from wiping all the gun, the gun and all the bullets, the extra magazine and then when I wiped all the bullets in the magazine, I put 'em back in but I didn't put a shell in the chamber 'cause I wasn't plannin' on using the gun anymore that's for sure because I was going to bury it so I went out and done that then I know I still had on that holster in the hotel there

Above: Dryman's confession, plaintiff's exhibit no. 5, January 6, 1953. *Courtesy of Toole County Clerk of Court.*

Opposite: *From the* Shelby Promoter and Tribune of Shelby, *April 12, 1951.*

Volume 43 Number 46 Shelby, Toole County Monta

Pellett's Killer Confesses

Frank Dryman, alias Frank Valentine, about 22 years old of Vallejo, California, confessed to the brutal slaying of Four Corner restaurant owner, Clarence E. Pellett, Tuesday night before County Attorney John C. Hoyt, Chief of Police R. F. "Smokey" Denison, Sheriff C. O. Dunstall, and Cedor B. Aronow, Shelby lawyer.

A hearing of further testimony and the possible passing of a sentence against the young killer will be conducted this afternoon at 2 in district court, Judge R. M. Hattersley, presiding.

Dryman pleaded guilty to a first degree murder charge Wednesday afternoon after six days of diligent questioning and investigation by Toole county authorities.

"He began to crack a little Monday morning," Shelby Chief of Police Denison said yesterday. Denison and Sheriff Dunstall were highly praised for their detailed work by County Attorney Hoyt.

Dryman led Hoyt, Denison, and Cut Bank Chief of Police Don Toay to the hidden .45 revolver and cache of ammunition at Coutts Monday afternoon. They also found the shoulder holster atop a telephone booth in the Coutts hotel.

All finger prints had been wiped off the revolver, bullets and door handles by Dryman, but Denison discovered prints on the lower part of the deceased's Plymouth sedan. Plaster paris casts of wheel tracks discovered in a field near Four Corners were made by Denison and proved of value in the investigation.

Pellett's bullet-ridden body was found Thursday night, of last week, near his restaurant. The body of the 59-year-old man had seven bullet wounds, and eight empty .45-calibre cartridge cases were found nearby.

The California hitch-hiker was arrested Thursday night north of Lethbridge, Alberta, by Royal Canadian Mounted Police and turned over to Toole county authorities.

The full confession of the slaying, events leading up to it, and Dryman's actions until apprehended by Canadian mounties is published herewith:

I guess I got in the car at Shelby. He started asking me questions, he didn't tell me where he was going. I guess neither one of us told where we was going until we got out to Four Corners, I guess, and he says this is where I stop, and I guess I pulled the gun, told him to keep going, turn off on the first side road out a ways, so he turned off the side road, first he was saying this and then he was saying that, don't do this, don't do that, I guess and we just driving until I guess we thought we were far enough off the road and I told him to get out of the car and he was begging for mercy, I guess. A man would be in that condition and I guess I was talking

CLARENCE PELLETT
Victim

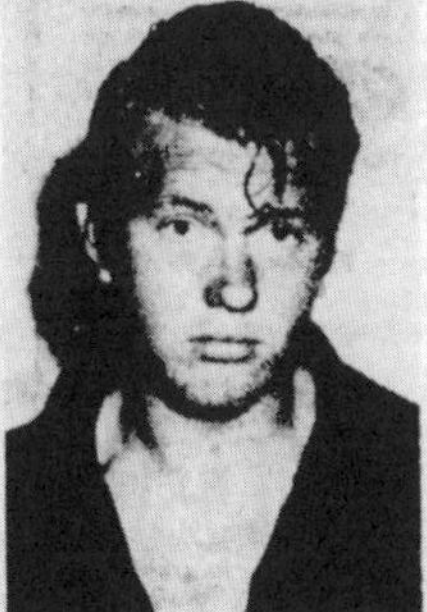

(Photo by Ted Jones)
FRANK DRYMAN
Murderer

P. J. Shea Named Country Club Prexy

Group Discusses Plans for Improvements

P. J. Shea was elected president of the Shelby Country club at the annual meeting of unit holders held last Friday.

Shea replaces Tom Gossack who served during the past year.

Principal business at the meeting, aside from the election, was a thorough discussion of building improvements contemplated for

That damned fool kid was so keyed up he didn't notice the parking brake was on. No wonder the car lugged; I'm surprise it didn't burn up."

Hoyt called Eva, his legal secretary. "I have ten disks of Dryman's confession."

"You got a confession! Congratulations! I'll transcribe it, it'll be on your desk first thing in the morning."

On Wednesday, April 11, 1951, Hoyt and Aronow met Dunstall at the Toole County jail. Dryman, seated at the desk, had just finished a steak and eggs breakfast. Pushing the dirty dishes aside, Hoyt set the typed transcript in front of Dryman. Before Dryman had a chance to read it, both lawyers again advised the teen of his rights. Dryman nodded. Following his finger, he read the copy line by line. In minutes, he was finished. He handed it back to Hoyt, who handed him a pen.

Aronow said, "You don't have to sign if you don't want."

Hoyt reiterated, "You will be in prison for the rest of your life. You could hang."

Dryman nodded. As he was signing, he said, "When I took apart the gun and wiped down all the pieces so there wouldn't be any fingerprints, I figured that was smart. I guess I should have thrown that handkerchief away. I guess a guy can't think of everything."

Sheriff C.O. Dunstall, Shelby Chief of Police R.F. Denison and attorney C.B. Aronow signed the document as witnesses. Hoyt walked the signed confession up the hill to the office of the Toole County clerk of court, Bernice D. Lutz, in the courthouse. Earlier, Eva had dropped off a copy of the transcript. Lutz remarked, "I see there were no changes from this morning."

Hoyt said, "No, that is his statement. I am hereby notifying Judge Hattersley that we have a notarized signed confession and that I am charging Frank R. Dryman with the crime of murder. I am requesting an information filing. Will you inform the judge?"

"Right away," Lutz answered. "I called him first thing this morning; he's aware of the confession."

An hour later, Lutz called Hoyt. "Mr. Hoyt, the judge has granted the information filing and will hold an arraignment hearing today at 2:00 p.m."

"I will be ready," Hoyt replied.

Chapter 7

THE SENTENCING

Few noticed Deputy Stromme as he led the handcuffed Frank Robert Dryman into the alley behind the jail at one thirty in the afternoon on April 11.

The courtroom was nearly empty when the bailiff called the arraignment of the defendant in criminal case 528 to order at precisely 2:00 p.m. Judge R.M. Hattersley presided. On the bench since 1929, he was considered a student of the law. The sixty-eight-year-old was born in Ohio but had called Conrad, Montana, a small town twenty-eight miles south of Shelby, home since 1909.

Hoyt presented the court with the document that charged Frank R. Dryman, also known as Frank R. Valentine, with murdering Clarence Pellett. After the citation was read into the record, Hattersley addressed the defendant.

"Your true name is Frank R. Dryman?"

"Yes, sir."

"You sometimes use the alias of Frank R. Valentine?"

"Yes, sir."

"Have you an attorney to represent you?"

"No, sir," Dryman said.

"Do you wish one?"

"No, sir."

The judge questioned Dryman closely about his decision to decline legal representation, but Dryman insisted that he did not want a lawyer. The judge then asked Dryman if he understood that he was being charged with murder and that the penalty was either life imprisonment or death. Dryman said he did.

The judge made sure that Dryman had a copy of the charges against him and then told him he could wait two days to enter a plea or make one immediately. Dryman said he was ready to enter his plea.

The judge again advised Dryman of the consequences of his plea and asked if he had been made any promises and whether he was in full possession of his faculties. Dryman's answer to both questions was, "Yes, sir."

The judge asked Dryman what his plea was. Dryman answered, "Guilty as charged, sir."

Despite Dryman's assurances, the judge was not satisfied. He decided he wanted to review the evidence and to hear from the witnesses in person. He also stated he was going to appoint a lawyer to represent Dryman regardless of his insistence that he didn't want counsel. He adjourned the proceedings until the next day at 2:00 p.m.

Top: Judge Hattersley twice sentenced Dryman to "hang by the neck until dead." *Courtesy of Toole County Clerk of Court.*

Bottom: William Black, Dryman's public defender in 1951. *Courtesy of Toole County Clerk of Court.*

By then, it was five o'clock. Clerk of Court Lutz phoned local attorney William Black at home. Seventy-three, a longtime resident of the Hi-Line, Black was a probate attorney with limited criminal experience.

"You have heard of the murder of Mr. Pellett?" Lutz asked.

Black replied, "Of course. Who hasn't?"

"Judge Hattersley would like you to represent the accused, Frank Dryman, in tomorrow's hearing."

Startled, Black said, "Me? Tomorrow?"

"Yes, at 2:00 p.m.," Lutz affirmed. "You are needed!"

"I'm in the middle of a considerable estate and preparing probate," Black told her.

"The judge has appointed you," Lutz said.

"Guess I can't argue with that."

The next morning, Black met with Dryman at the Toole County jail. Dryman wasn't interested in talking about his defense, so Black left before noon.

Word of the hearing spread across the Hi-Line like a chinook wind. Shelby businesses again shut their doors. Cars lined the streets from the bowling alley to the hospital. Long before the hearing began, the courtroom was overflowing. The crowd spilled out into the hallways, down the stairs and out the main entrance. People rotated, and whether they were sitting or standing, their places were immediately taken. High school students sat cross-legged on the floor below the judge's bench.

At 2:00 p.m., Judge Hattersley gaveled the court to order. He summarized the previous day's proceedings and then allowed Dryman to enter his plea. He told Dryman that he was willing to postpone the hearing, but W.M. Black, representing Dryman, told the judge the defense was prepared to proceed. Wearing a new dark green shirt, green fatigue pants and black jackboots, Dryman slouched at the defense table, uninterested.

Hattersley cited legal precedent for the day's bench trial. Then Toole County Attorney John C. Hoyt entered into evidence the possessions Dryman had directed him and the other two officers in Coutts, Alberta: sunglasses, a leather shoulder holster and the items found buried behind the Sunshine Motel, namely an M1911 Colt .45 pistol, serial number 250666; two loaded clips; and fifty-eight loose rounds of ammunition.

Hoyt then read Dryman's confession into the record. He finished his testimony by telling the courtroom that Dryman drove Pellett's car to Sweetgrass, abandoned it and walked across the border in the dark. Then the state called Toole County Coroner Dr. Stephen Adaskavich to testify.

Adaskavich told the court, "Mr. Pellett had been shot seven times. Death was due to injuries produced by the bullets tearing through the victim's flesh that caused a massive loss of blood. He didn't die instantly; his heart was still pumping for several minutes, as evidenced by the blood-soaked ground around where the body was found. The course of each of the bullets was from behind."

At three o'clock, Judge Hattersley called a fifteen-minute recess. After days of rumors and speculation, those in the gallery had heard firsthand about the brutality visited on their friend. Throughout the recess, the 150 people there sat in silence.

When court reconvened at three fifteen, Sheriff Dunstall took the stand. He testified that the scene of the murder was a sheep pasture and that Pellett

The gun Dryman used to murder Clarence C. Pellett. *Author's collection.*

was found face down in the dirt with bullet holes in his back and the ground around him.

Smokey was next to testify. The courtroom listened intently as he recounted digging four slugs out of the dirt.

Cedor Aronow was the state's last witness. He testified that Dryman told him he'd liked guns all his life. Dryman said he had carried a gun as long as he could remember because of how it made him feel.

Hoyt finished the state's case by introducing an affidavit from one Siegfried Sunbee of Reno, Nevada, stating Dryman had purchased a .45 army automatic pistol in Reno on March 31 and was seen leaving the city with it. With that, the state rested.

The court asked for testimony on behalf of the defendant. Attorney Black replied, "Your Honor, the defendant has no witnesses to call or evidence to introduce....The defense rests."

At 4:16 p.m., after two hours and thirteen minutes of testimony, the judge asked the defendant to rise to receive his sentence. Only then did the sullen, sandy-haired transient show signs of fear.

Noticeably nervous for the first time in his twenty-three years on the bench, Judge Hattersley, in a scarcely audible voice, uttered the words, "Frank R.

EXTRA

The Shelby Promoter

and Tribune of Shelby

Frank Dryman To Hang

A Packed court room of Toole county citizens heard Judge R. M. Hattersley, Conrad, sentence Frank R. Dryman, alias Frank K. Valentine, "to be hanged until dead" within tne next fifty days. The execution will take place at an undisclosed place in Toole county on June 1.

The unemotional Dryman, cold blooded killer of Clarence C. Pellett, Four Corners cafe operator, Wednesday, April 4, did not make any attempt to alter his plea of guilty during the 2 hours and fifteen minutes of testimony.

Ten witnesses were questioned, some several times, by County Attorney John C. Hoyt. Hoyt himself took the stand on different occasions to bring out details in the brutal slaying.

Dryman, hitch-hiking out of Shelby when picked up by Pellett near the 49'er Drive In, pleaded guilty to a first degree murder charge Wednesday afternoon after six days of diligent interrogation by Hoyt, Sheriff C. O. Dunstall, and Shelby Chief of Police R. F. "Smokey" Denison.

Dryman led Hoyt, Denison, and Cut Bank Chief of Police Don Toay to the hidden 45 revolver and a large cache of ammunition near Coutts Monday afternoon.

Dryman took eight shots at Pellett when the begging Four Corners oilman attempted to run away from the angry hitch-hiker. He missed the first time, then hit Pellett twice, and finally pumped four more shots into tne body before leaving the scene in Pellett's green 1951 Plymouth sedan.

Dr. Stephen Adaskavich testified in performing the autoposy that all the bullets entered from the back side. Six of the seven bullet wounds were fatal, the physician said. Hoyt then introduced two bullets which Adaskavich said he extracted from the dead man's body.

Cedor Aronow, Shelby lawyer, was called to the stand as the state's last witness and told of talking to the youthful killer. He said that Dryman had told him that he liked guns and that he carried a gun with him because of his fondness for revolvers.

Hoyt, in one of his appearances on the witness stand, told how Dryman had purchased the 45 army automatic pistol in Reno, Nevada on March 31, 1951.

First Death Sentence By Kindly Judge

Never before in 23 years on the bench had Judge R. M. Hattersley passed a death sentence. The kind, gray haired, soft spoken gentleman was noticeably nervous to the spectators as he passed the hanging sentence on Frank Dryman.

At 4:16 p. m., Judge Hattersley, in a scarcely audible voice, sentenced the 19-year old slayer to be "hanged by the neck until dead.

As far as is known, the hanging June 1, will be the first held in Toole county during modern times. Not in the 39 years that the Shelby Promoter has served this county has such a sentence taken place.

County officials were undecided following the sentencing whether to keep Dryman in custody at the Toole county jail or remove him to the state penitentiary at Deer Lodge.

SENTENCES

JUDGE R. M. HATTERSLEY

KILLER

FRANK DRYMAN

Hangs In Toole County June 1

Court Room Packed

People began milling into the Toole county District Court room about a half hour before the testimony which got underway at 2 p. m. By 1:55, all seats were taken and there was standing room only.

Many people couldn't stay for the 2 hour, 15 minute procedure and left intermittently with many taking their places, sitting or standing.

At 3 p. m., Judge Hattersley called a fifteen minute recess, which came as a welcome to the quiet crowd.

Many high school students took seats on the floor for the hearing.

Cars were lined from the bowling alley to the hospital, a distance of about a block and a half and were packed in every available spot around the court house.

Inside, spectators were quiet, until the passing of the sentence, when they rapidly filed out of the court room to gather and talk in groups in muted or excited tones, depending on their reactions.

FOR COMPLETE DETAILS SEE NEXT WEEK'S PROMOTER

JUSTICE IS DONE

In one brief week a killer has been tracked down and captured, a confession and complete evidence obtained, and sentence of death pronounced.

It was almost like the swift and terrible justice of the old Vigilante Days except this was within the formality of the law, with the prisoner being accorded council and also full access to a jury trial or change of venue—if he had asked for it. But he did not. He must have pre-judged in his own heart the black guilt in which he perpetrated the most dastardly deed in the history of Toole county. Either that, or as it appeared, he was so steeped in criminal tendancies that nothing could appeal to his warped and stony mind.

Killer Had Been In Trouble Before

Frank Dryman, alias Frank Valentine, was sentenced to juvenile court in his hometown, Hawthorne, Nevada at the age of 16 for robbing a liquor store, according to Mrs. C. J. Sharp, Hawthorne, Nevada, a sister of the deceased.

Mrs. Sharp was a neighbor of Dryman's at the time and had befriended him on many occasions, so much so, that she and other friends appeared in juvenile court to clear the sentence, that he might enter service.

It is understood that the ex-Nevadan was given an undesirable discharge, and while in the service his family moved to Vallejo, California.

Upon arrival in Shelby, Sunday, April 8, Mrs. Sharp went to the Toole county jail to identify a picture and Dryman as one and the same person. He denied knowing her, but admitted knowing her two sons, and then called them by name.

It's bitterly ironical that the slayer was a former neighbor and friend of Mrs. C. J. Sharp, a kind woman who was his friend on many troublesome occasions.

Dryman Unemotional

The 19 year old Dryman, with a Valentine alias, sat very still and unemotional throughout the proceedings. Seldom did he make any sort of a body motion, but once in awhile would whisper or nod his head to his appointed council, William Black.

Dressed in a dark green shirt, with light green fatigue pants, and black shoes, the tousle haired youth sat solemenly in his chair until told to arise before Judge Hattersley to receive his sentence.

Only then, did he began to show signs of fear, but he was apparently unshaken at the hanging sentence as he left the courtroom heavily guarded in handcuffs by Toole county deputies.

One of the 2,500 handbills the *Shelby Promoter* printed and circulated on the Hi-Line on April 12, 1951, the same evening Judge Hattersley sentenced Dryman to hang. *Compliments of the* Shelby Promoter.

Dryman, you are hereby sentenced to hang by the neck until dead. I direct the sheriff of Toole County to find some convenient place to carry out the warrant of execution in fifty days, on June 1."

Dryman was handcuffed. As Deputy Stromme and Officer W. Johnson hustled him from the courtroom, he shouted, "My hanging will be a good show for you all."

Speaking to reporters on the courthouse steps, Sheriff Dunstall said, "Dryman was cocky and wanted to be a big shot like 'Bad Man' Bill Cook. His Hollywood haircut proved to be the telltale factor when Dryman was apprehended in Canada."

Within hours, the *Shelby Promoter* printed 2,500 copies of a single-page report with "EXTRA" splashed in big red letters across the top. For days, paperboys hawked copies of it at trains arriving at the Shelby depot, on Main Street, at the Capital Café and at the Corner Barber Shop.

Sitting on the bunk in his cell, with impeccable penmanship, Dryman wrote:

> *Dear Mother & Dad,*
> *I really don't know how to begin this letter because I shall never write or see you again. I am in gail* [sic] *in Shelby, Montana, the reason; "Murder." I killed a man & now I must pay my debt to society....*
> *Goodbye, Love, as always,*
> *Frank*

Seven weeks till the execution, Toole County officials were concerned that they might not be able to prevent a lynching. To give the Hi-Line confidence that the sentence would indeed be carried out, Dunstall announced that he was calling around the state to find Montana's Galloping Gallows. Built in 1920, this scaffold could be disassembled, moved and reassembled. The gallows was last used on September 10, 1943, to hang a twenty-five-year-old Black man, Philip J. "Slim" Coleman, who was sentenced to hang after bludgeoning and stabbing Carl and Roslyn Pearson to death in Lothrop, Montana. The day he met his maker, he confessed to twenty-three other murders.

Dunstall tracked down the gallows 225 miles away in Missoula, Montana, where its pieces were stored in the basement of the county courthouse. Dunstall called Missoula County Sheriff R.D. MacLean and asked if Toole County might borrow the scaffold.

"You bet you can," MacLean replied. "I'd be happy to pull the trap door lever myself."

Charlie arranged for a local Shelby family, the Irwins, to pick up the equipment. The sheriff appeared before the Shelby City Council seeking permission to use the civic center building for the execution. The building was the only place in town large enough to accommodate twelve reputable citizens, the coroner, a physician and the sheriff to witness the hanging, as required by law. Fearing that the building would forever be branded as the site where a hanging had occurred, the newly elected city councilmen tabled the sheriff's request, so Dunstall drove north to Tom Peg's farm, about a mile outside of Shelby. Peg had a barn on a hill overlooking the town.

"Tom, the city council won't allow the hanging at the civic center," Dunstall told him. "Any chance we can use your place?"

"Clarence was a good man," Tom said. "I'm happy to oblige."

From the hill plus the thirteen steps of the gallows, Dryman's last vision on this Earth would be the spot where Clarence offered him a ride.

The barn had room for a much larger crowd than that required by law. At his desk, Dunstall made a list of invitees. The next day, he called a print shop in Great Falls and ordered fifty engraved invitations. However, it was an open secret that invited or not, the people of the Hi-Line were determined to attend the hanging.

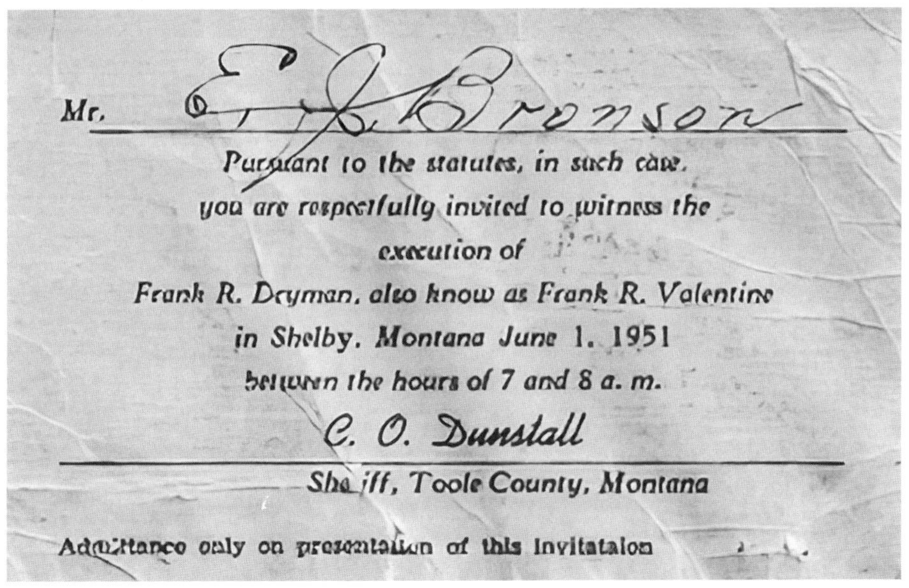

Mr. E. J. Bronson

Pursuant to the statutes, in such case,
you are respectfully invited to witness the
execution of
Frank R. Dryman, also know as Frank R. Valentine
in Shelby, Montana June 1, 1951
between the hours of 7 and 8 a. m.

C. O. Dunstall

Sheriff, Toole County, Montana

Admittance only on presentation of this Invitataion

An invitation to Dryman's June 1, 1951 hanging. *Author's collection, courtesy of E.J. Bronson.*

I guess I got in the car at Shelby. He started asking me questions, he didn't tell me where he was going. I guess neither one of us told where we was going until we got out to Four Corners, I guess, and he says this is where I stop, and I guess I pulled the gun, told him to keep going, turn off on the first side road out a ways, so he turned off the side road, first he was saying this and then he was saying that, don't do this, don't do that, I guess and we just driving until I guess we thought we were far enough off the road and I told him to get out of the car and he was begging for mercy, I guess. A man would be in that condition and I guess I was talking to him about killing him or something, telling him I was going to kill him and he kept getting worse and worse, I guess, and when I raised the gun he started running and I started shooting and then I guess I was going after him when I was shooting at him. When he finally fell over, I probably went up and emptied the gun into him. Went back to the car, put in another magazine, slammed it shut, pulled out of there back up the same road—I tried to find the same road, went into Sweetgrass, parked it there by the garage, got out, tried to catch a ride, got back in—or couldn't catch a ride, was freezing to death, got back to the car, decided to take it down to Cut Bank and not across the border, I was going to go down that road to Cut Bank. Something went wrong with the car, wouldn't run, something, I don't know what it was on the brake, or something, anyhow it's lugging the back wheels down and I could smell something burning so I managed to turn it back up and to about the same place anyhow, I got it on the first side road there and something was really burning. I jumped out of the car and looked under and there was flames or sparks from underneath and so I thought the car was going to burn and I took off out of there back down to

Above and opposite: Dryman's confession on the front page of the newspaper. *From the* Shelby Promoter, *April 12, 1951.*

After the *Shelby Promoter* published Dryman's complete confession on its front page, newspapers across the Treasure State portrayed Pellett's murder as one of the most significant cases in Montana history. Excerpts of the confession were carried not only across the front pages of Montana newspapers but also by papers of bordering states and Canadian provinces.

front of the hotel. I got back down in front of the hotel, waited around awhile and the car never caught afire or anything so I headed into the bar had a drink, fell asleep, bartender woke me up, told me to go across the border to the hotel beings this one was closed. I went out and didn't want to go over there, the car seemed to be in one piece, I went over there and started the engine up, no heat because the car wasn't moving, I guess, or something, so I guess I wiped the car off and went over to the hotel then decided to go to sleep in the chair when I couldn't get a room and then decided I'd better get rid of the gun—I was going to stay there overnight, anybody could come in and grab me—didn't want to have the gun on me, that's for sure so I just went outside and I couldn't see anything but crawled around some rocks there and lifted up a rock, oh, I wiped all the bullets off first, one by one, and took them all out of the bag and wiped them off one by one, poured all the bullets under the rock and took the gun apart and wiped it all down and everything with a handkerchief, in fact I guess you could take the handkerchief you could find the grease and oil or something black on it from wiping all the gun, the gun and all the bullets, the extra magazine and then when I wiped all the bullets in the magazine, I put 'em back in but I didn't put a shell in the chamber 'cause I wasn't planning on using the gun any more that's for sure because I was going to bury it so I went out and done that then I know I still had on that holster in the hotel there with all the lights, anybody could come into the lobby there so I didn't dare take off my coat, there was no other place to go, too cold outside to take off a coat so I just took my knife and cut the holster off, threw it up on the telephone booth there and I still had this other magazine in my pocket and I wiped it off and threw it up there. I don't know what in the heck made me throw my glasses up there but I threw that up there too. Then I went in, went to sleep and the bus driver woke me up and I got aboard the bus and went into Lethbridge, spent what money I had, then hitchhiked out of there, the Mounties picked me up, brought me back, that's the end of it.

So far, Dunstall had managed to keep a lid on the high feelings swirling around this cold-blooded murder. But the sheriff knew his community. Serious discontent was simmering just below the surface. That spring, families strolled up and down the alley behind the jail, hoping to sneak a peek at a real live murderer.

As the day of the hanging approached, excitement built. Old-timers recollected that not since Shelby hosted a world heavyweight boxing championship on July 4, 1923, had the town been so energized. The challenger, Tommy Gibbins, was an unknown, but defending champ Jack Dempsey was as famous as Babe Ruth. The fight put Shelby on the map. With the buzz surrounding the hanging, the little rural community was back in the limelight.

In Shelby, at Wilson's Grocery, the 49er Drive In and the Capital Café, the usual topics of conversation—the price of a bushel of wheat, oil production and the weather—took a back seat to the upcoming hanging.

Dunstall knew any delay of the execution could be the spark that ignited a powder keg of emotion. But the gallows was on the way, Tom Peg's was the site and invitations were in the mail. For the time being, he was satisfied that the people of the Hi-Line were confident swift justice would be done.

Chapter 8

THE PEOPLE'S VOICE

It was not so 170 miles south in Helena, Montana's capital. When news of the death sentence reached husband and wife Harry and Gretchen Billings, coeditors of *The People's Voice* newspaper, they were alarmed that a friendless teenaged boy alone in a "strange" land was being railroaded by a bloodthirsty mob set on vengeance.

Founded in 1939 by prominent left-wing Montana politicians, *The People's Voice* was financed by Montana labor leaders and farm co-ops that sought to counter the political dominance of the Montana Power and Anaconda Copper Mining Companies. Dubbed the Montana Twins, these two companies controlled most of the state's newspapers and, with their army of lobbyists, wielded substantial influence over the Montana legislature.

The Billingses, coeditors of this weekly publication since 1948, were dedicated to advancing progressive causes. Located across the street from the state capitol building, the crusading journalists considered themselves the watchdogs of state government, the mouthpiece for those who had no voice, advocates for the disenfranchised little guy. Others characterized the paper as a "left-wing journal of discontent which sets itself up in judgment as to who are the friends and foes of the people." Among the causes they promoted were labor unions, worker's compensation, national health insurance, Indian rights and mental health. But their particular passion was their vehement opposition to the death penalty.

Gretchen G. Billings was born in 1914 in Whitefish, Montana, but she was raised in Seattle. Harry, a year older, was born, raised and educated in Montana. He and Gretchen married in 1933 and soon welcomed three sons, John, Mike and Leon.

Gretchen G. Billings. *Courtesy of Montana Newspaper Hall of Fame.*

Self-avowed socialists, the Billingses were rumored to sympathize with the American Communist Party. Their Helena home was a hub of liberal thought in Montana. For the price of a bottle of whiskey and the promise of lively political debate, Harry and Gretchen opened their home and hospitality to "fellow travelers" roaming the Treasure State.

During the 1950s, the Cold War's Red Scare was sweeping the nation. Slogans such as "Better dead than Red" and "There's a Red under every bed" bolstered the belief that communist agents were secretly living in large and small towns, pitting regular Americans against progressives. Montana was not immune. The Billingses had a reputation for an uncompromising journalistic style that was at times intentionally contentious, earning the paper the nicknames "commie-rag" and "the Red Sheet."

The family was the target of frequent vitriolic attacks and anonymous phone calls. Their boys were often bloodied in schoolyard fights. After they found a bullet hole in their front window, they started closing the living room drapes at sunset. But even the threat of physical violence didn't deter them from their zeal to effect social change.

As one of the first female reporters of the era, Gretchen often felt like a "skunk at a picnic." On one occasion, a company lobbyist took a swing at her, despite her sex. Later, she mused, "I did what came naturally. I ducked."

But they weren't about to duck the Dryman case. It was the perfect vehicle to expose the failings of state-sanctioned execution and rural Montana's frontier justice. Politically well-connected Gretchen reached out to a colorful Montana Democrat, Willard Fraser. Known as the "Montana fireball," he had run for elected office numerous times with mixed results. He and Gretchen put their heads together and concocted a list of candidates for a brain trust to prevent this hanging.

Foremost on that list was attorney Dr. Myron Tripp, a political kindred spirit who also allegedly had Communist leanings. A representative in the state legislature for the Great Falls area, he had introduced an unsuccessful bill to abolish Montana's death penalty. Thus, he was the foremost expert on the politics associated with Montana's capital punishment law.

On April 17, Gretchen wrote to Tripp, "There is this young fellow in Shelby who committed a terrible murder." She asked for his ongoing consultation in a fight to save the youth from the gallows. Tripp was only too happy to join in. He advised her to write to Cedor B. Aronow: "I have worked with him in the legislature. He always has his ear to the ground up on the Hi-Line. If anybody can give you the straight dope, he can."

Gretchen wrote to Aronow, asking about the circumstances surrounding the "scheduled hanging of Frank Dryman" and suggesting that perhaps the boy was mentally deranged. She added, "There seems to be a feeling among the lawyers with whom I have talked that all the processes available by law have not been allowed him….I am sickened by the greatness of his crime….I could chuck this matter in the back of my mind…but after June 1st, if this boy is hanged, I am wondering how I am going to feel."

On April 20, Aronow informed Gretchen that Toole County Attorney John C. Hoyt had been his law partner since the previous August, and consequently, he was not only familiar with the facts of the case but was also well-versed in criminal case law and courtroom procedures. Knowing that Gretchen was relying solely on secondhand information, Aronow shared his eyewitness account.

"My observation of him [Dryman] and my conversation with him, I do not think he is deranged, but a very clever boy," Aronow told Gretchen. "I was present when Dryman admitted to the murder. When the weight of the evidence was shown to him…he confessed to the whole crime."

Aronow affirmed that the judge had "leaned over backwards" to warn Dryman of the gravity of his situation, cautioned him no less than three times to allow an attorney to help him and apprised him of the consequences of his guilty plea. "Dryman's rights were fully and amply protected in every respect and was not railroaded in any sense of the word."

Familiar with the reputation of *The People's Voice*, Aronow added, "This is no case of big interest pressing some weak and fallen individual. The man Dryman killed was just a poor working man merely getting along."

He reminded Gretchen that in Montana, a life sentence is, on average, only twelve to thirteen years. "That would make Dryman in his mid-thirties at his release, ready to kill again. In America people must learn to curb their impulses. We should be praising the officials of Toole County for the skillful manner [in which] they solved this brutal killing, rather than wasting time on this murderer."

THE PEOPLE'S VOICE
In the Shadow of the State Capitol Building
MONTANA'S ONLY STATEWIDE INDEPENDENT NEWSPAPER
Vol. XII—No. 21 HELENA, MONTANA, APRIL 27, 1951 Price 5c Per Copy

Shall Montana Countenance . . .

'Swift Vigilante-like Justice'?

By GRETCHEN G. BILLINGS

FRANK R. DRYMAN murdered a man in cold blood. He murdered a man who befriended him. Clarence Pellet was a poor man and all who knew him say he was a good man. It was a brutal, heinous crime which Frank Dryman committed, and he must answer to society for his crime.

JUDGE R. M. HATTERSLY has said Frank Dryman must hang.

For two weeks I have been struggling with mixed emotions over this sentence of death. I do not believe in capital punishment. I do not believe Frank Dryman should have murdered Clarence Pellett. I do not believe the State of Montana should murder Frank Dryman.

Shortly after the body of Clarence Pellet was found Dryman was apprehended. Law enforcement agencies worked diligently and efficiently in their search and final capture of the murderer. Public emotions were at a high pitch.

Then followed six days of questioning by the sheriff. chief of police, county attorney and his law partner. Dryman confessed on the sixth day. On the seventh day, in the afternoon, after refusing counsel, he pleaded guilty before the district judge. Local counsel was appointed and after a little more than two hours of presentation of the State's case he was sentenced to hang.

However, the people of Montana sanction capital punishment, and thus the killing of a man is made legal by the laws of this state. A controversy on the merits or demerits of capital punishment can not prevent the death of this boy. We must function upon the premise that it is legal to decree that we take the life of another and are therefore absolved of all consequences. So be it.

There I would like to be able to stop. There I would like to be able to draw an "iron curtain" over my mind.

But, no matter what I am doing, my mind is not free from the gruesome spectacle of man, sanctioned by law, taking a boy, on June first and hanging him by the neck till he is dead.

Why was such a harsh sentence imposed in this case?

Frank R. Dryman is 19. His 20th birthday would be the fourth of June

The SHELBY PROMOTER, in a red ink EXTRA after the sentencing, stated "It was almost like the swift and terrible justice of the old Vigilante Days except this was within the formality of the law, with the prisoner being accorded counsel and also full access to a jury trial or change of venue if he had asked for it. But he did not . . ."

Frank Dryman, after having been questioned for six days, in a strange country, an attitude of "lynch" prevailing, penniless and without friends or relatives to give him advice, has been allowed to literally commit suicide.

Within our system of government we have set up safeguards We have said that all accused men shall have access to full consideration under this system. One of our most important safeguards is trial by jury. Trial by jury means 12 men and a judge shall decide how a man shall pay for his crime.

Adequate legal assistance should be a prerequisite to the pronouncement of the death penalty. Adequate legal assistance is possible only when sufficient time is allowed for proper preparation and examination. Even the most able attorney would be helpless to assist in circumstances so frought with emotionalism and without proper time for preparation.

I can not free myself from the feeling that there is a moral responsibility upon us to see that our agents, when they decree that we kill someone, make certain that every safeguard has been afforded.

The sheriff apprehended and arrested Frank Dryman "in the name of the State of Montana." The county attorney prosecuted Frank Dryman "in the name of the State of Montana." The judge sentenced Frank Dryman to hang "in the name of the State of Montana." And the hand that springs the final trap will be acting "in the name of the State of Montana."

Who is "the State of Montana?"

These agents of ours are men to whom life has been good; men who have resisted the temptations of sin; men who have, by the grace of God found their feet embedded in the rock and not in the clay; men who must hope "law" written by men will supersede basic Christian tenets.

One man, albeit a judge, has decreed Dryman must die. To cooly appraising legal minds this is a responsibility no man should be willing to accept. This is a responsibility no man has a right to assume.

Are we the powerful State of Montana with the confessed murderer at our mercy, to be a party to an act as emotionally unstable as the one committed by Frank Dryman?

* * *

Frank Dryman gave Clarence Pellett no chance. He shot him in cold blood.

WHY?

Is there no one who is interested in finding out the answer to that question? Frank Dryman is not a citizen of Montana; he is penniless; he has no friends; where is his family?

It matters little, after all—June first he will be dead. The life taken from Clarence Pellett will have been avenged, and the agents of the State of Montana, protected by law, will have taken the life of 19-year old Frank Dryman. Swift, Vigilante-like "justice" under the formality of the law, and the judgment of one man will have been done.

This page and opposite: Billings's front-page editorial. *From* The People's Voice, *April 27, 1951.*

On April 23, Gretchen replied, "I appreciate the completeness, candor, and sincerity of your reply....I do not believe in capital punishment....To have this boy hang without a word of protest would find me without the courage to speak what is deep within me." She did, however, acknowledge, "This boy must not be allowed the chance to again menace society."

From the day the death sentence was handed down, lawyer Black visited his client three to four times a week. On Sundays, he'd see him twice.

Dryman had finally decided to become an active participant in his defense. On one occasion, he told Black: "My discharge papers were taken from me by the sheriff the night I was booked." Black went to the jail and retrieved the papers, on which he found Dryman's military serial number and navy ship number. He wired the U.S. naval hospitals at Bremerton, Washington, and Mare Island, California, for Dryman's service records.

That same day, April 25, Harry Billings drove north from Helena to Shelby to offer Black assistance and get a firsthand look-see. Over the following couple of days, he and the probate attorney hammered out a criminal defense strategy. Black confessed to Harry that though he was trying to "do right by this poor boy, I'm in over my head. Find a qualified trial attorney!"

During his time in Shelby, Harry, for reasons known only to him, saw no need to speak with Dryman.

Back in Helena the next day, Harry asked Gretchen, "Are you interested in taking the lead on this case?"

"Yes! I'll gladly take the lead," Gretchen told him. "I think this could potentially be one of the most enlightening experiences of my life!"

Twenty-four hours later, she fired off her first editorial salvo.

> The People's Voice
> *April 27, 1951*
> *"Shall Montana Countenance 'Swift Vigilante-like Justice'?"*
> *By Gretchen G. Billings*
>
> *Frank R. Dryman murdered a man in cold blood, he gave a man that befriended him, Clarence Pellett, no chance. It was a brutal and heinous crime for which Frank Dryman must answer to society....Judge R.M. Hattersley has said Frank Dryman must hang.*
>
> *For two weeks I have been struggling with mixed emotions over this sentence of death. I do not believe in capital punishment, but the people of Montana have sanctioned capital punishment, and thus the killing of this man is made legal....*

> *I would like to be able to draw an "iron curtain" over my mind but no matter what, my mind is not free from the gruesome spectacle of a man* [a boy of nineteen] *hanging from the neck until dead....*
>
> *The boy is a pitiful pauper, he has no funds for adequate and timely legal representation.*

Gretchen advocated "for the immediate replacement of Dryman's assigned public defender, William Black....Are we, the powerful State of Montana, with the confessed murderer at our mercy, to be a party to an act as emotionally unstable as the one committed by Frank Dryman?"

Judge Hattersley is an "aberrant judge," she wrote, "that has decreed Dryman must die. This is a responsibility no one man has a right to assume.... Swift Vigilante-like 'justice' under the formality of the law and the judgment of one man will have been done."

Chapter 9

THE DEATH PENALTY FIGHT

A line had been drawn in the sand. On one side were urban socialists defending a poor friendless boy, on the other side a rural blue-collar community dispensing swift frontier justice to a blackhearted murderer.

Brawls over capital punishment were not confined to Montana. As the Soviet Iron Curtain came down on the European continent, Cold War anti-Communist tensions in the United States escalated to a fever pitch. In the year 1951, liberals seemed to be losing on all fronts—but especially on the death penalty.

One example was the Rosenbergs. Convicted of passing classified atomic secrets to Russia, Julius and Ethel Rosenberg were sentenced to death on April 5, 1951. In Boise, Idaho, another setback occurred when a double hanging took place on April 13. Sentenced to death for the beating and stabbing death of an elderly grocer during a robbery that netted them twelve dollars, Ernest Walrath (nineteen) and Troy Powell (twenty) were the youngest to be executed in the Gem State.

In his latest update, Black informed Gretchen and Harry that he was working to obtain Valentine's navy records. "There is some question about his mental status. I think we can use them to get his guilty plea removed."

On April 30, Judge Hattersley advised Governor Bonner that "at the direction of his court," Dryman would be examined by three state-appointed mental health experts: Robert J. Spratt, MD, superintendent of Montana's State Mental Hospital in Warm Springs; Winfield S. Wilder, MD, of the

Examine Dryman At Request of Governor

This page and following: From the Shelby Promoter, *May 3, 1951.*

Two psychiatrists and a physiologist examined Frank Dryman, 19-year-old confessed slayer of Clarence Pellett, 59-year-old Four Corners cafe operator, in the county jail Wednesday afternoon for nearly three hours and again last night at the request of Governor John Bonner and District Judge R. M. Hattersley.

A copy of the results will be mailed to Judge Hattersley and Governor Bonner and the decision will rest in their hands.

Examining Dryman were Dr. Robert J. Spratt, superintendent of the state hospital at Warm Springs, Dr. Alice Baslow, head of the Butte mental hygiene clinic, and Dr. Winfield S. Wilder, Great Falls, head of the mental hygiene clinic there. Miss Baslow is a physiologist.

Governor Bonner gave the examination order to Judge Hattersley who was to select three doctors for the investigation. Hattersley was not in Shelby at the time of the interrogation by the three specialists.

Dryman is scheduled to hang June 1 for the Pellett murder, but the sanity examination may bring an alternation in the sentence if the report shows that he is insane.

Under the law of Montana, "If after judgment of death, there is good reason to suppose that the defendant has become insane, the sheriff of the county, with the concurrence of the judge of the court by which the judgment was rendered may summon from the list of jurors selected for the year, a jury of 12 persons to inquire into the supposed insanity, and must give immediate notice thereof to the county attorney of the county."

"The county attorney must attend the inquisition, and may produce witnesses before the jury, for which purpose he may issue process in the same manner as for witnesses, to attend before the grand jury, and disobedience thereto may be punished in like manner as disobedience to process issued by the court.

"If it is found by the inquisition that the defendant is sane, the sheriff must execute the judgment; but if it is found that he is insane, the sheriff must suspend the execution of the judgment until he receives a warrant from the governor or from the judge of the court by which the judgment was rendered directing the execution of the judgment. If the inquisition finds that the defendant is insane, the sheriff must immediately transmit it to the governor, who may, when the defendant becomes sane, issue a warrant appointing a day for the execution of the judgment.

Although County Attorney John Hoyt was out of town on business at the time of the examination and the first part of the week, a statement was released by him as to whom, and the number of people would be required by law to attend the hanging if it is held. Section 94-8016 of Revised Codes of Montana states: "Execution where to take place and who is to be present. A judgment of death must be executed within the walls or yard of a jail, or some convenient private place in the county. The sheriff of the county must be present at the execution, and must invite the presence of a physician, the county attorney of the county, and at least 12 reputable citizens to be selected by him; and he shall, at the request of the defendant, permit such priests or ministers of the gospel, not exceeding two, as the defendant may name, and any persons, relatives or friends, not to exceed five, to be present at the execution, together with such peace officers as he may think expedient, to witness the execution. But no other persons than those mentioned in the section can be present at the excution nor can any persons under age be allowed to witness the same."

It will be three or four days from the completion of the examination before a report will be in the hands of Governor Bonner and Judge Hattersley.

N other persons were present at the time of the examination and each specialist was alone with Dryman during their observation and questioning.

Great Falls Clinic; and Alice Barlow, a "mental hygienist" from Butte. On May 2, at the Toole County Jailhouse, these examinations were split into three-hour sessions, giving each expert several hours for their independent evaluation.

Satisfied that her recent discussions with liberal lawyers had made her fluent in the nuances of the Montana capital penalty statute, Gretchen walked across the street to the state capitol building for a face-to-face appeal to the governor. A fixture in the capitol building, she attracted no attention as she marched straight into his office. Without an appointment, she burst into the chief executive's office and launched into her plea.

"Governor Bonner, I'm here to discuss what is going on in Shelby, the Dryman case. I know the boy's attorney has submitted a plea for executive clemency.

"I'm here to save this poor boy from the gallows. You must consider the disposal of a boy whose whole background is one of great maladjustment. We are waiting for his service records that will show that at seventeen, he was discharged as mentally disabled.

"For weeks, I have been contacting lawyers around the state. I have learned a great deal about procedures in law as they pertain to capital punishment. Many feel not all legal procedures were afforded Dryman."

The governor asked, "Who were the lawyers?"

"I'm not at liberty to divulge names," Gretchen admitted. "Neither Republican nor Democrat would go on the record, but I assure you they are well-respected attorneys. I found that many liberal lawyers have tied their kites to the Democratic bandwagon and see no future in standing on principle in the face of gubernatorial disapproval."

Well acquainted with Gretchen's dogged persistence, Bonner knew it was better not to engage, just listen.

Gretchen railed on, "The law says when Judge Hattersley passed sentence, he was finished with his investigative authority. As such, when the judge ordered a sanity hearing for Frank Dryman, he was entirely without jurisdiction."

Politely, the governor thanked her for her concern. He reminded her that he was the attorney general of Montana before he joined the army, and therefore, she need not remind him of the law.

"I've read your recent articles; your view is abundantly clear. But I must remind you, Montana is a capital punishment state, and Judge Hattersley is an able jurist who followed the law. I'm sure you are aware that he notified me of his court's intention to conduct the mental exams; that was within the law. However, this was such a heinous and senseless crime—maybe this is one issue in which you and I disagree."

John W. Bonner ran for governor several times from 1948 to 1956. He was elected in 1948 but lost in 1954 and 1958. Research suggests that this poster was used in an election later than 1948. *Montana Public Library.*

Gretchen snapped back, "Silly me. It would be good to be able to recognize the strong and admirable qualities of mercy in the man we Democrats elected as governor."

On Monday, May 7, Governor Bonner issued a press release summarizing the reports of the two state-appointed psychiatrists and the psychologist who had examined Frank R. Dryman. The experts had concluded that Dryman "[knows the] difference between right and wrong, understands the nature of the charges against him and is able to act in his own defense. These independent examinations concluded that Dryman

Dryman Sane at Time Of Killing; Denied Clemency

Governor John W. Bonner denied clemency to Frank Dryman, 19-year-old California hitchhiker, who killed Clarence E. Pellett, Four Corners cafe operator, April 4, as a result of a report from two psychiatrists and a psychologist who examined the slayer in the Toole county jail Wednesday, May 2.

Bonner released a statement Monday at which time he said, "The defendant was given every opportunity to defend himself by the court, and that he is sane."

Dryman was sentenced to hang June 1, by District Judge R. M. Hattersley, Conrad, after he pleaded guilty to a murder charge.

Never during the court hearing did the light-haired transient make an attempt to defend himself. He was appointed a counsel by the court after he had continually refused to obtain his own counsel.

A copy of proceedings at the sanity examination, ordered by Judge Hattersley, was sent to the governor, who said he had been asked to commute the sentence.

Bonner ended his statement by saying, "There are no legal extenuating or mitigating circumstances in his favor. The defendant was sentenced by an able jurist, and in light of all the circumstances of the case, I find no reason why I should interfere with the judgment of the court."

Governor Bonner's full statement:

"Some citizens of this state have suggested that I commute the sentence of Frank R. Dryman from hanging to life imprisonment.

"From an investigation of the case, I find that Dryman confessed and plead guilty to murder. Before his pleas he did not want counsel, but after his plea, the court appointed counsel for him and then gave him every opportunity to present evidence or to change his plea. This the defendant refused to do, and after state witnesses were heard in the presence of the defendant and his counsel, the defendant did not desire to introduce any testimony in his behalf. The court then asked the defendant whether he knew of any legal cause why judgment should not be imposed upon him, and he replied he did not. The court then sentenced the defendant to be hanged.

"Recently the court had the defendant examined by two psychiatrists and a psychologist. These persons are highly qualified in their professions, and found that the defendant knows the difference between right and wrong and understands the nature of the charges against him and is able to act in his own defense. The psychiatrists and the psychologist also state after their examination that there is no reason to believe tha, given opportunity, the defendant will not repeat his recent or similar behavior.

"It appears the defendant was given every opportunity to defend himself by the court, and that he is sane. There is no question about the guilt of the defendant or the brutality of his crime. There are no legal exenuating or mitigating circumstances in his favor. The defendant was sentenced by an able jurist, and in light of all the circumstances of the case, I find no reason why I should interfere with the judgment of the court."

From the Shelby Promoter, *May 10, 1951.*

was sane at the time of the brutal killing." Thus, Bonner found "no reason why I should interfere with the judgment of the court."

On May 8, 1951, Willie McGee, a Black man accused of raping a White woman, was executed in Mississippi's traveling electric chair. Although his was the fifty-fourth death sentence carried out in the United States so far that year, this execution hit progressives particularly hard. For the last five years, McGee's legal case had been a cause célèbre for the left.

McGee was first convicted by an all-White jury that deliberated for two and a half minutes. The Mississippi Supreme Court reversed the conviction on the grounds that the atmosphere in the courthouse, which required National Guard troops to maintain order, prevented a fair trial.

McGee's second conviction prompted the Civil Rights Congress (CRC), a Communist-affiliated group, to rush to his defense. Characterizing the death penalty as a reflection of the repulsive racist and corrupt core of capitalism, they mounted a spirited two-pronged defense, part legal battle and part public relations campaign.

The Communist Party Civil Council raised $100,000 and hired celebrated attorney Bella Abzug, who managed, over the ensuing five years, to get McGee six stays of execution, two new trials and two venue changes.

As part of the media prong of the strategy, the *Daily Worker*, a newspaper published by the Communist Party USA, printed a series of anti–death penalty editorials. Concurrently, Rosalee Saffold (a.k.a. Rosalee McGee), a woman picked by the CRC to pose as McGee's wife, crisscrossed the nation pleading for her "husband" to be spared. Although in the United States, the PR campaign's success was limited to the East and West Coasts, the CRC's "Save Willie McGee" crusade gained international support.

Albert Einstein and William Faulkner were among the public figures who took the fight straight to the Oval Office. Not bowing to celebrity or international pressure and dodging "Red taint," President Truman refused to intervene on McGee's behalf.

On May 11, Gretchen Billings published another editorial titled "The Quality of Mercy":

> *Are we going to treat this boy like an unclaimed stray dog—and kill him?… Are you willing to participate in the hanging of a 19-year-old boy* [who] *was tried with "swift vigilante-like justice" and in the name of the State of Montana tie the rope around his neck? Is leading this boy to the gallows going accomplish a gainful purpose?*

HELENA

"The Quality of Mercy . . ."

Among the attributes of God, although they are all equal, mercy shines with even more brilliancy than justice.—CERVANTES

* * *

By GRETCHEN G. BILLINGS

I have learned a great deal about proceedures in law as pertains to Capital Punishment in the past month. I have hounded attorneys and looked at law books.

When Judge Hattersley ordered a sanity hearing for Frank Dryman I found that he was entirely without jurisdiction. The law says when he passed sentence he was finished with his investigatory authority. Why wasn't a sanity hearing called for before sentence? Why wasn't the boy's background investigated before the sentence? The judge then had it within his province to so do. It would have been proper for him to make such an inquiry even though Frank Dryman had no witnesses to offer. Isn't it possible that the court left such an investigation to be undertaken in a subsequent appeal for executive clemency?

When I heard that the Governor had been asked to grant clemency I again brow-beat attorneys into showing me the law. Therefore the Governor's press release on Sunday was a great shock to me. It has left so much to be desired and has left so many unanswered questions.

The press release indicated granting clemency would mean freedom for Frank Dryman. Few but attorneys realize the lack of truth in that implication.

The Governor reviewed the trial proceedings and found them "legally sufficient". He reviewed the state of sanity of Frank Dryman four weeks after the murder. The Governor gave a judicial review of the legality of the trial, which was not asked for or expected in a plea for clemency. Judicial reviews are intended for the Supreme Court. It is not the function of the executive to undertake a judicial review. Executive clemency is the granting of mercy by the Sovereign. The Governor is the executive representative of the Sovereign State. A plea for clemency is a plea to the executive to grant mercy.

Above and opposite: Gretchen Billings's op-ed "The Quality of Mercy." *From* The People's Voice, *May 11, 1951.*

On May 15, Black notified the Billingses that he was preparing a second petition for executive clemency based on the recently acquired service record of Frank R. Valentine. "Valentine was the name Frank used in the navy. Should the petition be accepted, I will ask for Dryman to be committed to the Montana State Mental Hospital in Warm Springs."

That being the case the Governor has completely avoided the intent of the plea which was intended to give him the opportunity to make an inquiry into the facts and circumstances and conditions in the life of the condemned which would determine whether under the existing circumstances the penalty of death was too severe. His press release does not demonstrate that he has given any consideration whatsoever to the elements which constitute a proper basis for effective inquiry.

Governor Bonner can yet assume the responsibility of his office as executive head of this state and hear evidence to determine whether this sentence is too severe. Governor Bonner can yet recommend an inquiry which will go beyond the question of technical sufficiency or insufficiency of the trial of Frank Dryman. Governor Bonner can yet recommend a commutation inquiry to the board of pardons which will allow an opportunity to present evidence that was not available, nor was time taken to find, at the "legal and sufficient" trial.

In the Governor's hands and heart rests not the question of guilt which has already been determined by the court, but the magnificient power of mercy and justice. This power has been given him in the high office he holds, by will of the people and by the grace of God in whose name he took his oath of office.

* * *

Once again I am asking you to think about Frank Dryman. I am asking you if you are willing to participate in the hanging of a 19-year-old boy who was tried with "swift, Vigilante-like 'justice'" with ten witnesses against him and no one to plead his case in a two-hour and fifteen-minute trial. A penniless, friendless boy whose home was in California, a good two-day trip from Shelby (if anyone had been interested in trying to get help to him); a 19-year-old boy who is being allowed to commit suicide because he has nothing in life that makes it worth his living; a 19-year-old boy who sat silently by and let a battery of competent legal authorities, in the name of the State of Montana, securely tie the rope around his neck. A silent, 19-year-old boy, who has never been sure who his father was, who refused to fight for his own life.

If this were your son would you be satisfied with the attempts made by the State of Montana to consider his case?

Are you satisfied that leading this boy to the gallows is going to accomplish a gainful purpose?

Is the State of Montana faced with such an inadequacy of law and such an inadequate prison, that we must kill a 19-year-old because there is no other alternative?

How many mature men do we have in the state penitentiary who have murdered and are serving life sentences because they pleaded "guilty" and were defended for a fee? At 19 life is not as valuable as it becomes with maturity. Must we take the lives of our immature 19-year-olds as examples?

Like a stray dog we are going to treat this boy—no one claims him—kill him.

* * *

After sentence was passed the attorney appointed by the state (and after the boy had pleaded guilty), had a chance to talk with him. He found a story so sad and so pathetic he was moved to ask for clemency from the Governor, who has the power of mercy at his command.

Only a few years ago Clifford Palin, condemned to die at Glendive, was given a commutation when Gov. Sam Ford recommended mercy.

Willie Cooke killed five people at one time, and one at another. A judge of the Federal Court investigated the background of that boy before sentencing and was merciful. Willie Cooke did not die.

But in the case of a 19-year-old, Montana, apparently unable to cope with such a situation says HANG!

Chapter 10

THE "LIFELINE"

From childhood, Frank was preoccupied with guns. He was in his early teens when, he claimed, he found his first two guns: a pistol out in the desert and a rifle he stepped on at the bottom of a lake while swimming with his brothers. The police confiscated the rifle because it had been used in a local murder. Said Frank, "The Valentine boys were on their radar after that."

During Frank's teens, he was always packing, even in school. At age sixteen, he was arrested for armed robbery of a liquor store in Hawthorne, Nevada. When he appeared in circuit court, the judge declared the Valentines unfit parents. The kids were to be removed from their home and sent to a reformatory for juvenile delinquents—all but Frank.

A marine colonel from the nearby Hawthorne Army Depot and neighborhood mothers came to his rescue. The officer asked the judge to remand Frank to an "industrial school" rather than the reformatory if Frank agreed to join the marines on his next birthday. Phyllis Sharp, Clarence Pellett's sister, volunteered to act as his foster parent in the interim.

In lieu of incarceration, Frank was directed to a conservation team surveying Elko County ranches in rural northeastern Nevada. At each ranch, he was given special permission to camp overnight—a rarity for a juvenile offender. Frank built up enough trust with his counselors that he was allowed to go solo into town to take in a movie.

On his seventeenth birthday, Frank took a bus to Hawthorne. As he rode, he couldn't stop thinking about the run-ins he and his brothers had had with gung-ho jarheads in Hawthorne. In Reno, he jumped off the bus and headed to the nearest navy enlistment office, where he filled out the paperwork as Frank Valentine. The recruiter said, "You'll hear from us in ten days, after we check your birth certificate."

Back in Hawthorne, Frank anxiously awaited the navy's call. The ten days came and went. He was getting concerned that the judge would send the sheriff to arrest him or drag him off to the marines. Finally, a letter from the navy arrived, asking why he tried to enlist under an assumed name. Frank didn't know the name on his birth certificate was Frank R. Dryman, not Valentine.

Indignant, Frank Valentine Sr. said, "Let's go straighten the U.S. Navy out!"

Frank Jr. paid for the two bus tickets to Reno. At the enlistment office, his father and the recruiter went into a room and closed the door behind them. Frank waited outside. When they emerged, he was officially U.S. Navy recruit Frank R. Valentine. It was not exactly the marines, but he hoped it would satisfy the judge's order to join the military. The judge never followed up.

On June 25, 1948, Frank R. Valentine took the oath of enlistment at the San Francisco recruiting station and became Seaman Apprentice (SA) Valentine, Service No. 799 16 42. After boot camp, on September 29, SA Valentine was assigned to the fire suppression unit on the aircraft carrier USS *Princeton*. He liked the "three hots and a cot" of military life but adjusted poorly to the rigors of the service. Valentine soon developed a reputation as a poor worker, a slacker. He concocted illnesses, even pled for a tonsillectomy, to get out of work—in navy jargon, "pulling a floozy." The teenaged sailor felt picked on by the boatswain's mate, who continually assigned him to the worst duties. While Frank was on shore leave at Pearl Harbor, he claimed, the boatswain's mate organized a gang of his shipmates to beat him up.

On April 4, 1949, two years to the day before Frank murdered Clarence Pellett, the *Princeton* docked in Bremerton, Washington. Dryman was assigned to a paint detail using zinc chromate marine paint in a cramped space within the voids—the spaces between the decks. He complained he felt woozy and was laid out on a stretcher, unresponsive. An exam was done, but no physical explanation for his unconsciousness was evident. However, when his gag reflex was tested with a tongue depressor, he opened his eyes and vomited.

Frank was taken by ambulance to the U.S. Naval Hospital at Bremerton, Washington, where he was admitted for "psychoneurosis hysteria." He was observed on a mental ward from April 4 to 16 and then transferred to an open ward unit until May 4.

"Finding no abnormality of behavior or mental reaction and fully recovered from the hysteric episode, he was returned to his ship 'fit to serve.' The night he was returned to his duties, he threatened his shipmates with a knife. The *Princeton*'s officer of the day demanded he be 'removed from my ship!'"

The sailor was escorted off the aircraft carrier by the Shore Patrol to the onshore hospital emergency room, where a junior medical officer declared him schizophrenic. At 2240, he was readmitted to the same ward where he had been found fit to serve twenty-four hours earlier.

On May 7, 1949, Frank appeared before a board of medical survey, by whose order he was transferred to the U.S. Naval Hospital at Mare Island, California, for further observation. Navy protocol required him to be straitjacketed and accompanied by a medical attendant. He was admitted to the U.S. Naval Hospital at Mare Island on May 10, 1949.

After further observation and psychiatric interviews, Frank was diagnosed as an emotionally immature seventeen-year-old who was torn between making a go of it in the navy and his impulse to escape. He claimed the boatswain's mate, who was in charge of him, thoroughly disliked him and restricted him at every opportunity.

After multiple interviews, navy psychiatrists concluded that the patient had pronounced immaturity and was frequently on the verge of tears and that "schizophrenic processes may be present, but they are not particularly conspicuous at this time." Frank Valentine was transferred to the open ward on May 15, 1949. On June 27, he was discharged by reason of permanent insanity from the hospital and the U.S. Navy.

Chapter 11

THE TRIP TO MURDER

Civilian Frank Valentine returned to Hawthorne, where he worked several dead-end jobs. Then he heard that there were better jobs in Montana. He left Hawthorne and hitched his way north. By August, he'd found work with the Western Chemical Fireproofing Company and as a busboy/dishwasher in restaurants around Great Falls. He joined the Waiters and Cooks Union and stayed the summer. Aimlessly hitchhiking across the country, he found himself homeless and hungry in Minneapolis. Missing the military's three hots and a cot, he decided to reenlist.

Still afraid of the marines, Frank figured the newest branch of the military would be looking for recruits. The U.S. Air Force had been a separate branch of the military for less than two years when he walked into a St. Paul Air Force recruiting office. Because he used the surname Dryman, his birth certificate was cleared in a matter of days.

After he was sworn in as Frank R. Dryman, he was sent to Lackland Air Force Base in Texas for basic military training. Given his affinity for guns, it's no surprise that he enjoyed weapons training. He especially liked the M1918 Browning automatic rifle and his favorite, the Colt M1911 .45 pistol.

After boot camp, the air force private boarded a train to San Antonio, Texas, where he trained as a telegraph operator. Assigned to Warren Air Force Base in Cheyenne, Wyoming, he found he didn't like the air corps any better than the navy. After a few months, he went AWOL. With the help of relatives, including his brother Jim, he managed to remain a fugitive for two months before he surrendered to authorities at an air force base near Los Angeles. He waited in the brig for two weeks before being flown to San Antonio.

At his court-martial, he explained his unauthorized absence as a search for his parents to end his confusion about whether to use Dryman or Valentine. Six weeks into his one-year sentence, his fingerprints came back from Washington, D.C. They matched his navy ID under the name Valentine and his discharge as permanently unfit for service. "I was immediately discharged," Dryman bragged.

A civilian once again, he went back to Los Angeles and stayed with his brother Jim. "It was the same day as the Korean War started," Dryman recounted, "when I started hitching across the country picking up odd jobs here and there." By midsummer, he was in Charlotte, North Carolina.

"I liked it there," Dryman said. He'd been working as a painter for three months when his boss had a mysterious accident. Immediately, he skedaddled. "I left right away and hitched back to Hawthorne. For two or three months, I worked at the U.S. Navy ammunition depot sending ammunition to Korea."

Frank spent the winter of 1950–51 in Los Angeles living with a friend of his grandmother, "Nana." "Mrs. Fred Smith, a very elderly lady, talked me into settling down. I stayed for six months; it was the longest I ever stayed anywhere."

That spring, he was back in Hawthorne driving a truck. At the end of March, he quit and went to Reno. There he stayed with a friend, Siegfried Sunbee, but it wasn't long before he wanted to get on the road again. Before he left, he went to a hockshop, where along with a shoulder holster and one hundred rounds of ammunition, he purchased his favorite firearm, a Colt M1911 .45.

From Reno, on April 2, 1951, he took a bus to Las Vegas and started hitchhiking north. "I wasn't sure where I was going. I had a vague idea of seeing my girlfriend in Canada." He later testified that she was his fiancée, which turned out to be news to her. Concealed under his secondhand split-tail sportscoat was the shoulder holster and the .45 pistol.

"I carried the gun out of habit," Dryman later testified. "I got a lift to an air base. While standing there trying to catch another ride, two APs [air policemen] walked up to me and asked for ID. I showed my navy discharge papers. They ordered me to lift my coattails and turn around slowly. I gathered up my gun under my coat, turned slowly waiting for the inevitable discovery—it never came."

Years later, in one of his applications for commutation of his sentence, Dryman wrote, "In the past nine years I've wished fervently that they had seen the gun! A life would have been saved and eighteen months in a federal penitentiary would have cured that kid of carrying a gun."

On April 4, Dryman was dropped off in Great Falls, Montana, early in the morning. He waited until ten o'clock and then walked up the steps of the Civic Center and went to the selective service office to register to receive his monthly disability check. Just before noon, he hitched a ride out of Great Falls. He was dropped off about ten miles north, close to Vaughn. In no time, he hitched a ride with three youths toward Shelby.

Chapter 12

THE COMMITTEE TO SAVE A POOR BOY

Although unsuccessful, the "Save Willie McGee" defense template inspired strong-minded liberal Montanans to rush to the killer's aid, forming the Dryman Clemency Committee on May 17. It was composed of businessman Francis E. Small, chairman; Gretchen G. Billings, secretary; and an anti-death penalty activist, Lucy T. McLemore, all from Helena.

Members of the committee launched a statewide petition drive, arguing that the killer's confession had been coerced, he had not received a fair trial and Montana was no longer a state of vigilante justice. Members of the Montana Welfare Association, never doubting the killer's guilt but stating they did not believe in the death penalty, helped circulate these petitions.

Attorney Black also dropped off petitions at Shelby-area churches, community meetings and local businesses. Most petitions were not returned, and those that were were unsigned or had "without comment" scribbled across them. Even a letter from the Montana Council of Churches claiming the boy must be saved in the name of Christ failed to stimulate meaningful public or political support.

Speaking to church parishioners on Sunday, May 20, Gretchen Billings assumed a higher moral posture and a superior intellect, alleging the Hi-Line's Toole County Court was railroading this "boy" in an atmosphere "but briefly removed from mob violence." Struggling to draw an "Iron Curtain" over her mental image of this young boy "hanging from the neck until dead," Gretchen beseeched congregations to pass collection plates to

Seek Clemency For Valentine With Petition

Request May Reach Governor's Desk By Week-End

A petition asking for executive clemency for Frank R. Valentine, alias Dryman, 19-year-old confessed slayer of a Four Corners Cafe operator, is being sought by William Black, Valentine's defense attorney appointed by the court for the trial on April 12.

Black reported that if word had not been received from the hospitals by the end of this week, the petition would ask for a stay of execution until the reports were received.

If Governor Bonner should grant executive clemency, the petition will ask that Valentine, alias Dryman, be removed to the insane asylum at Warm Springs.

He pointed out that all of the slayers service records listed him as Frank R. Valentine, and not Dryman, the name given at the time of the murder.

Attorney Black received a wire from John South, 23-year-old uncle of Valentine, stating that he would be in Shelby by the end of this week.

He was a radio operator aboard the USS Magoffin off the coast of Okinawa, when notified of his nephew's execution. No other relatives have been located.

Black said Tuesday, that the petition may be in Governor John Bonner's hands by the end of the week, depending on the arrival of service records.

The petition for executive clemency will be based on the killer's service record which shows that he received psychiatric treatment at two naval hospitals.

Telegrams were sent Tuesday to the U. S. Naval hospital at Bremerton, Wash., and the U. S. Naval hospital at Mare Island, Calif., for a copy of Valentine's service record.

Walter Coombs, Helena, a lawyer representing the state church affiliations, conferred with Black over the weekend and urged the petitions be on the governor's desk by the end of the week. He said that his organization will strongly support such a movement and are allegedly working in various towns about the state seeking a petition for executive clemency.

From the Shelby Promoter, *May 17, 1951.*

support hiring competent legal representation to stop this penniless youth from being lynched. The plates returned empty.

Undeterred, Gretchen tapped into the coast-to-coast underground word-of-mouth network of the nation's liberal political class. Known as the Whiskey Wire, it was used by those who wished to keep their Communist leanings out of the public eye. She lamented, "Sadly, the forces who cried out for Willie McGee are silent."

However, the committee did have successes. Letters of support arrived at *The People's Voice* with one- and two-dollar donations, and East Helena's VFW post passed a resolution imploring the governor to give all possible assistance to the nineteen-year-old veteran Frank Dryman, discharged from the navy for the mental condition of "dual personality." Despite being buffeted about in their quest for legal representation and monetary resources, the committee members remained fully committed to saving a boy they had never laid eyes on.

The blue-collar residents of the Hi-Line, among the poorest in the state, were too busy scratching out a living to pay much attention to politics. But this was the McCarthy era. Outsiders were coming uninvited to Shelby—commies, no less—using psychiatric mumbo jumbo to stand in the way of justice.

Curly Pellett was not about to let this meddling stand. He spearheaded his own petition campaign demanding that the death sentence be carried out. Unlike the mixed results of the Dryman Clemency Committee's petition drive, he gathered four pages, covered front and back with signatures.

On Monday, May 21, with copies of Valentine's navy record in hand, attorney Black drove three hundred miles to Billings, Montana, where he caught up with Governor Bonner, who was attending a veterans' convention. Black handed him the copies of Seaman Valentine's 1949 U.S. Navy hospital hearings and a second executive clemency application. He advised the governor that the transcript indicated his client was medically discharged for "the good of the service" due to his "split personality" and that while he hoped for clemency, a stay of execution for sixty days would give him time to prepare an appeal.

The governor thanked him for driving so far to deliver the papers and promised to let Black know of his decision not later than Friday. He then called each of the state's mental health experts, told them about the military transcripts and asked them to revisit their findings, telling them that time was of the essence and that he would be attending a convention on water rights in Bozeman and could be reached at the Baxter Hotel until Friday.

PETITION

To: Hon. John W. Bonner
Governor of State of Montana
Helena, Montana.

WE, the undersigned, residents of Toole County, Montana, are opposed to any commutation of the death penalty imposed upon Frank Dryman now in the Toole County Jail, the confessed and proven killer of Clarence Pellett. We feel that this crime is as brutal and cold-blooded killing as has ever happened and if it is ever [illegible]ified to impose the death penalty, this is the case when it should not only be imposed, but executed and carried out. We do not feel that the ends of justice would be served in any way whatsoever by confining the brutal killer, Frank Dryman, in any institution, either a prison or a mental institution, and that the death sentence should be carried out speedily.

NAME	ADDRESS
William J Corbett	Oilmont Mon.
Wayne C. Hilliard	Oilmont, Mont.
Lola Hoffman	Kevin, Mont.
[illegible]	Oilmont Mont.
Wm Halte	Sunburst, Mont.
Ted Bastian	Shelby Mont
Mrs Benj McGhie	Sunburst Mont
Benj S. McGhie	Sunburst Mont.
Floyd W Hader	Chester Mont
[illegible]	Ferdig, Montana
Ray [illegible]	Oilmont Montana.
Jess J Maxwell	Sunburst Mont
Harold McColley	Sunburst Mont.
[illegible]	Sunburst, Mont.

Petition to Governor Bonner circulated by the Pellett brothers, 1951. *Author's collection.*

Killer's Fate Rests On Governors Desk

May Have Decision By End Of Week

W. M. Black, defense counsel for Frank Robert Valentine, alias Frank Robert Dryman, is expected to have a reply on his desk not later than Friday in regard to a petition for executive clemency for the 19-year-old youth who shot and killed Clarence E. Pellett, Four Corners cafe operator, April 4.

Valentine, who was examined by two psychiatrists and a psychologist and found sane, is scheduled to hang Friday, June 1.

The petition asks the governor to grant Valentine executive clemency, "and suspend and stay the execution of the death sentence heretofore pronounced upon defendant (Valentine) until such time as a hearing may be had upon this Petition."

"It is urged further that defendant is not mentally normal, that his mental faculties are deranged, and have been for some time heretofore," the document said in part.

The psychiatrists named by Bonner to examine him on May 3, went into a huddle again yesterday for a further study of the situation.

Valentine's age, (he will be 20 June 4), has been an influence in efforts of churchmen and laymen to save the confessed slayer from the gallows. Others are opposed to capital punishment under any circumstances.

Black, in his petition, presented a transcript of Valentine's medical records while in the U. S. Navy, from which he received an honorable discharge, and the U. S. Air Force "as unfit and for the best interests of the Service, on account of his mental derangement."

The transcripts from the Bremerton, Wash., naval hospital and Mare Island, Calif., naval hospital diagnosed Valentine as suffering from schizophrenia, a type of psychosis characterized by loss of contact with environment and by disintegration of personality.

The petition said of the sanity examination held here May 3, "said Report is exceptionally brief and inconclusive and thereby indicates that insufficient time and study were given for a full and complete Examination of the said Defendant."

It also stated, in part, "said Report made on May 3d is incomplete, not conclusive, and misleading by reason of the inadequate study and examination made on said date. When the life of a human being is at stake, as in this instance, such examinations and Reports must be thoroughly scrutinized in all respects."

From the Shelby Promoter, *May 24, 1951.*

On Tuesday, Black wrote to the Billingses, telling them he'd received only one response to the petitions he sent to Shelby-area churches and that he had given the governor the transcripts and the clemency application. He ended by saying, "I prefer nothing be said about this matter until Bonner's decision comes thru [*sic*]. I am no longer going to discuss such matters over the phone; it seems there is a leak up this way."

The next day, the state's mental health experts confirmed that no matter what the military doctors concluded, they were confident that Dryman was sane. Bonner sent Black a telegram: "I hereby refuse to grant clemency or suspend or stay execution of the death sentence."

Dunstall, ever mindful of the mood in Shelby, summoned reporters as soon as he heard about the governor's decision, telling them, "In light of the governor's most recent statement, Dryman will be hanged as scheduled, June 1, Friday morning between seven and eight o'clock on Tom Peg's place."

On May 24, Black drove half an hour south to Conrad to see Judge Hattersley. He handed the judge a photostatic copy of the defendant's navy medical record. The judge quickly read the twenty-six-page report and told Black the records needed to be certified before they could be entered as evidence.

Black replied he wasn't sure how long it would take to get a certified copy from Washington, and Hattersley told him he was not going to stay the hanging for uncertified evidence. Black asked if the judge would at least set a hearing for Monday, May 28, and the judge agreed.

Black hurried back to Shelby and called Washington, D.C. It took a while to work his way up the chain of command, but eventually, he reached a naval officer who could help.

Black made clear the dire consequences should a certified copy of this sailor's record not be in his hands no later than May 27. The officer said, "I will be sending you the properly certified report as soon as the same can be gotten out."

> The People's Voice
> *May 25, 1951*
> *"Dryman Should Have Been One of Hitler's Mass Murderers"*
> *By Gretchen G. Billings*
>
> *Two hours before they were to die on the gallows last night for their major roles in engineering and carrying out Hitler's program of mass murder of millions of civilians, seven Nazi war criminals received reprieves, the judge didn't have the heart to permit their execution. Can we not find the same mercy for this young boy?*

Defendants Ex. #
Hearing May 29, 1951.

FILED
MAY 28 1951
Dep.

United States of America

DEFENDANT'S EXHIBIT "3"

DEPARTMENT OF THE NAVY

Washington, D. C., 23 May 1951

I hereby certify *that the annexed* twenty-six (26) photostats constitute the medical record of Frank Robert Valentine, 799 16 42, former Seaman Apprentice, U. S. Navy

on file in the Bureau of Medicine and Surgery

H. L. PUGH
Chief of the Bureau of Medicine and Surgery
(Official title)

OFFICE OF THE SECRETARY

I hereby certify *that* H. L. PUGH *who signed the foregoing certificate, was at the time of signing* Chief of the Bureau of Medicine and Surgery *and that full faith and credit should be given his certification as such.*

In testimony whereof, *I have hereunto set my hand and caused the Seal of the Navy Department to be affixed this* 25th *day of* May, *one thousand nine hundred and* fifty-one.

E. E. WOODS
ACTING JUDGE ADVOCATE GENERAL OF THE NAVY
FOR THE SECRETARY OF THE NAVY

U.S. Navy medical record of Seaman Frank Robert Valentine, defendant's exhibit 3, May 29, 1951. *Courtesy of Toole County Clerk of Court.*

United States Navy Says . . .

Dryman Discharged Because Of "Mental Disability"

By GRETCHEN BILLINGS

One of the firmest stands taken by the state administration was announced Thursday afternoon from Bozeman, when the Governor released his answer to Attorney William M. Black of Shelby, the state appointed attorney defending Frank Dryman, 19-year-old confessed killer sentenced to hang next Friday.

The Governor refused a stay of execution which would allow Mr. Black more time for preparation of appeals through the courts, and he refused clemency.

Those who interested themselves in the case after the hasty trial at the time of sentencing were disappointed when they heard the cursory dismissal of the case the second time.

Shortly after the Governor's first refusal, information was received by telegram which left little doubt that firm grounds for clemency exist. The telegram read in part:

"'PROPERLY DOCUMENTED COPY OF MEDICAL SURVEY AWARDED FRANK R. VALENTINE (DRYMAN), SN. USN FORWARDED VIA AIR MAIL SPECIAL DELIVERY. SURVEY AWARDED ACCOUNT MENTAL DISABILITY.

"SECRETARY OF THE NAVY, JUDGE ADVOCATE GEN."

In addition to the mental disability found to be present by the U. S. Navy closer examination of the boy's background made it seem incredible that we could take his life.

The argument most frequently advanced in favor of hanging this boy has been that our prison system and our state sanitarium are both a "fate worse than death." There is also the fact that our laws are so unsatisfactory and our facilities so poor that we have no alternative except to kill young fellows like 19-year-old Frank Dryman. Older men can be put in prison and kept until they are so old they wither away, but young men we must kill, because they might be paroled. Because of our insufficiencies as a state we will continue to deal with social problems by the process of elimination. These points no doubt figured strongly in the consideration of clemency, they no doubt took precedent over the 'mitigating" circumstances surrounding the boy's life and his mental disability. Why a little more time could not have been granted in the way of a stay of execution to present this newly acquired evidence in a court is hard to imagine.

From the political standpoint the decision was not difficult. The boy is from another state, a transient, he represents no constitutents, and shortly after June first none will

Dryman Should Have Been One of Hitler's Mass Murderers

Two hours before they were to die on the gallows last night for their major roles in engineering and carrying out Hitler's program of mass murder of millions of civilians, seven Nazi war criminals received reprieves from a District of Columbia federal court. The judge didn't have the heart to permit execution.

even remember his name. Hanging satisfies the thirst for vengeance of many who are unaware of the unfortunate circumstanees of Dry-

Continued on page four

Dryman Discharged—

(Continued from page one)

man's life, or who still abide by the codes of Hammurabi . . . and Moses. Yes, at this time when feelings still run high refusal of time and mercy is not difficult, it isn't likely to be a lasting issue.

Opposed to the hanging are those who do not believe in capital punishment and those who believe that the original hasty proceedings were a violation of the basic principle that greatest care should be exercised before the state executes the death penalty. . . . Those who believe that every reason and every motive of the condemned should be investigated and that the serious act of taking a life should not be done in haste, nor in the spirit of vengeance.

The fact that the boy may have been "legally" tried and accounted "legally" sane is apart from the forces that might go as the lawyers say, 'in mitigation" of the severe penalty.

Even though the law has confined the definition of "legal sanity," the mercy of the Sovereign is empowered to go further into the true nature of mental disabilities and surrounding circumstances. It is extremely difficult to understand why our chief executive insists upon confining his justification to the concepts of a court of review. The responsibilities which rest upon the executive power require an examination that goes beyond "legalisms" and calls for a greater depth of understanding. It is an entirely separate responsibility.

It seems apparent by now that Governor Bonner is not inclined toward mercy to others. In another few days 19-year-old Frank Dryman will be hanged, unless Lawyer Black can somehow get presented to a court the mitigating facts which in the few brief days past have been gathered.

Despite this disappointing refusal of the Governor to consider the naval record, the unfortunate background, and the mental discharge of Frank Dryman, I have not abandoned hope that somewhere in Montana there is a forum in which these factors will be considered, and hate, vengeance and expediency will not rule, somewhere the power of this state will face the future and not the past.

We can live without friends but not without our neighbors. — The Butte Miner.

This page and previous: Article by Gretchen Billings. *From* The People's Voice, *May 25, 1951.*

After the governor's second denial, the Dryman Clemency Committee in Helena changed its name to the Dryman Defense Committee. The Billingses took stock of their inability to attract a criminal attorney to take on this case. Put off by the lack of courage the lawyers they knew were showing, Gretchen and Harry speculated that they feared taking the case would be a political career killer.

"But I have high hopes! There is another attorney!" Gretchen exclaimed. Pausing for effect, she blurted out, "Jerry O'Connell has offered Black his services."

Chapter 13

MONTANA'S SNOLLYGOSTER PAR EXCELLENCE

A snollygoster: an unprincipled but shrewd person, especially a politician who is guided by personal advantage rather than by consistent, respectable principles.

When he answered Gretchen Billings's call to represent Frank Dryman, Jerry O'Connell was already a nationally known progressive New Deal politician, union activist and Cold War–era communist firebrand with a reputation for lying, larceny and skullduggery—in short, a snollygoster par excellence. With the kind of outlandish personality usually found only in fiction, O'Connell had already won and lost several prominent positions by the age of forty-two, often in spectacular style.

Born to Irish Catholic parents in Butte, Montana, on October 4, 1908, Jeremiah Joseph O'Connell lost his miner father to silicosis on April 24, 1917. For the rest of his life, O'Connell held the Anaconda Copper Mining Company and Montana Power responsible for his father's suffering. The experience instilled in him a lifelong radicalism against predatory big business.

Jerry attended St. Patrick Parochial School and Butte Central High, where he was elected class president, and Mount St. Charles College (now Carroll College), a Catholic school in Helena.

Short, squat and prematurely bald, O'Connell was not easy on the eyes, but friend and foe alike agreed he possessed not only an agile mind but also extraordinary oratorical skills. At the age of twenty-one, still in his senior year of college, O'Connell was elected to Montana's state legislature, making him

Jerry J. O'Connell. *944-193 MTHS Photo Archives.*

the youngest member of that body. He married Alena Smith, the daughter of a prominent Helena physician, soon after he graduated in 1931.

O'Connell embraced the ideals of communism, believing that capitalism was based on greed and that class struggle was the key to freeing workers. But his idealism was contaminated by a taste for the limelight and the good life.

O'Connell was reelected to the statehouse, and then Montana's voters elected him to the U.S. House of Representatives in the fall of 1936. That year, Jerry met Mazie Elizabeth Richardson, an entertainer at Helena's Placer Hotel, and began having an affair with her. O'Connell was soon hounding his wife for a divorce, but the devoutly Catholic Alena resisted until Jerry finally told her Mazie was pregnant. It was yet another lie, but on the eve of his planned wedding to Mazie, Alena agreed to divorce him.

The happy couple were married on January 2, 1937, in Mazie's childhood home in Great Falls, with a reception in the living room thereafter. It was a far cry from the grand wedding the couple had planned, but for Jerry, it all worked out fine. Alena never received a penny of alimony.

That same day, they traveled to Washington, D.C., where, four days later, O'Connell was sworn into the Seventy-Fifth Congress, making him the youngest member of yet another legislative body. That distinction is controversial, however, because O'Connell falsified his date of birth as June 14, 1909, which established him as the "Baby Member" of the Seventy-Fifth Congress by mere days and helped him rise above the obscurity ordinarily accorded a freshman congressman.

In early October, the Russian government sent the progressive phenomenon and his new bride on an all-expenses-paid trip to Spain to inspect the Abraham Lincoln Brigade, which was fighting the Nazis in the Spanish Civil War. Jerry's speeches and actions—which included raising his fist in the communist salute and shouting, "Viva Russo!"—persuaded FBI Director J. Edgar Hoover to add him to the Custodial Detention List of persons considered dangerous to the nation's security.

In Washington, D.C., despite his antagonistic style, O'Connell distinguished himself as an effective legislator by pouring Capitol Hill funds into the Treasure State. But the next chapter of his career was typically atypical. Montana's powerful senior senator Burton K. Wheeler had spearheaded the legislative fight that killed President Roosevelt's 1937 Supreme Court packing scheme, so FDR called on Montana Democrats to oust Wheeler. Not yet thirty and full of piss and vinegar, O'Connell answered the call. Wheeler's endorsement had helped O'Connell win his first congressional race, but with FDR's blessing, O'Connell barreled headlong into an attempted coup of the state's liberal leadership, thundering, "President Roosevelt instructed me to go beat Wheeler!"

A veteran of rough-and-tumble politics, Wheeler didn't bruise easily. He and his lieutenants recruited Butte native Jacob Thorkelson, MD, a Republican, to oppose O'Connell in the general election. Wheeler, a brilliant political tactician, successfully consolidated bipartisan constituencies, unions, the many Democrats who disapproved of O'Connell's antics and the Catholic Church to help beat O'Connell, who had been excommunicated after his divorce.

This David versus Goliath contest taught O'Connell a painful lesson about machine politics. Jerry attempted to win back his seat twice but lost, the second time to Republican Jeannette Rankin. O'Connell never held another elected office.

His ambition unabated and still a darling of the left, Jerry was recruited for several senior positions with labor unions and became a de facto lobbyist in D.C. for the American Communist Party.

Fellow New Deal young Turk Robert "Bob" Marshall, for whom O'Connell named his second son, appointed Jerry one of five trustees of his substantial estate shortly before his untimely death in 1939. This arrangement proved an important source of income for the O'Connells because Jerry demanded a fee for his services, although this was contrary to the provisions of the trust.

The FBI raised O'Connell's classification to "top functionary" of the Communist Party. Although Jerry never officially joined the party, it was common knowledge that he was a "concealed" or secret member. At a meeting of the central committee of the U.S. Communist Party at the Hotel Albert in New York City, he was appointed western regional director of the International Workers Order. This sinecure was welcome to the high-living O'Connells, who were always in financial straits.

Early in 1944, Congress of Industrial Organizations (CIO) leader Sidney Hillman recruited Jerry to be the assistant regional director for Washington, Idaho, Oregon and Montana and charged him with mobilizing Pacific Northwest union voters to back FDR's fourth term. Jerry and Mazie moved to the Queen Anne area of Seattle, near the CIO headquarters in the Smith Tower.

FBI agents broke into the CIO headquarters, rifled through Jerry's desk, opened his mail and forwarded their findings to J. Edgar Hoover. G-men also set up wiretaps and eavesdropped on meetings Jerry had with Communist Party leaders at Seattle eateries. They also made "pretext calls," using fake names to pry information out of Jerry on the telephone. "Hello, Mr. O'Connell," the agent might say. "This is the secretary of the Woodworkers Union. We need some information from you…"

In 1944, O'Connell proved instrumental in propelling Washington State Democrats to a statewide electoral landslide. Members of the Washington State Democratic Party, anxious to show their appreciation, unanimously elected him the executive secretary of the party's central committee at the December postelection convention in Ellensburg.

But Jerry just couldn't help being—Jerry. He repeated his Montana political faux pas by attempting to upend the leadership of the Washington State Democratic Party. On January 29, 1945, the *Seattle Post-Intelligencer* reported that O'Connell and his "goon squads" were seen scurrying from room to room in the capitol building, bursting in on meetings and attempting to force the appointment of communists and leftists to high state appointments.

In response, Harry Huse, chairman of the state Democratic Party, and George F. Yates, speaker of the Washington State House of Representatives, "ordered O'Connell to 'make himself scarce at the Capitol building.'" An FBI field agent sent a blunter assessment to Hoover: "Subject O'Connell has gotten himself in the 'bad graces' of the Democratic party of Washington State. Subject will be 'released' as Executive Secretary of Democratic party soon." After twenty-two short days, O'Connell's monumental overreach got him relieved of his plum posting.

Jerry then emerged as the head of Henry Wallace's Progressives. Wallace, FDR's vice president from 1941 to 1944, was dropped from FDR's 1944 reelection ticket as an anti-business communist. Harry S. Truman was named in his stead.

O'Connell was soon dismissed from the leadership of the Progressive Party. The politically radioactive Jerry announced his intentions to end political activism and sit for the Washington State bar in anticipation of opening a law practice in Seattle. He also said he would renew his Montana law license. In actuality, he had never passed the bar.

By early 1950, the O'Connells' flamboyant lifestyle had caught up with them. The FBI reported that they had a credit rating of D, they had not paid a phone bill for several months and, to avoid creditors, they had "fixed" their telephone to make only outgoing calls.

To make matters worse, the Seattle FBI office reported that O'Connell was accused of "knocking down on the funds passing through his hands and that he has misappropriated funds of both the Communist Party and the Civil Rights Congress, both have suffered accordingly from his activities.... O'Connell absconded with at least $3,000 of Progressive party funds."

Facing a cacophony of mounting allegations, Jerry and Mazie hightailed it out of Seattle for Great Falls in the predawn hours. Hoover was informed by his field agents, "The bear has gone over the mountain."

The O'Connells moved in with Mazie's mother. In spite of the circumstances of their hasty departure from Seattle, Mazie and Jerry immediately became the Electric City's couple about town. With no visible means of support, they were driving a brand-new Studebaker and were constantly out and about. One resident recalled, "They really thought they were something!"

The FBI reported, "The subject's finances are getting worse each day." Their money troubles were compounded when the IRS filed a tax lien against them. Jerry opened a jukebox business, only to have it fail. Desperation demanded they find an income.

Beyond his manufactured date of birth, several particulars of O'Connell's biography were loosely tethered to the truth. As a case in point, he claimed to have earned both undergraduate and law degrees from Georgetown University, but there is no record of his enrollment at that school. Furthermore, he had no law degree and was not a member of any state bar. No matter—O'Connell opened a law practice in Butte in 1940.

In March 1950, Robert Merrill named O'Connell co-defense counsel in a petty larceny case in Great Falls. Cascade County attorney William Swanberg asked Merrill for clarification of O'Connell's credentials. Merrill vouched for Jerry, stating that while O'Connell had not been admitted to the Montana bar, he was a member of the bar in the state of Washington.

O'Connell brashly submitted an application for Montana's bar exam that bristled with falsehoods, including the claim that he had successfully completed a full course of study at La Salle Extension School of Law at the University of Chicago and Columbus Law School in Washington, D.C. However, the FBI found that he withdrew from both schools during his first term, still owing on his tuition bills.

Inexplicably, Montana Bar administrators approved him to sit for the examination. Finally, after failing numerous times, twenty-six years after he claimed to have been appointed to the bar, O'Connell passed in June

1950, albeit through the influence of a politically sympathetic friend on the Montana Supreme Court.

Jerry was a longtime friend and frequent houseguest of Harry and Gretchen Billings. He shared their deep-seated antipathy toward the Montana Twins. O'Connell's résumé was right out of the McGee strategy. He was a vice chairman on the National Board of the Civil Rights Congress, he had directed money to the CRC from his position as a trustee of the Robert Marshall Foundation and he maintained a close relationship with the *Daily Worker*.

Gretchen and Harry agreed that by any standard, retaining a self-taught attorney unaccustomed to acting as defense counsel in such high-stakes litigation was a Hail Mary, but time was short. Official invitations for the June 1, 1951 hanging had already been circulated. The committee was out of options. Jerry got the job.

Chapter 14

THE MARATHON HEARING

As the sounds of workers hammering the sections of the mobile scaffold together echoed from atop Tom Peg's hill across Shelby Township, the certified naval records of sailor Frank R. Valentine from the U.S. Navy Bureau of Medicine and Surgery arrived via air mail express from Washington D.C., on May 27—just in the nick of time.

The next afternoon, at two thirty, in the Montana Ninth Judicial District Court Toole County Courthouse, attorney Black submitted an affidavit to Judge Hattersley stating that subsequent to the sentencing, the Department of the Navy declared that Dryman's mental condition rendered him unfit for service, was permanent in duration, had existed prior to his enlistment and was not caused by his service in the navy. The defendant was diagnosed as "permanently insane" and discharged on his own recognizance on June 17, 1949.

Black next asked that Jerry J. O'Connell be added as associate counsel for Frank Dryman. Hattersley agreed but added that Toole County would not pay for his services. He set the "hearing on petition to set aside judgment" for the following morning at ten o'clock.

Before he gaveled the court into session the next morning, Hattersley surveyed the overflowing courtroom. The gallery was packed with 150 citizens of the Hi-Line, a cross section of shopkeepers, waitresses, oil rig laborers, farmers, shepherds, cowboys, homemakers, students—young and old. The vast majority of the men in the gallery were veterans of either World War I or II.

A new face joined the defendant and Black at the defense table: attorney Jerry J. O'Connell, whose larger-than-life persona and reputation as a bombastic communist firebrand added fuel to an already combustible atmosphere. One area paper later reported that Dryman ought to hang—if only because O'Connell was his attorney.

Seated at the defense table, Frank Dryman sported a new haircut. He wore a green button-up shirt, dungarees, blackjack boots and a bored expression. Not once did he look up from the legal pad on which he was drawing gallows, guns and grisly depictions of shooting victims.

Hattersley called case no. 528 to order and announced that he had called the hearing after Black found new evidence: Seaman Frank Robert Valentine's navy medical records documenting how the navy discharged him back into civilian life after ten months of service with a diagnosis of schizophrenia (split personality). Valentine's lawyers, Black and O'Connell, intended to use these documents as the basis for Judge Hattersley to set aside his court's April 12 death sentence. Additionally, they petitioned the court to withdraw Dryman's guilty plea, replace it with a plea of innocence and submit a motion for a new trial.

Black was sworn in as a witness, and O'Connell asked him to explain how he became aware of Valentine's naval discharge. O'Connell walked him through the defense's issues with the previous trial. Dryman had no representation during the six days of interrogation that preceded his confession, he was without counsel when he pled guilty and, lastly, Black was compelled to represent the youth after he'd already been convicted, the evening before the sentencing hearing, leaving him little or no time to prepare.

Hoyt then began to cross-examine Black. He asked Black a question about the hearing on April 12, 1951, to which O'Connell immediately objected—and furthermore, he moved to strike any questions about that hearing because they were "irrelevant, immaterial and downright incompetent as far as this hearing is concerned!"

The judge fired back that he wanted to hear everything both sides had to say and that he would offer a ruling after he had done so. He added that he planned to, "in almost every instance, overrule objections made."

Hoyt continued to cross-examine Black, specifically on the question of whether Hoyt had sufficient time to prepare an adequate defense. Black pointed out that he was appointed on the morning of April 11 and that the hearing was at two o'clock the next day. Hoyt insisted that Black could have asked for more time. Black didn't recall having been told that. He also explained that he didn't ask to have the guilty verdict set aside on the grounds of insanity because he didn't have the necessary information at the time.

When the judge called a recess until eleven o'clock, the Pellett boys and their friends blocked O'Connell's exit from the courtroom. Curly stood nose to nose with Jerry. "You are not welcome here. This is none of your business. Dryman should hang!"

"Why are you defending a murderer?" Riley demanded. "He's a dirty rotten coward who shot an unarmed man in the back!"

Curly added, "If you know what's good for you, leave Shelby now, you commie fink!"

Promptly at 11:00 a.m., Hattersley gaveled the court back to order. Hoyt moved to enter the transcripts of the hearings on April 11 and 12 into evidence. O'Connell objected, Hattersley overruled him and the transcripts were so entered.

Hoyt then called Marjorie Boe, the teenager who described picking Valentine up when she, Dorothy Holeman and Kenny Sammons were about ten miles north of Great Falls. She said they dropped him off in Shelby by the Snack Shack. Prompted by Hoyt, she stated that they sang, talked and acted like "normal" young people.

O'Connell objected that Boe wasn't qualified to judge whether anyone was "normal," but the judge allowed her testimony to continue. When O'Connell cross-examined her, he grilled her mercilessly about how she determined Valentine was "normal." He succeeded in making Boe cry, at which point he dismissed her from the witness stand.

Hoyt then called R.F. "Smokey" Denison, the Shelby chief of police, to the stand. Despite O'Connell's objections, Denison testified that in his opinion, the defendant was capable of deciding for himself the consequences of pleading guilty to a charge of murder and that he was mentally competent to stand trial.

Denison further testified that Valentine's recollections of the events from the time he left Reno, Nevada, about a week before he was dropped off at the Snack Shack in Shelby, until he got about ten miles north of Shelby were very clear. According to Denison, Valentine then "faked a blackout until he got to Sweetgrass some two hours later that same evening. His recollections were very clear from then on, on every item."

"Did you not say at that time, to Dryman, 'You are pretty good at talking your way out of things'?" Hoyt asked.

"I did," Denison replied.

"What did he say?" Hoyt asked.

"He said, 'I am,'" Denison answered.

Denison proceeded to describe Valentine's behavior when he showed the officers where the holster, clip, sunglasses, gun and cartridges were hidden at the hotel in Coutts, Alberta. He stressed that Valentine was very clear in his explanations and that Denison had no doubt he was of sound mind when he confessed to murdering Clarence Pellett. Hoyt then ended his questioning.

All eyes turned to O'Connell. Whereas previously he had paced around the courtroom, he now sat still, tapping his pen on a legal pad. Finally, he asked Smokey how he determined that Valentine faked a blackout.

Denison repeated his previous testimony. O'Connell then asked if Denison thought it was possible for someone to actually know right from wrong and still not keep from doing wrong. Denison replied that he thought a person could do that. O'Connell asked if Denison had experience with people suffering from psychoneurosis, and Denison said he had taken several people to Warm Springs when he served as deputy sheriff of Toole County.

O'Connell asked Denison if the defendant told him about his naval record. Denison replied that Valentine told him he was given a medical discharge for "some question about mental stability," but he added, "In my opinion, the navy couldn't find anything wrong with him." Denison refused to engage with O'Connell's questions about the navy's diagnosis, instead describing Frank's attitude as "very cocky, from the first, very cocky!....Very sneering; he looked at you with a sneering grin on his face." He also admitted that Sheriff Dunstall hit Valentine on the wrist with a sap, although he denied vehemently that he struck him on the head.

On redirect, Hoyt confirmed with Denison that throughout his questioning from the April 6 to 11, Valentine was treated fairly and kindly, well fed and provided with cigarettes.

After another brief recross-examination, Smokey was excused, and the judge recessed the court for lunch. As the gallery filed out, Dryman stood up and leaned over the bar. Smirking, he handed Nellie a grisly sketch of himself shooting Clarence. As he was taken away by officers, he snickered.

At 2:00 p.m., Judge Hattersley gaveled the session to order. "The usual minute entry, if you please, Mr. May: 'The parties are all—'"

A commotion at the back of the room interrupted the judge. A soldier in an army dress uniform was walking down the center aisle. His name tag read, "Valentine." It was Frank's younger brother, Corporal Jim Valentine, who learned of his brother's plight while in Korea with the Seventh Infantry Division, which was fighting Chinese communists near the thirty-eighth parallel. He was granted a thirty-day furlough, and on May 24, he flew from Hong-chon to Tokyo, on to Midway Island, over to Honolulu, stateside to

Los Angeles and then to Billings, finally landing in Cut Bank at noon on the fifth day of his journey. His appearance completely surprised the defendant. The brothers greeted each other, and Jim took a seat directly behind Frank.

Judge Hattersley pounded his gavel. "Order in the courtroom! Mr. Valentine, I wish to extend this court's welcome and thank you for your service to your country. Mr. Hoyt, you may proceed with the state's presentation."

Hoyt then called Winfield S. Wilder, MD, and asked O'Connell if he was willing to accept Wilder's qualifications as a psychiatrist. O'Connell said he wanted the doctor's qualifications reviewed. Hoyt walked Wilder through his extensive background, including time spent practicing at the Great Falls Clinic. O'Connell agreed that Wilder was qualified as an expert in mental health.

Dr. Wilder testified that he examined Frank Dryman a little over three weeks prior at the Toole County jail along with Dr. Robert Spratt and Alice Bastow, a clinical psychologist at the Mental Hygiene Clinic in Butte. Each had conducted two two-hour sessions with Dryman alone, one in the morning and one in the afternoon. Over O'Connell's objections, Wilder testified that Dryman was capable of comprehending the consequences of a guilty plea—in short, he was sane, and he was not schizophrenic. He disagreed with the navy's diagnosis of Dryman's mental state, testifying,

> *Mr. Dryman has a psychopathic personality—that is, an individual who has little or no consideration for the feelings or well-being of other people, completely concerned with gratification of his own immediate desires no matter whatever the cost to other people and lacking sufficient moral standards. In other words, he is a moral imbecile.*

Jim's presence in the courtroom had given Frank Dryman fresh interest in the hearing. He was bright-eyed and attentive, conversing frequently with his attorneys.

Hoyt then called Dr. Spratt, who rebutted the navy's findings, testifying that the defendant was a "psychopathic personality": someone with little regard for others' rights. He also emphasized that the defendant was emotionally immature but had normal intellectual capacity and knew right from wrong.

With that, at seven o'clock, the state rested its case. The judge asked O'Connell if he wanted to make his closing arguments, but O'Connell said he wanted to talk to Jim Valentine first, so the judge declared an hour's recess.

As the gallery filed back into the courtroom at eight o'clock, Dryman passed a note to Hoyt. It said, "My brother Jim was threatened by one of the Pellett boys."

Hoyt asked, "Which one?" Dryman pointed to Curly, who was sitting in the front row.

Hoyt said, "I will personally see that no harm of any kind will come to your brother."

The judge asked, "Is the defense prepared for closing arguments?

"Yes, your honor," O'Connell replied.

"Proceed," Hattersley instructed.

O'Connell then argued that Dryman's sentence should be set aside because attorney Black had not had sufficient time to prepare an adequate defense, Black didn't have in his possession the navy's records of Dryman's mental condition, Dryman had been coerced into confessing to murdering Pellett and the state's witnesses who testified to Dryman's mental condition were not qualified to do so. He therefore asked that the judgment be set aside, the plea of guilty be changed and Dryman be granted a new trial.

At the court's invitation, Hoyt disputed O'Connell's assertion that the guilty plea was made without counsel. Hoyt stated that Dryman understood the consequences of entering a guilty plea and insisted on doing so anyway. He also asserted, "The medical officers who examined the defendant were convinced that the defendant was not insane but faking in order to be relieved of duties and achieve a discharge from the service." Furthermore, "Interviews with his shipmates disclosed that they were of the opinion he was a poor worker who frequently reported to sick bay: in their words, 'Trying to pull a 'floozy.'"

Hoyt argued that although some people opposed capital punishment, it was the law in Montana. "Our community lost a good and decent man. The Pellett family's patriarch was taken to the gun, leaving behind a widow. There has never been a case of a more heinous, more dastardly crime committed in this or any other state where capital punishment should be mandatory and meted out. Your Honor, justice demands it should be done so here."

"Mr. O'Connell, do you have anything further to say?" the judge asked.

"Your Honor, I want to object just as vigorously and strenuously as I can to the oratory that Mr. Hoyt just finished!" O'Connell exclaimed. "Counsel for the state referenced the height of this crime and the denunciation of the defendant without any consideration of the fact that this record from the navy does show a diagnosis of insanity, does show a diagnosis of schizophrenia, does show a diagnosis of psychoneurosis with all the associated symptoms.

"It is true that at times while in the service, the defendant tried to avoid work, just like all the boys in the army or navy would have done from time to time. The state's argument fails to recognize that the diagnosis of insanity found in the navy record is presumed to continue from his discharge to this day.

"Further, I resent the implication that Mr. Black was derelict in his duty! In his statement, Mr. Hoyt implied that Mr. Black was appointed immediately following the arraignment and had a full twenty-four hours to interview his client. This is not true!"

Hattersley interrupted, reminding O'Connell that despite the defense's entry of the Navy Department medical records into evidence, other mental health experts' testimony had rebutted that military record. Based on those rebuttals, he denied the motions to grant a new trial, to withdraw the guilty plea and to substitute a not guilty plea. However, he did grant sixty days in addition to the ten days allowed by law "within which to prepare, serve, and file the Bill of Exceptions." When he adjourned the trial, it had been in session for eleven hours.

As Dryman was handcuffed and led away, Hoyt tapped his brother, Corporal Jim Valentine, on the shoulder. "It's been a long day. What do you say I take you over to the VFW club?"

Jim looked at Black and O'Connell as they were gathering up their papers. Black said, "I'd take John up on his offer. You heard the judge; Jerry and I need to get this appeal filed pronto. We're going to be busy all night."

Jim followed Hoyt through the front door of the VFW club just as the VFW Club Meeting started. Hoyt introduced Jim: "Gentleman, this is Army Corporal Jim Valentine, brother to Frank Dryman. He's on furlough from the front lines of Korea. Let's welcome him in the best traditions of our Western hospitality."

In unison, half a dozen veterans extended their hands in welcome. Said a member, "We have no beef with you, but your brother shot a man in the back for no reason. For that, he should hang."

Hoyt intervened: "Remember, he's our guest."

Hoyt stayed close to Jim, but he could see the local vets were hungry for firsthand information on the ongoing "police action" in Korea. By the end of the evening, Jim was a brother in arms, swapping war stories. Walking to the car, Hoyt asked, "Jim, are you concerned about the threats? You're welcome to stay at my place." Jim replied, "Thanks, I can take care of myself."

On May 30, attorney Black wrote to Harry Billings, describing the hearing the previous Monday in Shelby and reporting that he and Jerry had filed notices of appeal, which would stay the death sentence. "Jerry has done a bang-up job on this," Black wrote. "He is a horse to work, and he knows the procedures. His statement to the court at the conclusion of the evidence was really fine." He urged the Billingses to find a way to come up with one hundred dollars to compensate O'Connell for his services.

HISTORICAL SOCIETY OF MONTANA HELENA

The Shelby Promoter

and Tribune of Shelby

SHELBY Capitol Montana's Oil Industry, Natural gateway to Alaska. Adjacent to Glacier Park. Focal Point, Railroads-Highways. Future Prospects Unlimited!

Volume 44 Number 1 | Shelby, Toole County Montana, Thursday May 31, 1951 | 5c Per Copy

Execution Of Frank R. Valentine Delayed

Valentine Denied Motion For New Trial; Petition For Plea of Not Guilty

A motion for a new trial and petition for a plea of not guilty against Frank R. Valentine, entered in District Court Monday, was denied by Judge R. M. Hattersley in a night session Tuesday.

Defense counsels, W. M. Black and Jerry O'Connell, immediately entered an appeal to the supreme court. A Bill of Exception will be prepared and presented before the high chamber within the next 70 days.

The customary recess of the supreme court may throw the hearing into the middle of September.

Frank R. Valentine, alias Frank R. Dryman, will not swing from the gallows somewhere in Toole County early Friday morning, as a result of district court proceedings Tuesday.

A petition entered before District Judge R. M. Hattersley Monday afternoon, then postponed until Tuesday morning, asked that Valentine be permitted to substitute a plea of not guilty for one of guilty.

On the morning of May 31, 1951, the *Shelby Promoter* reported that the district court had delayed Frank Dryman's hanging. That same morning, Smokey found "3-7-77" painted on the door of the Toole County jail. He recognized it as the calling card of Montana vigilantes: a lynching was in the offing. Smokey immediately called Dunstall.

The origin of this set of numbers is lost in Montana lore, as is their exact meaning. They may indicate the amount of time vigilantes gave their subjects to leave town (three hours, seven minutes, and seventy-seven seconds) or the dimensions of a grave. Others have speculated that the Masons originated this signal. However, there is no denying that the numbers are intended to be a warning that a group of citizens are about to take the law into their own hands.

As Dunstall feared, the postponement of the hanging had blown the lid off the area's emotional powder keg. The Hi-Liners didn't hide their frustration. Why should they? They had all come to the aid of a friend and a neighbor's family. But now it appeared this young punk with the Hollywood haircut was going to get away with cold-blooded murder.

By Friday, June 1, the horse was out of the barn: Toole County was exploding. Adding to the general frustration was the irony that instead of hanging that morning, Dryman was going to be around to celebrate his twentieth birthday on Monday, June 4.

the motion entered by Defense Counsel W. M. Black and Vice Counsel Jerry J. O'Connell, Great Falls lawyer, a trial by jury to decide whether Valentine is sane or not will be held sometime in July in District Court. If Judge Hattersley denies the motion, the lawyers said they would appeal to the Supreme Court.

Few people were present at the morning session, but many streamed in and out during the afternoon. At this writing, Dr. Robert J. Spratt, superintendent of the state hospital at Warm Springs, was on the stand as a witness for the state.

W. M. Black was the only witness to testify for the defendant. Marjorie Boe, Cut Bank, Chief of Police R. F. Denison, and Dr. Winfield Wilder, preceded Spratt.

Hattersley said during a fifteen minute recess he hoped to finish the hearing Tuesday, even if it meant continuing with a night session.

James Valentine, 18-year-old brother of the confessed slayer, arrived from the Korean battlefield, completely surprising the defendant who had no knowledge of his whereabouts.

The returned war hero had heard of his brother's plight while fighting Chinese Communists around the 38th parallel on May 24. Within five days he was out of the battlefield and in the courtroom. He flew from Hongchon to Tokyo, then to Midway, Honolulu and Los Angeles, arriving in Cut Bank around noon Tuesday.

The veteran of 8½ months of overseas duty did not know of the trouble his brother had got himself into until he received a letter from his uncle, John South, who had been here two weeks ago to see the 19-year-old slayer.

He was serving with the 7th Infantry Division when he received his 30-day furlough and had been in the hospital on two occasions as a result of battle wounds.

Frank Valentine was very bright-eyed and attentive during the sessions. He conversed frequently with his attorneys and showed immense interest at several bits of testimony given by the parade of witnesses.

Black and O'Connell said the petition "is based upon the . . . medical records of the defendant duly certified by the chief of the bureau of medicine and surgery of the navy department."

The petition also stated in part that the guilty plea "was entered by the defendant without consultation with counsel or attorney whatsoever . . . was not made voluntarily nor intelligently by the defendant, and was made under circumstances over-reaching the free will and judgment of this defendant."

Psychiatric and psychological phrases were tossed around rather freely during the testimony of Wilder, Spratt and Miss Alice Bastow, psychologist at the Butte mental clinic. The three agreed on the findings reached here May 3 when they each examined Valentine.

During the hearing, Wilder said Valentine had a psychopathic personality which indicates little or no feeling for the welfare of other people, but not a form of insanity. He also said the defendant had no control over what he does and that he gave way to sudden impulses.

Spratt's finding was in accordance with Wilder's and they all agreed that Valentine could determine between right and wrong and was mentally competent.

County Attorney John C. Hoyt asked for a recess at 5:50 and the court convened again at 7 o'clock.

This page and previous: From the Shelby Promoter, *May 31, 1951.*

Opposite: Frank Dryman's mug shot. *Montana Department of Corrections.*

Hi-Liners assumed that the remoteness of rural Montana insulated them from the Red Scare of the 1950s that was sweeping the nation. But out of nowhere, an uninvited communist attorney, backed by commie outsiders, had materialized to defend the blackhearted murderer of one of their own. The Red Menace had landed on their doorsteps.

Residents of Shelby, Oilmont, Kevin, Ferdig and Cut Bank organized a protest they called "doorbelling against the Reds." At six o'clock on the evening Dryman had been scheduled to hang, people

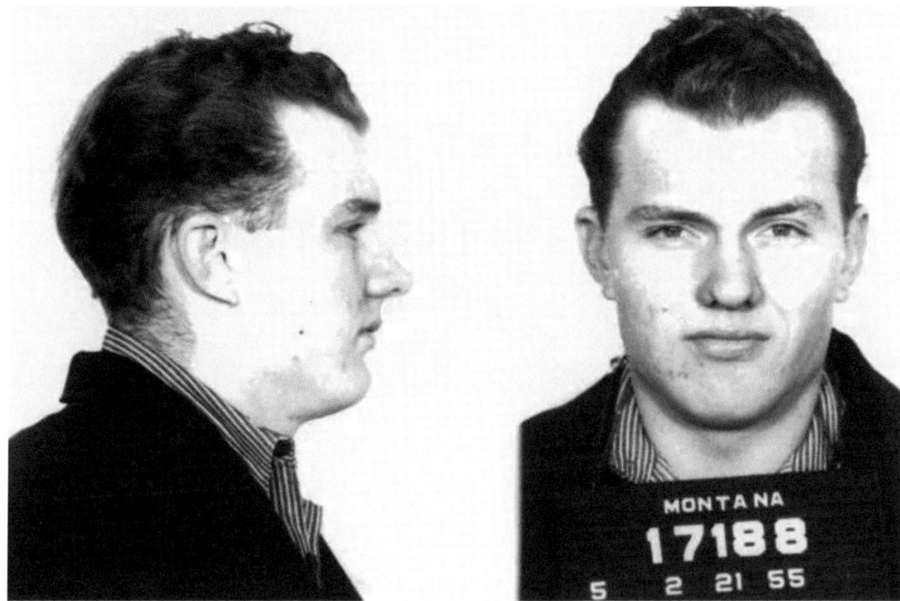

opened their front doors, stepped out on their front porches and rang their doorbells for five minutes.

Smokey and Dunstall had to act quickly to prevent a lynching. Moving Dryman to an adjacent county, as was the custom, would be far from adequate. The only option was to move him to the state prison in Deer Lodge, over two hundred miles south.

Dunstall went straight to Judge Hattersley, who immediately wrote an affidavit supporting Dunstall's plan to move the killer. The sheriff also penned a petition to the State Board of Prison Commissioners for permission to move the prisoner to Deer Lodge.

While Smokey and Deputy Stromme stood guard around the clock at the jail, Sheriff Dunstall hopped in the squad car and drove to Helena to testify before the state prison commissioners. There, on June 6, at three o'clock in the afternoon, Dunstall told the commissioners, "My presence is not to save a cold-blooded murderer, only to prevent a lynching and to prevent a blot on the citizens of the Hi-Line." He submitted the affidavit and petition, signed on June 5, 1951, by himself and attested to by Judge Hattersley. Acting on the sheriff's request and under pressure from Toole County's State Senator George W. Wilson, Governor Bonner, Attorney General Olsen and the prison board chairman signed a resolution accepting custody of Frank R. Dryman.

Chapter 15

TRIALS AND TRIBULATIONS

O'Connell was confident he enjoyed an advantage with the Montana Supreme Court. After all, not only had this court facilitated his bar appointment, but Associate Justice Lee Metcalf was also cofounder of *The People's Voice* and a close friend of the Billingses.

Knowing that this greenhorn attorney was learning on the job, the high court was extraordinarily lenient in granting him three extensions. Chief Justice H. Adair accepted "overworked, too busy and printing delays" as excuses that stretched the seventy days Hattersley had granted to four months, triggering speculation that legal shenanigans were afoot.

Rather than shenanigans, Gretchen Billings interpreted these postponements as "resistance to the passion of the mob." Her fiery commentary in *The People's Voice* matched Jerry's scorching rhetoric. Her involvement in the case grew from writing editorials to drafting appeals and devising legal strategy.

Finally, in November, O'Connell filed appeal briefs with the Montana Supreme Court. He ignored Hattersley's order to lodge his written appeal with him and serve a copy on Toole County Attorney Hoyt, who only learned of the filing through the United Press.

Feeling Hoyt had been "Pearl Harbored" escalated the high feelings across the Hi-Line. "Why they kept the county attorney in the dark must have some sort of significance," speculated the *Shelby Promoter*. "Several have been wondering about the shenanigans down at Helena."

Jerry accused Hoyt of withholding evidence and doctoring the defendant's confession. He also accused the citizens of the Hi-Line of acting like a "hot-blooded mob."

The new year was filled with legal proceedings. First, on January 15, O'Connell and Hoyt addressed the Montana Supreme Court. Harry Billings sat in the gallery.

Addressing the justices, O'Connell avoided talking about the crime. Instead, he directed his remarks at the Toole County attorney and the U.S. Navy. In addition to alleging that the defendant was beaten into confessing, O'Connell accused Hoyt of withholding evidence of the defendant's navy record at the initial arraignment and of doctoring Dryman's confession. He bitterly criticized the U.S. Navy for returning an "insane" man to civilian life. "The U.S. Navy should be in the penitentiary for releasing [Valentine] into his own custody…and for declaring he does not constitute a menace to himself or others."

Hoyt countered, "The defendant was not denied due process, knew the consequences of the guilty plea and…the boy's desire to kill anyone who irritated him was proof of his sanity. The boy was treated kindly; the sap was used in the manner as a mother would tap a child who had been in the cookie jar."

Letters to the editor flooded state newspapers stating that Dryman was the responsibility of the navy, not the hangman.

On Friday, January 18, Gretchen Billings wrote,

> *As the shadow of the gallows loomed, Jerry J. O'Connell entered the Dryman case. Mr. O'Connell's appearance in the high court chambers lost nothing by the absence of a fee for his services. Without material or mental resources, the defendant had no inclination to defend himself. Without money, should anyone be allowed to commit suicide? The laws of Montana do not ensure "life" imprisonment for a boy of 19, but should we then condone euthanasia?*
>
> *"You shall not take the life of your fellow man," said Moses. It must not apply to county attorneys putting a man to death—Mr. Hoyt, when the roll is called up yonder, what will you say?*

Three days later, the Billingses' friend and political ally W.P. Pilgeram, former Democratic speaker of the Montana House of Representatives, wrote to Gretchen that he was "somewhat alarmed" by her support of Dryman, whom he characterized as "a cruel, vicious, inhuman individual who killed his benefactor, Mr. Pellett, deliberately....I cannot sympathize, nor do I agree with you that this individual should be shown mercy. After all, how much mercy did he show Pellett?...I am afraid that this stand that I am going to take in regard to this man Dryman is going to break up a beautiful friendship that existed between us."

Gretchen replied, "Bill, it is now my turn to be 'consternated and alarmed.' Friendship, like my convictions, Bill, are based on sterner stuff." She insisted,

> *It is absolutely ridiculous that that point* [about "beating the rap"] *should be raised every time the hanging crowd starts talking. At no time has anyone interested in this case even remotely suggested that this boy should be allowed freedom. I would have been horrified and sickened had you or my husband been in Clarence Pellett's place. But I still would not want to see Frank Dryman hang. If fate had decreed Frank Dryman to be my son or yours, Bill, would he have been sentenced to die in three hours?*

She then accused Bill of being an active member of an organization that supported a foreign policy that taught boys the fine art of killing. "We cannot allow them [juveniles] to commit deeds of violence upon the peaceful citizens of our own country, even if they will be expected to perform these same deeds on the homes of people of other races and colors."

On February 15, Montana's high court unanimously ordered the Toole County District Nine Court to allow the defendant to withdraw his guilty plea, thus requiring a new trial. Justice Freebourn wrote, "The evidence raises grave doubt that the defendant had the mental capacity to appreciate and understand what he was doing and the consequences thereof.

In March, Toole County Attorney John C. Hoyt sent a ten-page petition to Attorney General A.H. Olsen to file with the Supreme Court for a rehearing of its ruling. Hoyt offered up three punishments: first, to be hanged as sentenced; second, a life sentence served in Deer Lodge; and finally, to commit Dryman to the state hospital at Warm Springs. Hoyt warned, "Dryman had already repeatedly threatened certain residents of Toole County. If any further murders are committed by the defendant, the court itself will have to accept its share of the responsibility." Within a week, the high court brushed aside Hoyt's petition.

On October 29, a hearing on a petition for a change of venue was held at the Toole County Courthouse. Over that day's proceedings, the state submitted twenty-five affidavits, two from clergy, and called multiple

Old Montana Supreme Court chamber, Helena, Montana. *Author's collection.*

witnesses. All of them save Shelby resident Edwin Adams were confident that Dryman could get a fair trial in Toole County.

O'Connell stated that his conversations at the Capital Café, the Snack Shack and other places throughout Toole County had convinced him that everyone on the Hi-Line was biased against the defendant, certain of his guilt and convinced that he should be hanged. But in his travels around other parts of the state, including Helena and Butte, he had heard some doubt about whether Dryman did kill Clarence Pellett. Mrs. Pellett's swift remarriage to a man younger than her only child, Marion, heightened suspicions that she might have been involved in C.C.'s murder. O'Connell also complained that the *Shelby Promoter* was advocating for the state to carry out the hanging. The next day, Hattersley denied the motion.

In November, William Black was elected Toole County attorney, replacing Hoyt. Since Black could not represent both the defense and the prosecution in the same murder case, Lewis P. Donovan was appointed Toole County special prosecutor. This left O'Connell as the lone attorney for the defense.

In December, "Bad Man" Bill Cook was executed at San Quentin, although his defense team used the same arguments as Dryman's, contending that Cook was emotionally unstable due to a poor upbringing and that he was not sane enough to understand the consequences of his guilty plea. Strapped to the chair in the gas chamber, he clenched his fists, showing the letters "H-A-R-D L-U-C-K" tattooed on his fingers. His last words were, "I hate everybody's guts, and they hate mine!"

A week later, Donovan turned down O'Connell's proposed plea deal for a life sentence. The judge also denied the defense's request that the state pay for medical experts and set a trial date of January 5, 1953.

The Dryman Defense Committee, encountering as much resistance as they had in retaining an attorney, struggled to find a psychiatrist willing to support an insanity plea. With the trial date looming, Gretchen Billings and Charles Huppe, former first assistant to Montana State Attorney General Olsen, phoned the Missoula County auditor, LaVerne Taylor, a friend of psychiatrist Gladys Holms, MD, director of the Mental Hygiene Clinic at the University of Montana. All three on the call agreed that Dryman was being railroaded. They decided that the auditor, Taylor, would be the best one to approach Dr. Holms to testify on Dryman's behalf.

Taylor explained to her friend Gladys that as a psychiatrist and the director of a mental health clinic, her expert testimony for the defense could prevent a potential injustice. Aware that Superintendent Spratt had already found the killer sane, Dr. Holms stressed that she was not inclined to involve herself.

By January 1953, the case was in the national news. *Special Detective Magazine* detailed the international manhunt, the capture, the confession and Dryman's new trial.

In Shelby, on Monday, January 5, jury voir dire commenced. By evening, twelve jurors had been sworn in. At nine thirty the next morning, before an overflowing gallery, the trial began. Special Prosecutor Lewis P. Donovan, assisted by his son Pat, called mostly the same witnesses who had testified in 1951.

Donovan introduced plaintiff's exhibit no. 10: the April 12, 1951 letter Dryman wrote to his parents. Donovan pointed out to the court that "the defendant wrote, 'I am in jail in Shelby, Montana, the reason: "Murder"....I must pay my debt to society....I did it....Me, I'm done for.'"

On Wednesday, O'Connell informed the court, "My heart is fluttering." John A. March, MD, was summoned at eight thirty that morning to examine him. Finding his heart normal, March advised Judge Hattersley that the trial could resume immediately. O'Connell requested additional rest. Hattersley granted a continuance until the following morning.

That same morning, at eleven o'clock, in Missoula, Gladys Holms was served a subpoena directing her to appear in Shelby prepared to testify for the defense. "It came as a great shock," Holms recalled.

While Jerry prepared his client for his upcoming testimony, Holms used the afternoon to "glance through" Dryman's navy record. That Thursday evening, she examined Dryman at the Toole County jail for three hours.

The following morning, Frank R. Dryman was called to the stand. O'Connell asked the defendant why he had two names. Frank explained that his mother was still married to Dryman when he was born, so the birth certificate was filled out "Dryman" even though Valentine was his biological father. He testified that his mother was "a word I'd rather not say; she went with other men when my father wasn't home."

O'Connell limited his direct examination of Dryman to certain parts of the timeline. Adroitly, he omitted asking his client about hitching a ride with Pellett, the gun, the murder, the confession or how he crossed the border into Canada.

When Donovan began to question Dryman about how he got the weapon, O'Connell objected, pointing out that the information had not been developed in direct examination. Hattersley sustained the objection on the grounds that cross-examination was limited to what had been brought out in direct examination. By omitting salient points surrounding the murder in his direct examination, O'Connell severely constrained the prosecutor's questions.

Donovan attempted to introduce the transcript of the signed confession into evidence. Again, O'Connell objected, and his objection was sustained. Frustrated, Donovan said, "Well, that is as far as I can go at this time."

Judge Hattersley called a recess to study the transcript of O'Connell's direct examination and case law. On returning to the bench, the judge stated, "There is no question in my mind that the cross-examination is proper if limited strictly to the matters brought out in the examination in chief."

At midafternoon, Dr. Holms was called to the stand. She testified that after three hours of examination, she had arrived at a diagnosis: "A schizophrenic of paranoid type, and [he] had been for a number of years."

As she did when she taught a class at the University of Montana, Holms wrote definitions of mental conditions on a blackboard to help the jury understand the word salad of psychiatry. Emphasizing that Frank showed no signs of mental derangement and that he had nothing specifically against Pellett, she testified, "Mr. Pellett just happened to be there when he exploded. He was antagonistic and bitter towards everybody on the earth."

That same day, after weeks of unsuccessfully scouring the state for medical experts willing to testify for the defense, Dryman Defense Committee member Lucy McLemore finally persuaded a psychiatrist to appear in court. On Custer Hotel stationery, McLemore wrote to Gretchen that Marin Albert Rouna, MD, of Billings, agreed to testify for the defense only after he was issued a cashier's check as a "good faith" initial payment.

The next morning, Saturday, January 10, O'Connell notified the court, "We have another witness, Dr. Rouna, who will arrive this afternoon by plane. I now ask leave of the court to call him out of order."

Judge Hattersley answered, "Of course, the court will grant that leave! We can't wait until he gets here."

The defense rested temporarily. The state called Drs. Spratt and Wilder, who both testified that in preparation for this trial, they had re-examined the defendant on December 10, 1952, at the state prison in Deer Lodge. Each testified that their opinion had not changed: Dryman was not insane or schizophrenic, and he knew right from wrong.

Next, Alice Bastow, a psychologist at Butte Mental Hygiene Clinic, testified for the prosecution. She had examined Dryman in both Shelby and Deer Lodge. Using inkblot and other tests, she concluded that Dryman had above average intelligence, was hostile and rebellious and had disregard for the rights or feelings of others.

Around noon, the state rested its case. O'Connell drove to Cut Bank to meet Dr. Ruona's two o'clock flight. In Shelby, over the next four hours, O'Connell advised this expert witness of the status of the case and the defense's strategy. At 6:00 p.m., Rouna walked to the Toole County jail, where he examined the defendant. At 6:50 p.m., O'Connell and Dr. Ruona walked up the hill and up the steps to the Toole County Courthouse. Court reconvened at 7:30 p.m.

After Dr. Rouna finished his lengthy description of his credentials, O'Connell asked, "Was your examination of less than an hour sufficiently long for you to make a diagnosis?"

The doctor answered, "Definitely! My personal examination of..." Pausing, the doctor asked, "What name is he going by?"

Hattersley answered, "Mr. Dryman."

The doctor resumed his testimony. "Mr. Dryman is insane and...he is suffering from schizophrenia, paranoid type."

Although his diagnosis was word for word the same as Holms's, his diagnostic methods were a far cry from hers. "When I asked him to lay on his bed in the nude, he had certain postural mannerisms which we see in schizophrenics," Rouna said. The doctor went on to describe using a needle all over Dryman's body to test his reactions. "When I touched him with something sharp, he would say, 'Dull,' and vice versa." This pattern of responses indicated to Rouna that Dryman was insane.

Late that Saturday night, at eleven o'clock, jury deliberations began. At two thirty on Sunday morning, January 11, jury foreman Roland Myers announced, "We the jury in the above-entitled case find the defendant guilty of murder in the first degree and leave his punishment to be fixed by the court."

"I'm going to kill you all!" shouted Dryman.

The following day, Gretchen Billings wrote a letter of thanks to Dr. Rouna. "As I am just a working gal, Mr. Rouna, may I ask if it will be all right if I pay this money to you by the month. I would like to commit myself to twenty dollars a month. Enclosed please find my check for the first twenty dollars."

On January 13, Dryman again stood before Judge Hattersley to receive his sentence: "hanged by the neck until dead." A warrant of execution instructed Sheriff Dunstall that the sentence was to be carried out on Friday, February 13. As before, O'Connell informed Judge Hattersley of his intention to file an appeal with the Montana Supreme Court. Again, the judge granted an extension of the stay of execution for an additional sixty days.

When a death sentence is handed down, both the judge and the clerk of court are required to sign the death warrant to make it legal. Clerk of Court Lutz walked out of the courtroom to her office, cleaned out her desk, left the building and never returned, never to sign the warrant. Three months later, a new clerk of court signed the warrant.

In early April, Judge Hattersley petitioned to move Dryman back to the state prison, citing Dryman's threats of "personal violence" against Toole County officials and the fact that he had "threatened to break jail and in fact from his statements and actions has become a dangerous person to be confined in the county jail." His petition was granted.

On June 19, those opposing state execution suffered yet another setback when the Rosenbergs were electrocuted in New York's Sing Sing prison.

The remainder of 1953 was filled with more filing delays. Even Montana's Attorney General A. Olsen requested a postponement because O'Connell had not filed "certain" papers.

O'Connell requested that the high court grant a new trial and a change of venue. In a point-by-point brief alleging twenty-three errors in the Toole County trial, O'Connell wrote, "I had taken this case convinced of Dryman's guilt, but…in the course of his defense [I] was convinced that Dryman did not commit the crime and was 'framed.'"

Three weeks later, L.P. Donovan resigned from the case. John "Luke" McKeon of Anaconda, Montana, applied and was hired by the Toole County commissioners as special prosecutor. The twenty-five-year-old recent graduate of the University of Montana Law School was the third attorney to represent the state in this case.

The situation in Montana had caught the nation's attention. On a coast-to-coast radio broadcast, one announcer concluded, "If you want to get away with murder…go to Montana."

In April, citing "high feelings" and deep-seated beliefs in Toole County that the defendant was guilty, Montana's high court handed down a 3–2 ruling:

> *The judgment of conviction is reversed and set aside, and the case is remanded to the district court for a new trial, with directions that the change of venue and place of trial be granted from Toole County in some other county not adjacent thereto.*

Soon after, Judge Hattersley notified the high court that he would preside over a new trial to be held in Choteau at the Teton County Courthouse. Teton County is separated from Toole by one county, Ponderosa. The trial was set for August 30, and the names of eighty prospective jurors were drawn.

Claiming that Judge Hattersley was prejudiced, and his client couldn't get a fair trial in the Shelby area, O'Connell filed a writ of supervisory control with the Montana Supreme Court on the grounds that Judge Hattersley was not in compliance with the ruling. O'Connell argued that although Teton County does not adjoin Toole County, it is "adjacent," according to the legal interpretation of the word. On September 24, the Supreme Court summoned Hattersley to show why the jury trial should not be transferred "to a court not adjacent to Toole County."

> Independent Reporter, *Helena, Montana*
> *November 22, 1954*
> *"Montana Supreme Court Sets Aside Toole County District Court Order Moving Site of Dryman Trial"*
>
> *A 4–1 decision: the word "adjacent" is of Latin derivation, from "adjaceo": to lie at, or nearby. It has been said that the word* adjacent *has no*

Ban Trial Of Dryman In Teton

HELENA—The Montana Supreme Court Monday ruled that Teton county is adjacent to Toole county and in effect apparently ordered the murder trial of Frank R. Dryman to be held outside of the Ninth Judicial District.

The ninth district presided over by Dist. Judge R. M. Hattersley takes in the counties of Teton, Pondera, Toole and Glacier.

Dryman has twice been sentenced to hang for the hitchhike gun slaying of Clarence E. Pellett, Four Corners cafe operator, near Shelby in 1951.

Dryman's counsel, Jerry J. O'Connell of Great Falls, appealed to the Montana Supreme Court from each sentence. The high tribunal first ordered a trial on the basis of errors the first time Dryman appeared in court when he pleaded guilty and was sentenced to hang by Judge Hattersley in Toole County District Court.

Dryman changed his plea to innocent. A Toole County District Court jury then convicted him and Hattersley again sentenced Dryman to hang.

Before the sentence was carried out however, O'Connell again appealed to the State Supreme Court claiming Dryman could not get a fair trial in Toole county.

The high court ordered a new trial to be held in a county not adjacent to Toole county. Judge Hattersley set a new trial for Teton county, separated from Toole county by Pondera county.

However, Dryman's council asked the State Supreme Court for another change of venue, claiming that Teton county is adjacent to Toole, even though it is separated by Pondera. He said the Legislature placed counties that are adjacent in the same judicial districts. He also said that Hattersley was "completely prejudiced in the matter."

Telephone Co. Builds New, Large Garage

The William L. Kappes Construction Co., of Shelby will construct a $10,500 garage-storeroom for the Mountain States Telephone and Telegraph Company here.

Telephone Company manager, L. G. Bucklin said that the contract for the new building was let recently, and work was begun this week. The one-story building will be built of pumice block at the rear of the present telephone building, and will house three vehicles and serve as equipment storage space.

Former Shelby Man Named As Capitol Aid For Orvin Fjare

Orvin B. Fjare, Congressman Elect from Montana's second congressional district, has announced that Waldo N. Spangelo of Billings would be his administrative assistant in Washington, D. C.

Spangelo, a former Shelby resident, is a 33 year old native of Box Eler, Montana, and the son of Mr. and Mrs. N. M. Spangelo of Great Falls. He is married to the former Evelyn Scharfe of Havre, and they have one son, James. Spangelo attended St. Olaf College at Northfield, Minnesota and in

From the Shelby Promoter, *November 25, 1954.*

> *arbitrary meaning, but the term is a relative and not a definite and absolute one, the exact meaning of which in any particular case is determinable principally by the context in which it is used....*
>
> *Under all the facts and circumstances of this case...Teton County must be held to be a county adjacent to Toole County.*

On Sunday, February 13, Dryman was transferred from Deer Lodge to Havre, 260 miles north. On February 14, Valentine's Day, the second jury trial of the convicted murderer, who had twice escaped the hangman's noose, was called to order at the Hill County Courthouse.

Neither Hill nor Teton County shares a border with Toole County. Each is separated from Toole by one county, yet Teton had been ruled "adjacent" to Toole and Hill had not. The difference? Hill County was out of Judge Hattersley's jurisdiction.

Judge C.B. Ewell presided over the six-day trial. Every day, throngs of people packed the courtroom, spilling into the hallways. Special prosecutor Luke McKeon was assisted by Hill County attorney Edward Ober Jr. O'Connell was the lone defense counsel.

In the first few moments of the trial, O'Connell argued to move the proceedings to Helena in Lewis and Clark County. Judge Ewell overruled him. Jury selection and voir dire took all day and resumed at nine thirty the next morning. By eleven o'clock, a jury of seven women, five men and two alternates had been empaneled.

Both the prosecution and the defense called the same witnesses and introduced the same exhibits as in the previous trial. Each side's witnesses reconstructed their view of the events surrounding April 4, 1951.

Young McKeon used Donovan's notes for each witness. Uninterested in the proceedings, Dryman sat silent, chewing gum and doodling.

On February 16, the same day Congress voted to admit Alaska and Hawaii as the forty-ninth and fiftieth states, McKeon called FBI Agent Robert M. Zimmerman, one of only six FBI agents trained in the new science of ballistics, to the stand. Zimmerman testified that the two bullets found inside Pellett and the four that passed through his body and lodged in the ground beneath him were fired from the pistol found buried in Canada.

By the fifth day, the trial had taken on now-familiar strong psychological overtones. Not surprisingly, each side's mental health experts disagreed about the defendant's sanity. Speaking coherently and deliberately, Dryman testified,

> *I goes into dreams at any time, and their recurrence can catch me unawares. I suffer a mental block which leaves me in a semiconscious or abstracted state. I do not remember taking the life of Pellett or of the man's begging and pleading to spare his life. If I had shot and killed the man or had met and spoken to the motorist who had given me a ride, I would have remembered.*

On Friday, February 18, both sides presented closing arguments. For the state, Edwin Ober explained,

> *The navy records recited in court never said Dryman actually was not sane, just not fit for service. Dryman shot Pellett because he was incensed by not having hitchhiked a ride earlier in the cold night and…he was antagonized by Pellett.*

O'Connell was next. For three hours, he rhetorically laid waste to the state's witnesses. Frank Dryman, he said, was beaten so badly by Dunstall that Chief Denison left the room in disgust. This brusque handling colored the defendant's confession.

If Dryman really were sane, as the prosecution charged, he would have been nervous or frightened when he was picked up by the RCMP. Instead, he gave his statement to an officer clearly and calmly. Nothing in that statement implicated him in the murder of Pellett.

O'Connell decried ballistics as more a matter of opinion than science, but he conceded that Zimmerman did prove Dryman's gun was the murder weapon.

Luke McKeon took an hour to rebut the defense.

Closing arguments concluded at 1:15 p.m. Judge Ewell then gave instructions to the jury. The jurors filed out to deliberate, taking the navy record with them. Four hours later, the jury reassembled to ask Judge Elwell if the defendant would have to serve the whole of his natural life if he was sentenced to life imprisonment. The judge explained that under state law, a life sentence did not ensure imprisonment for one's entire natural life.

One hundred people, including the victim's family, held vigil in the courtroom. After eight hours and ten minutes, at 9:15 p.m. on Saturday, February 19, jury foreman Murvin Hanson handed the verdict to bailiff E.G. Wood, who read it to the courtroom.

> *We the jury in the above-entitled action find the defendant, Frank R. Dryman (a.k.a. Valentine, 24 years, of Vallejo, California) guilty of murder in the 1ST degree and fix his punishment at imprisonment in the state penitentiary for the term of his natural life. Dated this 19TH day of February AD 1955.*

Judge Ewell then polled the jurors, asking if they agreed to the guilty verdict and punishment imposed as read by the bailiff. All replied, "Yes."

O'Connell waived the statutory time for sentencing, and the judge sentenced Frank R. Dryman to be imprisoned in the state penitentiary of the state of Montana, at hard labor, for the term of his natural life. He was remanded into the custody of Hill County Sheriff R.C. Timmons, and court was adjourned.

Convicted for the third time of first-degree murder and twice sentenced to hang, Dryman was all smiles as the sheriff escorted him out of the courtroom. For the Pelletts, there was no justice, only pain and sorrow that a murderer had beaten the rap.

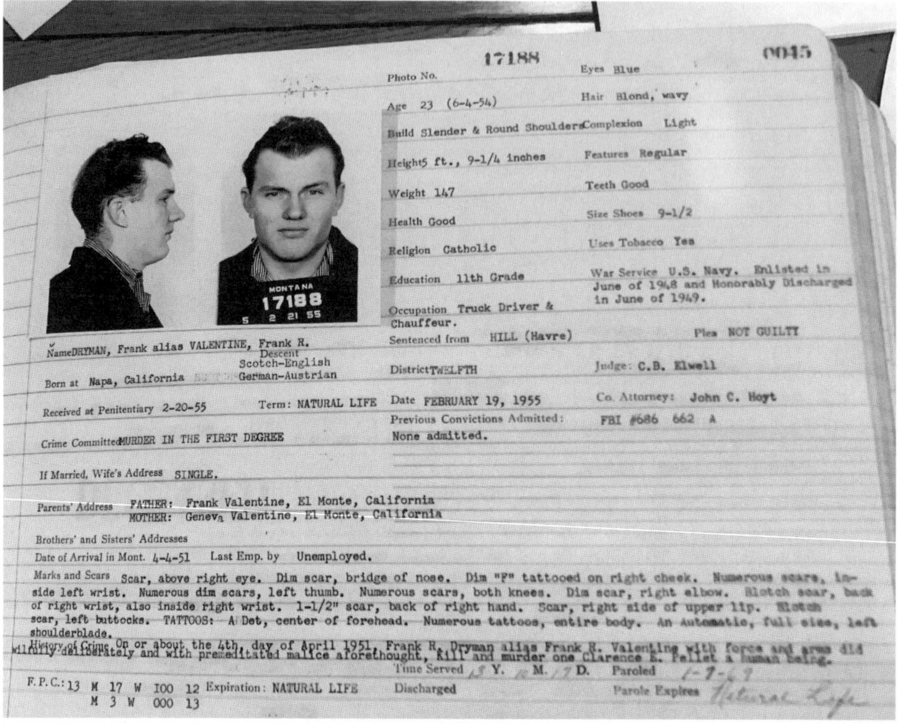

17188 0045

Photo No.
Eyes Blue
Age 23 (6-4-54)
Hair Blond, wavy
Build Slender & Round Shoulders
Complexion Light
Height 5 ft., 9-1/4 inches
Features Regular
Weight 147
Teeth Good
Health Good
Size Shoes 9-1/2
Religion Catholic
Uses Tobacco Yes
Education 11th Grade
War Service U.S. Navy. Enlisted in June of 1948 and Honorably Discharged in June of 1949.
Occupation Truck Driver & Chauffeur.

MONTANA 17188 5 2 21 55

Name DRYMAN, Frank alias VALENTINE, Frank R.
Sentenced from HILL (Havre)
Plea NOT GUILTY
Born at Napa, California
Descent Scotch-English German-Austrian
District TWELFTH
Judge: C.B. Elwell
Received at Penitentiary 2-20-55
Term: NATURAL LIFE
Date FEBRUARY 19, 1955
Co. Attorney: John C. Hoyt
Previous Convictions Admitted: None admitted.
FBI #686 662 A
Crime Committed MURDER IN THE FIRST DEGREE
If Married, Wife's Address SINGLE.
Parents' Address FATHER: Frank Valentine, El Monte, California
MOTHER: Geneva Valentine, El Monte, California
Brothers' and Sisters' Addresses
Date of Arrival in Mont. 4-4-51 Last Emp. by Unemployed.
Marks and Scars Scar, above right eye. Dim scar, bridge of nose. Dim "F" tattooed on right cheek. Numerous scars, inside left wrist. Numerous dim scars, left thumb. Numerous scars, both knees. Dim scar, right elbow. Blotch scar, back of right wrist, also inside right wrist. 1-1/2" scar, back of right hand. Scar, right side of upper lip. Blotch scar, left buttocks. TATTOOS: A Dot, center of forehead. Numerous tattoos, entire body. An Automatic, full size, left shoulderblade.
History of Crime On or about the 4th, day of April 1951, Frank R. Dryman alias Frank R. Valentine with force and arms did wilfully deliberately and with premeditated malice aforethought, kill and murder one Clarence E. Pellet a human being.
Time Served Y. M. D.
Paroled
F.P.C.: 13 M 17 W IOO 12 / M 3 W 000 13
Expiration: NATURAL LIFE
Discharged
Parole Expires Natural Life

Montana State Prison record. *Courtesy of Powell County Museum and Arts Foundation.*

Harry Billings marked the saving this murderer from the Galloping Gallows as one of Gretchen's "most notable achievements." Blue-collar rural Montana saw it differently. The sentence not only allowed a teenaged drifter to get away with cold-blooded murder but also meant he would likely be paroled back into society before age forty. That was a frightening proposition, considering how frequently this remorseless killer had lobbed taunts at prosecutors, jurors and the victim's family. They all remembered that Dryman had said, "I started killing the Pelletts. When I get out, I'll finish the job."

Chapter 16

INMATE TO ABSCONDER

In June 1951, Frank Dryman was driven 230 miles from the Toole County jail to the Montana State Prison in Deer Lodge, Montana. He was held there in protective custody throughout the four years of legal wrangling surrounding the murder case of Clarence Pellett.

For the first six months, Dryman was housed in a special section of a cell block reserved for "fresh fish." As he did during his short time in the navy, he whined about various ailments and poor treatment and claimed he was being poisoned by a strange white dust in his cell: talcum powder. Filling his idle time, he sketched, painted and fabricated a miniature gallows with toothpicks he pilfered from the cafeteria, complete with a string noose.

With no appeals pending, his protective custody status was changed to "prison inmate" on February 20, 1955. Inmate 17188—twenty-three years old; five feet, nine and a half inches; 147 pounds; slender, with rounded shoulders; shoe size nine and a half; blue eyes; wavy blond hair; and good teeth—was assigned to building no. 2, cell no. 309. Immediately, Dryman petitioned for his four years in protective custody to be credited against the thirteen years and nine months till he would be eligible for parole. A judge denied this out of hand.

Dryman started serving his sentence in the garment factory and as an orderly in the prison hospital. But it was when he was assigned to the sign painting and print shop that he flourished. He was talented, with a good eye for sign design.

Overcrowding and mismanagement led to three prison riots during Dryman's stay in Deer Lodge. By far the worst occurred in April 1959, when Alcatraz alumnus Jerry Myles and his accomplice Lee Smart threw gasoline on a guard and threatened to set him on fire. The guard turned over his keys and a .30-30 rifle.

After thirty-six hours, the national guard reclaimed control of the penitentiary by firing two rounds from a World War II bazooka into a prison tower. All told, inmates murdered Deputy Warden Rothe and held twenty-five hostages, including sixteen guards and Warden McCormick. Instigators Myles and Smart died in a murder-suicide pact.

The extent of Dryman's involvement in the riot is not certain, but in the upside-down hierarchy of prison culture, having been twice sentenced to hang for first-degree murder and then beating the rap with a life sentence, he was held in high standing, part of the "con boss" network that ran the prison. He later claimed that he turned down an offer from ringleader Myles to carry one of the firearms inmates confiscated from the guards. However, witnesses testified to seeing Dryman participating in reprisals against "stool pigeon" inmates and holding hostages at knifepoint.

Meanwhile, on the outside, Jerry O'Connell, Dryman's erstwhile defense attorney, was up to his elbows in troubles that seemed peculiarly Jerry-like. In June 1955, he was called to appear before the House Committee on Un-American Activities (HUAC). Although the FBI had classified him as a "top functionary of the party," O'Connell adroitly sparred with the HUAC questioners, stoutly asserting, "I am not now, and I have never been a member of the Communist Party. I'm an old-fashioned American liberal."

To the committee members, the thin line between liberalism and Communism was a distinction that made no difference. O'Connell died of a massive heart attack at the age of forty-six on January 16, 1956, sparing himself being called to appear before HUAC again.

Throughout his time behind bars, Dryman was relentless in his attempts to reduce his sentence. Given his eleventh-grade education, his multiple letters requesting commutation were surprisingly eloquent—and they were written in near perfect penmanship.

On May 1, 1960, Dryman wrote to parole board director W.A. May:

> *A Catholic priest visits me daily. In prison I have learned to live with my fellow man. To work beside him, to share with him and most of all pray with him. I was a bad boy nine years ago. Now I'm a sorrowful, mature man.*

Montana State Prison, Deer Lodge, April 16, 1959. *Courtesy of Powell County Museum and Arts Foundation.*

GUN MAN'S FATE

Gather around boys and listen to me well,
I'll tell you a little story before I go to Hell.

Now I was a man with a heart of gold, and a
Disposition to match or so I've been told.

But way out in old Montama when the goin' got rough,
I pulled my .45 and they got tough.

Now the sheriff tried hard to stove in my head
And the Judge said hang by the neck till dead.

Then they took me down to the Montana pen
Lock me in a cell and told me where I'd been.

Now I stayed right there for a year or two
Because I didn't have much to do.

Then they took me out and hanged me high
And I soon found out that I could die.

Then they cut me down and shooked me loose
And filled me up with embalming juice.

They put me in a wooden box, covered me up
With the dirt and rocks,
And all went well for about a week
And then my coffin began to leak.

My eyes fell in, my teeth fell out and the worms
Played pinochle upon my snout,
And after all was said and done, nothing was
Left but my skeleton.

Now if I could come back to see my Hannah,
I'd damn sure stay away from Montana.

Frank Dryman

Poem written by Frank Dryman, inmate 17188, circa 1958. *Author's collection.*

Although the Board of Pardons and Parole denied commutation, it did grant him another hearing the following year after his mental status was evaluated at the Montana State Hospital in Warm Springs. Evaluations that fall found no psychosis.

That April, Dryman, an avid reader of law citations, penned a *forma pauperis* writ of habeas corpus to the Montana Supreme Court. In it, he maintained that the 1960 U.S. Supreme Court ruling in *Blackburn v. Alabama* was identical to his case. Like Seaman Valentine, Jesse Blackburn was discharged from the armed forces while suffering from "schizophrenia reaction of the paranoid type" and, because of this "permanent mental disability," was deemed unfit for service.

Civilian Blackburn was arrested for robbery. Subjected to "sustained interrogation and intimidation, he signed a confession." The U.S. Supreme Court ruled that he was not mentally competent and that his confession should not have been admitted in evidence. Dryman claimed the ruling established a new precedent regarding confessions that made his inadmissible. Furthermore, he wrote, "The court erred in admitting my confession for the reason I was a person of limited mental ability. I was beaten and struck with a sap while six or more officers held me in the chair."

Montana's high court said Dryman's account of his confession "was not supported by the evidence." The court also quoted Dryman's letter to his parents, "I did it....It was cold-blooded murder. I put seven .45 slugs in him." It reminded Dryman that he'd had ample access to the state's judicial system: multiple trials, a change of venue and four favorable Montana Supreme court appeals. Said the state's high court, "We do not believe any of the statements of defendant were improperly admitted in evidence....It is ordered that the petition for writ of habeas corpus be denied."

On July 1, 1961, Dryman applied yet again for commutation, claiming he should be credited for having served thirteen years and nine months of his sentence. Five days later, in its denial, the board reminded him that his life sentence started the day he was received at the prison after the jury imposed a life sentence in 1955—not on June 4, 1951, when he was taken into protective custody. "Prison records show you have served 6 years and 3½ months."

In July 1962, although they had never spoken or laid eyes on each other, Dryman wrote to Gretchen Billings, asking for her support in his quest for commutation of his sentence.

> *Mr. O'Connell never explained to me who you were, cuz I was a crazy mixed-up bitter kid incapable of understanding that someone was trying to help me. Now that kid has grown up. I've earned a high school diploma and am an accomplished sign painter....While studying my case I came*

across the last letters written to me by my Mr. O'Connell before his death. He wrote, "I have talked to the ministers, to Mrs. Billings, Mrs. McLemore and others who have been interested in you and they are already doing the things that have to be done in order to accomplish that which I have suggested." That letter prompted me to seek your help, Mrs. Billings. I'm asking for it now. Please hear my plea!

Gretchen wrote back,

I am not just sure what we can do or just how to go about doing anything. Don't want to give you false hope but will start some inquiries and see what develops.... We are happy to hear you have not wasted the intervening years. Eleven years ago, you weren't a very encouraging prospect, you know.

Five days later, on August 20, 1962, Dryman wrote back to Gretchen, asking if she or her representative would meet with him about the court actions of the previous two years. Gretchen Billings, a self-proclaimed activist for mental health in Montana, served under two state executives as a member of the Governor's Committee for Mental Health. However, neither she nor her representatives visited this "permanently insane, mentally disabled" boy in prison, nor did they advocate for his psychiatric care while he was in prison.

When Dryman was named the 1964 Junior Chamber of Commerce prisoner of the year, prosecutor Luke McKeon accepted Dryman's invitation to present the award to him. The award "ceremony," also attended by Lieutenant Governor Ted James, was held in the prison cafeteria over coffee and donuts.

On April 1, 1966, the parole board notified the Toole County commissioners that Frank Dryman's sentence would be on its agenda at its hearing on April 22, 1966. This sparked immediate responses from Toole County. The Board of Toole County Commissioners, Toole County Sheriff E. Pierson, Judge R.D. McPhillips of the Ninth Judicial District, Theron Pellett and Marion Pellett all objected strenuously to the prospect of Dryman being paroled. Consequently, the parole board rejected Dryman's request for commutation. "You will appear when eligible [in the fall of 1968] without further consideration."

Notification of "review for consideration of granting parole to inmate 17188, Frank R. Dryman, a.k.a. Frank R. Valentine" was sent to the inmate's family a month prior to the fall of 1968 board hearing. However, the board failed to notify Toole County officials or the victim's family of the upcoming hearing.

On November 22, 1968, Mr. Martinson, chairman, called the hearing to order. The chairman addressed Dryman: "I see you were involved in the 1959 riot. Tell us about that."

"Inmate Myles offered me a .30-30 rifle, but I turned him down," Dryman explained. "I didn't want any part of that."

"Your record indicates you started carrying a gun as a youngster."

"I used to like guns. I no longer have a desire to have one; no good can come from carrying one. I've given up on guns."

Asked how he would support himself if paroled, Dryman said, "Before, I waited tables, painted houses and drove a truck, but during my time here I have earned my high school diploma, taken drafting and highway engineering courses, was named prisoner of the year by the JCs—and I'm told I'm an accomplished sign painter."

Chairman Martinson asked, "Before we render a decision, Mr. Dryman, do you have anything more you would like to say?"

"Yes sir, I am most desirous to become a productive member of society."

Martinson reminded board members that under Montana law, although this inmate had served sufficient time to qualify for parole eligibility, it was solely at the board's discretion whether to grant it. Because the parole board hadn't notified the victim's family and Marion Pellett had passed nine months earlier, none of the victim's family members were present to object. Dryman was granted parole and released into his brother Jim Valentine's custody in Chino, California.

Martinson asked, "Do you have anything else you would like to say to this board?"

"Yes sir, I want to be home for Christmas after eighteen years."

The board immediately notified the warden of Montana State Prison at Deer Lodge of its decision. It also sent a letter to California's Interstate Compact Unit, Sacramento, to the attention of deputy administrator Milton Burdman, requesting acceptance for supervision of Montana parolee Frank Robert Dryman.

On January 3, 1969, Supervising Agent J. Allen in Ontario, California, notified the board that he had visited James Valentine at his residence in Chico. He reported that Mr. and Mrs. Valentine confirmed they would sponsor and house parolee Frank Dryman and that Frank's half-brother Hank and sister Ginger both resided in the Los Angeles area and were willing to help. Jim also confirmed that the owner of South Garey Furniture had agreed to employ Frank.

Residents of the Hi-Line felt they had again been "Pearl Harbored." Robert Tomsheck, chairman of the Board of Toole County Commissioners, sent the parole board a very stern letter objecting to Dryman's release. "Mr. Dryman has made numerous threats against certain witnesses; these threats should not go unheeded."

Dryman was released the next day. Before he walked out of prison on Tuesday, January 7, he was required to sign an agreement that outlined the terms of his parole. After signing, Dryman was provided a bus ticket and was free to travel on his own recognizance. There were no guarantees that he would not head north to Shelby to make good on his threats.

The Pelletts were caught off guard, too. Lyle Pellett, the fourth of the five siblings, wrote, "To the Board of Pardons, we, the family of Clarence Pellett, were informed by TV news that Frank Dryman was paroled to California. Please send details and reasons for this release of Frank Dryman."

Dryman had been in California for over two weeks before board of parole director Fred White Jr. responded to the Hi-Line's concerns.

> *To: Honorable R.D. McPhillips, Judge*
> *Cc: Lyle Pellett*
>
> *I am sorry that the interested people of the Shelby area did not receive the information of the parole hearing on Dryman. Our files indicate that notice was sent to Judge Thomas* [Ewell's replacement], *the sentencing Judge. Mr. Kalbfleisch* [the Toole County attorney] *states he did not receive notice. I am positive we sent it.*
>
> *Mr. Martinsen, board chairman, told me that they arrived at this* [granting parole] *from recommendations of people who have known and supervised Dryman since his incarceration in June of 1951.*
>
> *You may be assured that California will pay very close attention to Dryman. He will be returned to Montana State Prison at the first indication that his parole performance is not satisfactory.*

From the jump, the parole plan unraveled. Frank's brother Jim had moved, and the owner of the furniture store thought better of hiring a convicted murderer. In his "Progress and Conduct Report, Form No. 4," Parole Officer J. Allen informed Montana parole director Fred White Jr. that parolee Dryman would seek a sign painting job and had been instructed to get a California driver's license.

That August, Dryman met and married Bryle Cahill, a divorcée with five young children. He explained to his parole officer that he wanted to marry using his "true" name, Frank R. Valentine.

Over the next year, parole officer J. Allen paid "close attention," contacting his charge every two weeks. In his May 3, 1970 report, Allen informed White that parolee 17188 had married Bryle Valentine. The parole officer summarized Dryman's work history: "Worked at Kaiser Steel but was laid off; has sign painting business out of home."

Two weeks later, there was a major overhaul of California's interstate parole compact personnel. Allen was replaced by M.D. Hanlon, and B.C. Miles came on board as the state's new administrator. Following Hanlon's first visit to Frank Valentine's new family home, he wrote a report dated May 21, 1970, to the new administrator, B.C. Miles: "Wife and subject operate sign shop in newly rented house in Rialto. Overall adjustment—satisfactory—no problems anticipated."

After that, due to "vacation and large case load," monitoring of parolee 17188 dropped off significantly. Hanlon merely drove by: "Subject has been seen at a distance to be on the property."

This lackadaisical monitoring continued for five months until December 1970, when Hanlon met with Dryman. Two months later, on February 11, 1971, Hanlon forwarded an update to Montana, reporting that the subject's sign painting business was flourishing and his adjustment continued to be "excellent."

Two weeks later, Hanlon found "marital strife—wife has moved to San Bernardino." The following month, he reported, "Subject sent to psychiatrist, Dr. Campbell. Subject was thoroughly interviewed—found nothing organically wrong—subject is very hardheaded after eighteen years in prison—he has found it very difficult to adjust to outside living especially with a wife and five kids."

In July 1971, Hanlon reported, "The couple has reunited, took a vacation to Texas, continued adjustment seems good."

Then, in December, Hanlon reported his parolee was nowhere to be found. Bryle Valentine reported she thought he was "living in the desert as he purchased camping equipment and clothing." Immediately, a case conference was called in Sacramento. Unit supervisors J. Naghshineh and S. Harwell took charge of tracking down Dryman.

California's Interstate Compact investigators were able to find only a single lead. "Subject is driving a red 1971 Maverick—CA license 772—DIZ." But with a two-month head start, he could be anywhere.

Finally, on March 27, 1972, eight months after he was last seen, the State of Montana Department of Corrections and Human Services Probation and Parole Bureau issued an arrest warrant with no bond for parolee Frank Dryman. He was ordered returned to the custody of the warden of the Montana State Prison.

In no time, word got out that Dryman was on the loose. Hi-Liners feared he would make good on his threat to kill everyone in Shelby. Loaded guns were kept at the ready, especially after sunset. Law enforcement was flooded with calls. Northcentral Montana became a hitchhiking desert—no one offered rides or stopped to help stranded motorists.

Dryman emerged from the desert using various birth dates, Social Security numbers and aliases. He used "Edwin O. Adams," the name of the Shelby resident who testified on his behalf, and cities such as Dallas as aliases before settling on "Victor Houston." He got married for the first time as Houston to a woman named Georgia in Albuquerque, New Mexico. She repeatedly threatened to turn him in. It was rumored he shot her in the back of the head, dug a deep hole near their trailer, dumped her corpse into it, filled it with dirt and planted a tree on top. No proof of this has ever been found.

Over the decades, there was but one lead. On December 15, 1972, a private investigator reported seeing Dryman's red Maverick in the Las Vegas area. Finally, on March 29, 1977, Frank Adams reported in the *Great Falls Tribune* that Montana officials lost track of Dryman after he was paroled to California.

The publicity stimulated George M. Cuff, a member of the parole board, to activate the parole revocation system, which sent bulletins to Montana police departments and entered Dryman into the National Crime Information Center (NCIC).

In Shelby, Toole County Attorney Kalbfleisch consulted Judge McPhillips, who advised him to contact the FBI and demand they assist in apprehending this absconder. Soon after, the FBI issued an Unlawful Flight to Avoid Prosecution warrant.

Blissfully unaware, Vic Houston carried on with his new life. He painted a cartoon image of the Pink Panther on either side of his red Maverick and drove down Highway 25, pulling into every truck stop along the way. With the windows rolled down and his eight-track tape boom box blasting the Pink Panther theme song, Vic circled each truck stop, drumming up business customizing the cabs of eighteen-wheelers for one hundred dollars. He also used "Pink Panther" as his handle on his CB radio. The irony of a fugitive

STATE OF MONTANA
DEPARTMENT OF CORRECTIONS AND HUMAN SERVICES
Probation and Parole Bureau
1539 11th Avenue, Helena, MT 59620
(406) 444-4913/4916-Phone / (406)444-4920-Fax

ARREST WARRANT - NO BOND

This is a warrant for the arrest of DRYMAN, FRANK Montana # AO17188 an inmate of Montana State Prison, sentenced from TOOLE County, on the 19TH day of FEBRUARY, 1955 for the crime of MURDER IN THE FIRST DEGREE. He was granted a parole on the 7TH day of JANUARY, 1969.

Pursuant to Sections 46-23-433 and 46-23-1023, Montana Code Annotated, the Department of Corrections and Human Services hereby demands the return of the above named inmate to the custody of the Warden of Montana State Prison, or to any other suitable detention facility designated by the Department, because DRYMAN, FRANK has violated the conditions of his release.

Under the authority granted by the above statutes the Department of Corrections and Human Services hereby authorizes and directs any peace officer or parole officer to apprehend, take into custody, and hold the above-named person and to return such person to Montana State Prison or to any other suitable detention facility designated by the Department.

Dated this 27TH day of MARCH, 1972.

Mike Ferriter
CORRECTIONS DIVISION

** If parolee is arrested in Montana, subject is entitled to a Preliminary Hearing prior to being extradited to Montana State Prison pursuant to 46-23-1024 MCA.

Updated 6/8/95

Dryman disappeared in the fall of 1971 and was officially declared an absconder the following March. An arrest warrant was issued. *Courtesy of Montana Board of Pardons and Parole.*

from justice using the theme from a movie featuring an inept police detective was not lost on him.

At a Standard Oil truck stop near Albuquerque, Vic met a teenage cashier, Debbie "Kay" Barker. An aspiring cartoonist, she admired Houston's talent. The next day, she left her husband and ran off with Vic. "He said he wanted to get something off his chest, be up front with me," Kay later said. "He told me he had killed a man in a bar fight and asked if that was okay."

Using both the Dallas and Houston aliases, the couple drove up and down the West Coast. "It was exciting being on the run," Kay said. "When we needed money, we'd pull over and work the truck stops....When it came to the law, he thought he was untouchable; he definitely thought he was smarter than everyone else. But we had a big fight, he pulled a gun on me, so I left and went back to Albuquerque."

At the Silver Bells Wedding Chapel in Las Vegas in August 1978, "Houston" got married for the second time, to a prostitute twenty years his junior, Cynthia Robin Hughes. A friend of hers who witnessed the ceremony reported, "When they returned from their 'honeymoon' to a trailer next to an Albuquerque truck stop, they had a 'big fight.' Hughes wasn't seen after that. When Cynthia's sister came looking for her, Vic told her that 'she had run off with a trucker.' It wasn't long after that the sister vanished."

Vic reconnected with Kay Barker. The trio—Vic, Kay and her infant daughter, Wendy, by her first husband, whom she never divorced—moved to the remote desert town of Arizona City, Arizona. They bought two acres and lived in a trailer on the property. As Victor Houston, he applied for and obtained an Arizona driver's license and a license to perform marriages. As a State of Arizona–ordained officiant, he became deacon of the Cactus Rose Wedding Chapel. He also kept up his sign painting business and sold pottery and cacti. He and Kay were married in the Little Chapel of the Flowers in Las Vegas in 1981. Not long after, their daughter, Cathie Houston, was born.

Two years later, in 1983, a third round of Montana and federal violator at large warrants was issued. Frank R. Dryman, a.k.a. Valentine, was again entered into the Criminal Justice Information Network and the NCIC.

As the years turned into decades, Dryman swept the memory of the murder under the rug and embraced hiding in plain sight. He took on the persona of a Western hero, dressing in Western wear, a stovepipe hat and cowboy boots, affecting a handlebar mustache and carrying a holstered gun. Said one sheriff, "Vic, someday I'm going to find out why you always wear a gun."

Vic reveled in the notoriety that came with being a colorful character in this tiny snowbird community. When he walked into Duffers Restaurant, the local hangout, everybody knew him as Vic, Rattlesnake Jack, Cactus Jack or Deacon Houston. A member of the NRA, he was always packing one of his forty firearms.

Bragging was another habit he couldn't break. He spun yarns of hitchhiking across the country, catching a ride with Marilyn Monroe. As a chapel deacon, he claimed, he had so many groups that wanted him to preach to them that "I had to turn them down, just not enough time."

Victor Houston wore a gun and posed as a Western hero while hiding in plain sight for thirty-eight years in Arizona City, Arizona. *Author's collection.*

He inserted himself into the community, volunteering for civic committees and attending PTA meetings. He posted signs all over town. At the gate to the Cactus Rose compound was a sign reading, "ID required, so we can notify next of kin."

Above: Victor Houston was the deacon of the Cactus Rose Wedding Chapel. *From the* Casa Grande (AZ) Dispatch, *April 2010.*

Left: Deacon Houston was licensed by the State of Arizona to officiate weddings. *Author's collection.*

Opposite: Pinal County Sheriff Roger Vanderpool (*left*) presents Victor Houston with a Citizens On Patrol (COPS) certificate. *From the* Casa Grande (AZ) Dispatch, *2002.*

ABOVE: Dryman shows off his certificate at the sheriff's academy in Arizona City. **RIGHT**: Dryman wears his badge.

Vic registered for a post office box in Arizona City as Frank Valentine. Every month, he picked up his navy disability check.

Year after year, Victor Houston made a point of ingratiating himself with local law enforcement. He campaigned for several sheriff's elections, was part of the sheriff's department's security details, volunteered for the Pinal County posse and joined the search and rescue team. But his crowning achievement was graduating from the Citizens On Patrol program. Pinal County Sheriff Roger Vanderpool presented him with an impressive certificate, a uniform and a badge to pin on it.

As an experienced fugitive, Dryman was an expert in the finer points of being on the lam, never filing state or federal tax returns and using birth dates and Social Security numbers close to the real ones to make them easier to remember.

Vic divorced Debbie—unlike his previous four wives, who either disappeared or from whom he just walked away. Vic and Debbie's relationship was fiery: they fought like cats and dogs and pulled guns on each other. According to Debbie, "He's a cold-blooded chameleon, he has such a temper—he just explodes. I should have killed him that day. But that's not why I left him. He had been doing lots of bad things to Wendy. The rumors that he was molesting her were true." Debbie packed up and moved to Portales, New Mexico.

Never considering that they were aiding and abetting a fugitive, the Valentines had family reunions. Cathie's aunt Ginger called him Frank. Little Cathie would say, "Why do you keep calling him Frank? His name is Vic." He also attended navy reunions using his "navy name"—Frank Valentine.

In 2001, Deacon Houston officiated the wedding of Cathie, seventeen, and Nathan Rose, nineteen, in the parking lot of a Walmart in Portales, New Mexico. After a fight involving fisticuffs, Cathie threatened her new husband: "My dad is a fugitive murderer. He'll kill you. He's done it before." A year later, Nathan was found dead in the couple's apartment under mysterious circumstances.

On March 26, 2004, Vic drove to Phoenix, where he was commissioned and bonded as a notary public. Imagine: a fugitive, living under an alias, verifying signatory identities!

Unlike Kay, Wendy and Cathie, Vic never succumbed to drugs, but the years of scotch took their toll. His neighbors Pat and Jack Lindholme, whom he had married, watched as his health deteriorated.

Despite Vic's nasty disposition, the Lindholmes felt it was their duty to look after him. They arranged for Meals on Wheels and bought him groceries.

However, the couple kept their guard up around Vic. Pat recalled, "He may look like a harmless old man, but he was a dangerous person. He has a temper....He loved his guns; he was always armed."

Vic thought his disguise was impervious, but only a few years later and just forty miles to the north, his perfect disguise began to unravel—when his victim's grandson picked up his trail.

Chapter 17

THE CITIZEN DETECTIVE

In the spring of 2009, a neighbor in Sun Lakes, Arizona, found my thrice-married, widowed eighty-two-year-old mother, Jo, semiconscious on her living room floor. A chain-smoking alcoholic, she had suffered a stroke.

After we settled Jo in a long-term care facility, my wife and I cleaned out her trailer. We shipped numerous items to our condo in Bellevue, Washington, including a cardboard box filled with her keepsakes. Despite Cynde's encouragement, for months, I ignored that box.

One quiet Sunday afternoon, finally I decided to open the box. I found it filled with items Jo had accumulated over eighty years: awards, report cards and special occasion Hallmark cards. I also found an odd assortment of objects whose significance had long been forgotten. At the bottom were some frail, yellowed newspaper clippings that I carefully unfolded.

"Wide Search," "Foul Play," "Slaying of Montana Man," read the 1951 headlines. These articles reported on the murder of a man who was shot in the back by a teenage hitchhiker he picked up during a blizzard. The victim was Clarence Chester Pellett, my grandfather. At the time of the murder, he was fifty-nine, the father of six and grandfather of sixteen. I thought, *A big family, and I don't know them.*

I learned the shooter, who conspicuously sported a duck's ass–style "Hollywood haircut," was captured on April 5, 1951, the day after he shot his benefactor. Notwithstanding the teen's confession, his lawyer successfully appealed his multiple death sentences, arguing his client was permanently insane. Each execution was stayed, replaced by a life sentence. Despite public

Frank R. Dryman, 19
For Murder of C. E. I

-spondent

12—Frank R.
Frank Valentine,
vas sentenced to
hanging for the
ce E. Pellett.
ttersley of Conra
sentence after
, hearing testimo
reading Dryma
on and question
wo hours.

he hanging was s
ley, who order
O. Dunstall to sel
place." Dunstall s
ng will be held

who lived previou
lif., and Hawthorn
calm through toda
and failed to cha
n even on hear
ntence.
an pleaded guilty
murder yesterday
3,000 men.

Youth Clings To Denial of Shelby Death

SHELBY, April 6 (AP)—Weary authorities still hammered this morning at a youthful hitchhiker's story that he had nothing to do with the murder of Clarence E. Pellett, 59-year-old northwestern Montana cafe owner and oil pumper.

The bullet-riddled body of Pellett, seen when he picked up a hitchhiker near here Wednesday, was found in a muddy field where he ran a restaurant at Corners about 6 p. m. (MST) day.

Corner is 18 miles north of on the road to Sweet Grass the Canadian border where car was found yesterday. d billfold was in the back

C. O. Dunstall said the arrested between Leth- MacLeod, Alta., by the dian mounted police late claimed to be 20 years

he suspect answers the of a man seen getting car, adding: riding in a green like Pellett's

maintaine

Suspect Officers Pistol Ca

SHELBY, April 9 (U.P.)— old hitchhiker charge murder of a Montana c north of here last wee officers to a hidden .45 r a cache of ammunition a dian border town of Cou

Frank R. Dryman, a "Valentino," of Vallejo, been charged with the s Clarence E. Pellett.

Dryman led Toole Cou John C. Hoyt, Shelby Chi lice R. F. Denniston and D police chief at C hidd

birthday.

tanan Brutally Murd riff at Shelby Says Af

BY, April 5 (AP)—Clarence ett, 59, whose bullet-riddled was found in a muddy field his home today, was "brutally ered with a .45-caliber six ter," Sheriff C. O. Dunstall said

"I think Pellett wa and jumped from his have been shot from t body was 45 feet fr marks. Then the kille to the body and emp of his shells into it.

Clippings I found among my mother's keepsakes that led me to track down my grandfather's murderer. *Author's collection.*

entenced to Hang
lett, Cafe Owner

nnocence
breaking

ds

raised the gun he
ning and I started
when he fell over,
went up and empt
into him . . ."

Rumors that Dryma
been connected with
George H. Monroe, 42,
bartender who was fo
his home Tuesday, we
today by Dunstall and
pointed out Monroe diec
bullet wound, not a .45,
Dryman's movements prc
not in this vicinity at
Contrary to rumors, Pe
was found in front of th
Sweet Grass, not in Mon

Hanging of Dryman wou
first in Montana since
1943, when Philip J. Coler
to the gallows in Missoul
for murder.

him and others $2,800,000.

With 6-Shooter,
Viewing Body

he is 20 years old, said he had been in a hospital at Vallejo, Calif.

MOUNTIES CATCH SUSPECT

By Tribune Correspondent

The suspect, Frank R. Dryman, alias Frank Valentine, about 23, was arrested by Royal Canadian

Officers Fear Foul Play in Disappearance

A general alarm was spread over Montana and western Canada today for Clarence Pellett, 59, who disappeared Wednesday night after picking up a hitchhiker near Shelby.

Sheriff C. O. Dunstall of Toole county said foul play is considered "a very definite possibility."

Dunstall said three airplanes and about 100 cars joined the search for Pellett this morning. "We'll stay on the search until we find out what happened to him," the sheriff said.

Pellett's abandoned car was found near some tourist cabins in Sweet Grass about 8 o'clock this morning.

Dunstall said Pellett's billfold, which had been ransacked, his coat and his watch were found in the back seat of the car. The sheriff said there was no evidence of a struggle.

Dunstall said a man who knew Pellett saw him pick up the hitchhiker at a drive-in restaurant north of Shelby about 7:35 p. m. Wednesday. He said Pellett had left Shelby and was driving to his home at Four Corners, about 18 miles north of Shelby. Pellett operates a restaurant at Four Corners.

Joan Pellett, daughter of Mr. an
Mrs. Byron Clem of Great Falls,
the missing man's daughter-in-lav
She marriet Pellett's son, Mari
who is a Montana repr
Stauffer Chemi

outcry, after serving less than fourteen years, the killer was paroled. Learning this for the first time stunned me.

An only child, I was raised in Montana in my family of three. We never spoke of the murder of my grandfather. I was eleven the one and only time my dad talked about it. We were sitting in our car, in front of the Ben Franklin store on the west side of Great Falls, Montana. He told me his father was murdered in cold blood by a hitchhiker. I recall his solemn tone as he described how, in spite of my grandfather's begging, the hitchhiker shot him in the back.

"The killer got away with it because no one could find the gallows to hang him!" That was the version I had lived with for forty-five years. Perhaps I'd been given a simplistic explanation of a very complicated story, just enough for an eleven-year-old to grasp.

My father went on, "Just months later, my mother, your grandmother, married a man a year younger than me. I went to Oilmont High School with him. He was a buffoon. She and I had words. We have never spoken since, and we never will." He added sternly, "You are never to pick up a hitchhiker. Say it. Promise!"

Taken aback by his stern tone, I obediently answered, "I promise." Abruptly, Dad stopped talking. The subject was closed, not to be reopened. As it turned out, it never was. My father died not long thereafter.

As brief as that conversation was, the message was unmistakable: I was never to contact the Pellett family. I honored my father's intent.

I reread the articles. I saw the name of the murderer, Frank Dryman (a.k.a. Frank Valentine). I went to my computer, typed in D-r-y-m-a-n, F-r-a-n-k. Immediately, the website of the Montana Parole Board popped up. A few clicks brought me to a list of dozens of those who had skipped out on parole. Dryman had been missing for thirty-eight years, the longest of anyone on the list. He was the only one with no photo. I yelled to Cynde in the other room, "The guy who murdered my grandfather is a fugitive!"

Peering over my shoulder, Cynde said, "Let me see."

"Paroled in 1969 and absconded in 1972."

Ever the realist, Cynde declared, "You've never cared about this before; why now? What are you going to do—look for him? Where would you start? Besides, that was so long ago, there's no way he's still alive. I don't see the point." With that, she left the room. Feeling a bit deflated, I had to agree: the chance of learning any more was remote.

The next thing I knew, I was starting another search. This time, the Montana Historical Society's website came up. I thought, *I just stumbled upon four original articles—there's a good chance a historical society would have more.* I sent emails to the historical society and the parole board asking for assistance in finding information on the April 4, 1951 murder of Clarence Chester Pellett.

On June 2, 2009, I received a four-page letter from the historical society's research center director, Molly Kruckenberg: "This was a big case. To date I have found sixty pages of newspaper articles, miscellaneous handwritten notes, as well as nearly one thousand pages of materials from the Supreme Court docket filings. Much too much material to copy and send you. It would be helpful for you to come to the Montana Historical Society library here in Helena and review the materials on-site."

She suggested the best way to start was to contact newspapers and ask them to search their archives. "Included please find a list of Montana publications."

Not anxious to take time away from my oral surgery practice on what could be a wild goose chase, I concentrated on that list. I recognized all the publications but one, *The People's Voice*. Little did I know how big a role that unknown weekly paper would play in my quest.

Over that summer, I contacted newspapers across the Treasure State, so many that I developed a patter: "Hi, my name is Clem Pellett. I'm researching the 1951 murder of my grandfather, Clarence Pellett. I realize that is some sixty years ago, but I would be most grateful if you would take a look at your archives for any articles your paper might have that could help me in my research. I will be happy to compensate you for any copying and mailing fees. I look forward to working with you."

Although it took a special effort for them to rummage through their archives for sixty-year-old editions of the countless publications I contacted, the folks at each and every paper were not only cooperative; they were also downright enthusiastic. "Good luck to you," they said, one after another. "Let us know if we can help, and keep us updated!"

Each week, manila envelopes filled with dozens of copies of articles landed on the reception desk of my surgery center. I took them to my office, where I annotated each article and then printed out my notes and placed the pages in a three-ring binder. It was a laborious process, made slower because I did all this in between patients. After all, I had a practice to run.

In no time, I had a mountain of articles still to be annotated. After I ran out of space at my surgery center office, I took copies home. Soon my home office was filled to the brim.

But space wasn't the only problem. The articles were not sent in chronological order; they documented a sentencing here, an appeal there, mixed in with the occasional editorial. It was all a mishmash, with no coherent storyline. Not to mention the names—so many names! It was impossible to keep them straight! Dunstall, Hattersley and "Smokey"! I fashioned a "case character list" that included the names of the victim's family, the Pelletts.

Cynde and I marveled at how the people involved in this saga were so colorful: the communist lawyer with no law degree, the self-avowed socialist reporter and the one-eyed sheriff.

My daily routine was to swim over my lunch hour. I'd beat the monotony of counting laps by mentally reviewing what I learned that morning. There were times, staring at that black line on the bottom of the pool, when my mind wandered to that question: "If I found Dryman, what then?" Would I sit down and talk with him man to man, spit in his face, forgive him? I knew Cynde was right; there was no way he was still alive, so what was the point of my investigation?

As the months rolled by, Cynde and I had several discussions about "my little project," as we had come to call it. She asked me that same question, and I didn't have an answer. However, I was sure of one thing: as the story of my grandfather's murder came into focus, I could feel the saga drawing me in, deeper and deeper. I was obsessed.

Summer gave way to autumn. I had a reasonable idea of the political and social firestorms the murder had ignited. The next logical step was to learn the details of Dryman's release. Since the parole board hadn't bothered to answer my initial email, I decided to contact them the old-fashioned way. I picked up the phone and called.

With a pleasant greeting, Janet answered. In no time, we were just two Montanans getting acquainted. I broke into my patter, but she interrupted me. "I know all about this! I have that file on my desk; I'm looking at it right now!"

"Really?" I asked.

Excitedly, Janet explained, "I was just looking through his file yesterday. I've been on the Internet looking for obituaries over this past week. I've found no obits—I think he's still alive!"

"I'm not too sure about that," I answered. "I'm just curious to find out what happened to him. Did he start a family, take up golf, what? My intent is not to track him down; most likely he's dead. What's in the file?"

"Oh," she began, "addresses, names, warrants—we almost apprehended him in Las Vegas—all sorts of stuff!" I was sensing the same enthusiasm from Janet as from the newspaper people.

Energized, I asked, "Can you send me a copy of the file? I'd really appreciate it!"

"Sure!"

"Great!" I was about to give her my address when she paused. "I'm thinking perhaps I should check with my supervisor to be sure it's OK. But I don't see why there would be any problem."

"I understand. I'll call you tomorrow morning!" I was on cloud nine. This was real progress!

However, the thought crossed my mind that it was curious that after decades, she just happened to have that particular file on her desk. Perhaps she'd caught wind that I was contacting newspapers across the Treasure State. I quickly dismissed that thought, elated at the prospect of finding out what was in those records.

The following morning, I called back. Again, Janet answered, but her greeting was decidedly less cordial.

"Did you check with your boss?" I asked.

"Yes," she said coldly.

"What did your supervisor have to say? Can you send me a copy of the file?"

She gave a one-word answer: "Nothing."

Not believing my ears, I repeated, "Nothing?"

"Nope, nothing."

Scrambling, I said, "But Janet, there's so much good informa—"

She interrupted me. "My supervisor told me that I can't give you any information whatsoever, let alone the whole file."

"Oh, right, I get it," I said. "I'm just a voice on the phone. You don't know me. I'm happy to send you my driver's license. I'll even fly out and meet you in per—"

"No," she interrupted, "that wouldn't matter." She took on a tone of bureaucratic authority. "We here at the Montana Parole Board cannot release any information whatsoever. We have a duty to protect the prisoner's rights."

I was taken aback. *What about the victim's family's rights?!* flashed through my mind. *He's not a prisoner anymore—you lost him! He absconded!*

I pleaded, "Please, at least tell me again what's in the file."

Her tone turned sympathetic. "Well, OK, there are letters from Dryman, addresses, parole reports and much more. I'm sorry I can't help. Good luck with your search." She hung up.

I wanted nothing in the world more than that file. But how to get it? Worse yet, I now knew that information existed, but it was out of my reach. For now, I had to accept that the parole board file was a dead end. I comforted myself, knowing I still had dozens and dozens of newspaper articles piled up. Perhaps I would find what I needed in them.

By mid-September, I'd exhausted the list of newspapers the Montana Historical Society provided, with the exception of *The People's Voice*. I'd never heard of it. Frankly, the name sounded a bit grand. I wasn't optimistic that a small, obscure weekly publication would be of much help, but it was my last resort.

Unlike the other newspapers, *The People's Voice* had gone out of business four decades previously, and coeditors Gretchen and Harry Billings were deceased. With a bit of sleuthing, I found an email address for Mike, one of their three surviving sons.

In my email to Mike, I introduced myself as the grandson of Clarence Pellett. I emphasized that my motive for the inquiry was not to judge the past but to discover it. Would it be OK if I asked some basic questions?

Mike replied that he would be happy to answer my questions—by email only, no phone calls. He volunteered, "I might be able to give you leads/names," adding, "Over the years, my parents talked many times about the Dryman case, and they were: (1) against capital punishment, (2) very concerned there weren't fair trials. They never doubted that Dryman was the killer…but they thought that he was being railroaded to the gallows with no investigation."

Using what I had learned about the case, I emailed a dozen or so background questions. I had low expectations that this insignificant paper would be much help. However, I did assume I would get the same wholeheartedly cooperative response I'd gotten from so many others over the past months.

In a few days, Mike replied, "I have read your questions and interest in what my brothers might remember about the Dryman case.…My brothers and I have talked it over. I have to tell you that we are not interested in further communications on this matter.…What memories there are are generally unpleasant…unpleasant in the 1950s, unpleasant now.…We now have productive lives.…None of us choose to dwell on the negative. Good luck with your search."

His tone dumbfounded me. How did he go from willing to help to this? Had my questions insulted him? Desperate not to lose another source, I immediately sent a reply. "I apologize if I have in any way offended you. If so, it was unintentional. Please reconsider."

I reread Mike's email, line by line. Why was he so curt? The brothers' reaction seemed disproportionate to my inquiry. I was also struck by the lack of common courtesy. Why, after they'd taken the time to talk it over, didn't they think to inquire about the Pellett family? Yet they felt free to tell me about their family: "What memories there are, are generally unpleasant… unpleasant in the 1950s, unpleasant now."

Unpleasant? For you? I asked myself. *Are they seriously attempting to frame themselves as victims?*

Had they ever considered the impact the murder had on the victim's family? That seemed doubtful. The Billings family didn't care a whit about how the murder affected the Pelletts in the 1950s, and they don't care a whit now.

I reflected on the tenor of the email. It seemed narcissistic: "We now have productive lives.…None of us choose to dwell on the negative." Clearly, they had given themselves permission to move on. That seemed easy for them; it wasn't one of their own who'd been murdered. The fog of my desperation lifted. They were hiding something! It was time to do a deep dive into *The People's Voice*.

Both the parole board and the Billingses were dead ends for the moment. I did an in-depth Internet search on *The People's Voice*. I found that three years earlier, Anne Elizabeth Pettinger, a University of Montana journalism student, had written a master's thesis titled "Harry and Gretchen Billings and *The People's Voice*."

I studied the thesis from beginning to end. Throughout, Pettinger was a cheerleader for the two crusading journalists. She did an outstanding job of chronicling the inception and impact of the Helena-based weekly on Montana's political landscape from 1939 to 1969.

Pettinger devoted a chapter to the Billingses' opposition to capital punishment. I read with interest the section on their defense of Frank Dryman. The thesis made it clear that Gretchen Billings was not simply involved; she was the hub from which all the spokes of Dryman's defense strategy radiated.

Pettinger cited Harry and Gretchen's pride in saving a "mentally deranged transient youth" from hanging. Their youngest son, Leon Billings, bragged it was their efforts that made the difference. "They saved a life; how many people can say that?"

I noted Pettinger's citations, particularly the footnotes. She had conducted telephone interviews with the same Billings brothers who "wished to have no further communication." I learned that the Billingses' papers had been donated to the Montana State University Library Special Collections in Bozeman, Montana—Cynde's and my alma mater.

I also found that Anne Pettinger lived in Bozeman, and as chance would have it, MSU's homecoming was only a few weeks away. I contacted Pettinger and arranged to meet her over coffee. Prior to leaving for Montana, I also made an appointment to conduct research at the MSU Library Special Collections.

On October 7, Cynde and I met Anne Pettinger at a coffee shop in Bozeman, where we introduced ourselves and complimented her on her thesis. I launched into my newspaper patter, emphasizing that my motive wasn't to judge history but to uncover it. Although she had readily accepted our invitation, Anne's flat affect led me to suspect she had contacted the Billingses prior to our meeting. I braced myself to hear, "I want no further contact regarding this matter."

But no—she was very open. I explained that we had an appointment at the MSU Library in an hour. Anne passed along some tips about using the research library.

At the appointed time, Cynde and I arrived at MSU Library Special Collections. We were met at the door by the director of the section, Kim Scott. He was straight out of central casting for a John Wayne Western. Tall, with a handlebar mustache, he wore a black Western shirt, a bolo tie, a big belt buckle, black pants and cowboy boots.

In a deep, gruff voice, Scott gave us his official instructions: "Sign in here; we have your requested materials over on the table. No food, liquids or ink pens allowed. No folding, creasing or bending of the papers. Take only one folder at a time and then replace it back in the box in the order you found it! I'm going to lunch." Without pausing, he donned his five-gallon hat, put on a full-length black duster and pushed open the door as though he was leaving the Long Branch Saloon.

For hours, Cynde and I pored over *The People's Voice*, handwritten notes, PV issues and other materials. It was beyond my expectations, a treasure trove of information. With each discovery, Cynde walked to the copier across the room. As they had the previous summer, the stacks of copies added up: we had to commandeer a couple of extra tables.

Before we knew it, it was five o'clock. We each gathered up armloads of copies. On our way out, we passed Kim Scott. "I've been watching you two all afternoon—what on earth are you researching?" I gave him a short version of the story. He answered, "Now, that's one of the best reasons I've ever heard to do research!"

On the morning of October 8, Cynde and I drove in a snowstorm from Bozeman to Helena to visit the Montana Historical Society. After all the emails, letters and phone calls, it was nice to finally meet Molly Kruckenberg in person. As we followed her up a short flight of stairs to the research area, she said, "We've been looking forward to you looking through our materials."

When we reached the top of the stairs, we spotted two tables covered with stacks of file boxes. "For us?" I asked. Molly nodded. It was no surprise that she prepared for our visit by not only collecting what I had requested but also pulling additional documents. It was obvious that she, too, was invested in the story.

Again, we spent the day poring over and copying documents. During the course of the day, Cynde found trial transcripts of one of the defense's mental health experts' testimony. Cynde leaned across the table and whispered, "Listen to this: Dr. Rouna had Dryman strip naked, then lie down on the jail cell bunk. Then the doctor pinpricked him all over his body. From the pattern of Dryman's responses of 'sharp' or 'dull,' he concluded that Dryman was suffering from schizophrenia."

Amused by this novel approach to evaluating mental health, Cynde jotted down the doctor's description of Dryman's numerous tattoos, including the letters L-O-V-E on the fingers of his right hand.

By November, I was making headway on other fronts, but without Dryman's parole board file, my confidence in finding what became of the murderer was fading. Little did I know that providence was about to smile upon me.

We went out to dinner with friends that holiday season, including their daughter Emily, who had recently passed the California bar. Along with celebrating the season, we toasted Emily's success and her new job with the Santa Clara public defender's office.

Well into the evening's conversation, the subject turned to my little project. As I talked about the Billingses' overreaction and the stonewalling by the Montana Parole Board, I noticed a change in Emily. Eager to ply her new vocation, she jumped in. "As a family member of a murder victim, you have the right to see that file! I don't start my new job till after the first of the year; I'd be happy to help you with the parole board!"

Emily became animated as she laid out a rapid-fire list of ideas about how to get the board to turn over the file. "First, we'll email the board and put them on notice that we mean business. Next, I'll research Montana law and compose a demand letter. And once we have the records, I know the public defender's office in Santa Clara has access to private investigators! We can do this!"

As happy as I was to see if she could pry that file from the board's hands, I saw no need to go in with guns blazing. "Why not just call the board? I think if you identify yourself as a lawyer seeking release of all or a portion of the file on behalf of a member of the victim's family, you have a good chance of getting further than I did with my call. Let's hold off on involving a private investigator. I don't see a need to add more expense just to find a headstone."

On November 15, Emily called the Montana Interstate Compact Unit in Helena, the agency that oversees parolees from Montana who are being supervised in another state. She emailed me a summary of the call.

> *First, I got the same answer you did. "The records belong to the offender." I reminded the compact administrator, Kathy Gordon, that according to the "victim's rights" on the parole board website, starting in 1999, victims have the right to attend parole hearings. It's only fair, as the family member of a victim, that you should have the same access to the file. While we were on the call, Ms. Gordon was looking at the file; she assured me that she would review it and will get back to me with answers to our questions.*

On November 21, Kathy Gordon left Emily a voicemail: "There isn't a report in there [the file] stating the reason why he was paroled. And while incarcerated, he did have several psychiatric exams. I'm sure you understand that the results are confidential."

Emily emailed me that she had done some preliminary research into Montana law and that the Montana constitution guarantees the public the right to access and make copies of an inmate's parole records. "Bottom line: you have a right to inspect and copy every document in the file," she wrote. "However, the board can still determine if Dryman's right to privacy outweighs your right to know. Clem, we are going to ask for everything! Have a happy Thanksgiving!"

Happy Thanksgiving indeed! I thought.

That evening, I showed Emily's email to Cynde. She was pleased and impressed with Emily's legal work. But she again asked, "Why search for him? It won't bring back your grandfather."

"But I've come this far. I have to see it through!"

"I get that," Cynde said, "but if you're going to keep investigating, you need to tell your family what you're doing. They should hear it from you."

"I hear what you're saying," I replied, "but what if I tell them about my little project and they say, 'Stop investigating; we don't want you dredging up painful memories'—you know, like the Billingses. I'm not going to stop. I don't want my first contact with my family to be an argument."

Emily composed two formal letters to the Interstate Compact Unit. The first was a five-page legal authority letter regarding "Victim Request for Access to Parole Records." Quoting sections of the Montana constitution and case law, she stated that Dryman's records were not protected by law. In an additional letter on December 3 titled "Access to Parole Records," Emily included a list of questions designed to hold the ICU's feet to the fire.

> *Once he was declared an absconder, what steps were taken to find him?*
> *Do you a have a list of aliases?*
> *Is 6/4/31 his correct birth date?*
> *Does the file contain any letters, declarations, or expressions of remorse?*
> *Is the Interstate Compact actively pursuing Dryman?*

She concluded, "You can answer in writing or by phone, whichever is more convenient."

On December 9, Kathy Gordon replied, "The BOP has agreed to release parts of parolee Frank R. Dryman's record. The cost for copying this file will be $40 made payable to MT DOC, P.O. Box 201301, Helena, MT."

I couldn't make that check out fast enough.

On January 5, another manila envelope landed on the reception desk. I spotted the return address: Montana Interstate Compact Unit, Helena, Montana. I scooped up the thick envelope and hustled back to my office.

Excited, I opened the envelope like a kid opening a present on Christmas morning. As I read the first report, my enthusiasm faded. It was heavily redacted—unreadable.

Over the following days, I serpentined my way down each page between the redactions, searching for legible text. After two days, I hadn't found even a morsel of useful information. I was resigned to the fact that I'd hit yet another brick wall. I knew the information existed, but it was just out of my reach. It was maddening.

On the third day, I was at my desk, waiting to see my next patient. I wondered, "Should I ask Emily to go to a judge to force the parole board to fork over an unredacted file?"

I looked around my desk and realized that the answer was sitting right next to me: the hot light, an intensely bright light used to backlight X-rays to bring out details.

I held the first page up to the light—eureka! I could see all the information through the redactions! What was once a brick wall was now a gold mine! I jotted down phone numbers, addresses, the license plate number of Dryman's red 1971 Ford Maverick and the pièce de résistance—a Social Security number!

As if the ink on the pages was about to magically evaporate, I frantically typed an email to Emily. "Emily, now we have something a private investigator can use!" When I pushed "send," I thought, *Surely, this information will lead us to Dryman, or to his grave.*

The following day, Emily called to let me know she had passed the information on to a private investigator. She also informed me that the investigator didn't want any direct contact with me. This I understood. For all the investigator knew, I was a crazed, vindictive descendant of the murder victim. I was content to use Emily as the go-between.

A couple of days later, Emily called me with bad news. The SSN I provided turned out to be a dead end. While on the call, I retrieved the report, held it up to the hot light and recited all nine numbers one by one. I told her the last number was smudged. "It could be a nine or a seven."

"I'll pass that along to the PI."

A week later, all progress came to a screeching halt. On January 13, I was having a CT scan of my lungs to identify the source of a persistent cough. The X-ray tech was a Seahawks fan, so as the scan was underway, we chatted about football. Immersed in conversation, the tech let the X-ray equipment continue to scan below where it should have stopped. When the test was finished, the technician said, "Don't leave; the doctor will want to see you."

I could tell from the doctor's expression that it was bad news. After almost thirty years in practice, I had delivered bad news to patients lots of times, but now I was on the opposite side of that conversation. "Your lungs are clear, but the scan picked up a large tumor on top of your left kidney," the doctor explained. "It's cancer."

The instant he uttered the C-word, I had an out-of-body experience. My world went into slow motion. His voice was white noise. His last words to me were, "Good luck." *Good luck? This is serious!*

I called Cynde. "I've just been diagnosed with kidney cancer."

"Oh my God, no—not the same cancer that took my father!" she exclaimed. Our daughter, Reed, flew up from Los Angeles the next day.

On January 20, in a five-hour surgery, my diseased kidney was removed. I spent five days in the hospital, five days I hope never to repeat. The pathology report came back. It showed that the tumor was found before the cancer had a chance to spread. No further treatment was needed. That extended scan saved my life.

According to the surgeon, recovery would take six weeks. All I had to do was rest. I could do no work and nothing physical—not even a push-up.

How was I to fill that much time? Of course—my little project! Back home, my schedule quickly fell into line. I got up at three o'clock in the morning, put on a pot of coffee, spent the next eight hours annotating, took a two-hour nap and then got back at it for several more hours. Instead of working piecemeal in between patients, I was annotating full time.

Yes, I was making substantial progress, but the volume of information was staggering. Much like the inspiration of the hot light, one morning, it struck me: I needed a timeline to organize this mountain of information.

Obviously, the place to start was the day of the murder. I shuffled through the stacks of paper and the Post-it notes stuck on the wall and set aside the copies dated April 4, 1951. In a week, I had the first day of the timeline completed. Day after day, I repeated this process. Gradually, the stacks of paper became organized. With each Post-it I removed, the underlying wallpaper emerged. When I found information that might be helpful to the investigator, I sent it off to Emily, who forwarded it on to the mystery PI. I eventually learned her name was Sheila Klopper. Using Dryman's correct Social Security number, I tried my hand at investigating, but all I managed to turn up was a vacant lot in Glendale, Arizona.

On February 15, Emily forwarded an email from the private investigator, who had found a post office box registered to a physical address in Arizona City, Arizona, a small snowbird community sixty miles south of Phoenix.

Emily asked me, "What do you want to do? Would you like to check out that address, or would you rather someone else go?"

I imagined myself ringing the doorbell and asking, "Are you Frank Dryman? The guy that murdered my grandfather?"

"Emily, I can't do that. Have someone else do the knock and talk. Please!"

Chapter 18

THE CAPTURE

On March 20, at seven thirty in the evening, I was home alone in our nineteenth-floor condo in Bellevue, Washington. Cynde was in Manhattan Beach, California, visiting our daughter. Not yet fully recovered from my surgery, I was in my usual position, in front of my computer.

A message scrolled across my screen: "CLEM, OPEN THIS EMAIL, READ IT AND THEN CALL ME IMMEDIATELY! EMILY."

It was a report from PI Patrick Cote.

> *Today, March 20, 2010, at 4:00 p.m. I went to 16206 S. Desert Park Drive in Arizona City. This is the location for the Cactus Rose Wedding Chapel, Cactus Jack's sign painting and a notary public business. Driving up to the gate in a red golf cart, I met Victor Houston, owner and deacon of the chapel. He said he had lived there for 30 years, then he recanted—no, wait, 20 years. I told Deacon Houston that a PI in Phoenix had sent me to find a man by the name of Frank Valentine. I asked him if he knew of Frank Valentine or had he ever lived at this address. Deacon Houston looked surprised. But then he denied knowing anyone by that name, asking, "Why are you looking for this man Frank Valentine?"*

Phoenix PI Patricia Shaughnessy had forwarded Cote a description of the L-O-V-E tattoo on Valentine's right hand. During the conversation with Houston, Cote noted stars where the letters should be. An experienced investigator, he recognized the stars as prison tattoos used to cover up the letters. Deacon Houston was eager to give Cote a personal tour of the wedding chapel compound, "Just to be sure that this person Frank Valentine wasn't there."

Sensing danger, Cote politely declined, telling Houston, "Looks like I got some bad information."

Victor H. Houston handed Cote his business card, "Just in case you have more questions."

Driving north, once he was clear of Arizona City, Cote called Patricia Shaughnessy, shouting, "That's our guy!"

Back at home in Casa Grande, Cote checked out the information on Deacon Houston's business card: "A licensed deacon and a bonded notary public." He noted that Deacon Houston's birth date was June 6, 1931. Frank Valentine's was June 4, 1931. "That's too much of a coincidence!"

It was the report's final conclusion that left me stunned: "Victor Houston and Frank Valentine are one and the same."

Immediately, I called Emily. "Can this be true?!"

"Yes, I think it is. I've looked at this Cote's background; I think he's legit!"

"What do we do now?"

"I've looked at the old warrants," Emily told me. "They say to contact the Montana Highway Patrol. Do you want to do that?"

"*No!* I wouldn't know what to say. Plus, you're an attorney; they'll listen to you."

"OK, I'll get back to you."

My mind was buzzing. Waiting for Emily's call seemed to take an eternity, but only five minutes passed before the phone rang. I answered. "So what did they say?"

"They are very excited!"

"And?"

"They don't know what to do either," Emily said. "They told me to contact the Montana Parole Board. It's the weekend, so it looks like we'll have to wait till Monday."

"What happens next?"

"Well," Emily said, "he'll be arrested, and if this man Deacon Houston is Dryman, he'll be extradited from Arizona. What happens once he's in Montana, I'm not sure."

It was looking like we had accomplished what I set out to do: to find out what happened to my grandfather's killer. We agreed to accept that going forward, whatever the legal system decided was out of our hands.

My hands were shaking as I hung up the phone. I called Cynde and Reed, but I got no answer. I was bursting to share this news with someone, but I was on my own. So I did what anyone would do: I poured myself a glass of wine. Then I sat down in one of our living room chairs. The enormity of what was happening began to sink in. From the beginning, I'd honestly thought that the best-case scenario would be finding a headstone. I was not prepared for this outcome.

Over the months, as I endlessly annotated documents; combed through newspaper articles, court transcripts, personal letters, handwritten notes and FBI files; and interviewed witnesses, Cynde would remind me, "You do know this is about the murder of your own grandfather, don't you?" I wasn't hearing her. When I started my little project, I was detached; I felt no emotional connection. I wasn't even sure of my grandfather's first name.

But now, those words—"Victor Houston and Frank Valentine are one and the same"—echoed in my head. As I gazed into the blackness of the night, in that moment, I made an emotional connection to a man I'd never known: my grandfather. I imagined the terror of the last moments of his life, on his knees begging. Then Dryman raised the .45 pistol. In a panic, my grandfather scrambled to his feet and ran. Overweight and elderly, he hadn't covered much ground when that first bullet zipped past.

In the next instant, the second bullet entered the nape of his neck and exited his left eye. Stunned, he stopped and stood briefly, then collapsed. I wondered if, as he lay face down in the mud, did he hear the killer's footsteps approaching. Could he sense Dryman standing over him? I prayed he couldn't feel the pain of any of those slugs tearing through his body as Dryman emptied the gun into his back. I hoped he lapsed into unconsciousness as he lay dying that bitterly cold night, his blood staining that piece of Montana prairie red.

At 8:26:58 Pacific Daylight Time on Monday, March 22, 2010, before my first patient, I emailed PI Cote's report to the Interstate Compact Unit in Helena.

"Ms. Gordon," I wrote, "below please find an email re: Frank R. Dryman—your urgent attention is appreciated!"

Her reply came within minutes. "This is fantastic! We will contact the Arizona authorities and get back to you."

In Arizona City, Pinal County Sheriff Paul Babeu responded to Gordon:

Ms. Gordon, this warrant is decades old, are you sure it's active? I know Pat Cote, he was a chief of police and is a good PI, but if all you have

> *is his report that your fugitive and Victor Houston are one and the same, I think that is a bit thin. Vic has lived in Arizona City for decades. He paints signs, he's on the PTA, is a deputized COPs grad, helps us out with security, he's on the search and rescue team. Christ, he's a notary public, and he's been on a posse. Granted, he's a bit of a character, but he is a part of the community. Besides, he has macular degeneration, legally blind—this has to be a mistake. Vic, a murderer? I just don't see it.*

Emily wrote to Babeu, "I checked this out with the parole officials in Montana; I assure you the warrant is good. Dr. Pellett is the grandson of the victim; he's concerned that Dryman is going to run. If you have the time, would you be so kind as to let us know what's happening or going to happen?"

That afternoon, a sheriff's deputy drove out to the Cactus Rose and advised Vic that Montana had a warrant to arrest a Frank Dryman/Valentine for a parole violation. By that evening, with still no word from the parole board, I feared we had lost him. If this was our guy, he had been on the lam for more than thirty-eight years, and as an experienced fugitive, he most certainly would have developed survival instincts. A PI snooping around asking about Frank Valentine, a name he hasn't used for decades, would have set off alarm bells. It wasn't a great leap of logic to think that immediately after the PI's visit, Deacon Houston would have thrown a few belongings into a bag and hightailed it the short distance across the Mexican border, just as he had crossed over the Canadian border the night of the murder.

The next morning, before I started my workday, I resent the email with PI Cote's report to Gordon in Helena. Her reply was immediate: "We're not sure why we have not heard from Arizona. We will try to see what the holdup is."

Not long after, Cathy Gordon emailed me: "I found out that nothing happened yesterday. Just sent more info. Hopefully something happens today!"

An hour later, I checked in: "Ms. Gordon, status? Clem."

"I have contacted that area, and they will get him picked up and questioned."

Finally, that afternoon, Pinal County dispatcher Anna Lucas advised Sergeant Villegas, "We have an active warrant from the Department of Corrections (DOC) in Montana, regarding a homicide suspect possibly living in the Arizona City area. I'm sending photocopies of paperwork from the State of Montana regarding Frank R. Dryman DOB 6-4-31, along with felony warrants as a parole absconder for past homicide."

The Arizona City home of Victor Houston, a.k.a. Frank Dryman. *From the* Great Falls Tribune, *April 4, 2010. © USA TODAY NETWORK.*

Villegas contacted Gordon: "Deputy Compact Administrator Gordon, can you give more information regarding this warrant?"

Reading from Cote's report, Gordon replied: "Subject Frank R. Valentine lives at 16206 S. Desert Park Place, Arizona City, Arizona—using the name Vic Houston."

"Ms. Gordon, how did you come across the information on the subject being in Arizona City, of all places?" Villegas asked.

Gordon answered, "A descendant of the victim's family hired a PI to track the subject's location. Patrick Cote had contact with the subject and confronted him and questioned him about a subject identified as Frank Valentine—one of the subject's past a.k.a.s" ("also known as").

Although Villegas remained doubtful that Deacon Houston was a murderer, he proceeded cautiously because it was well known that there were numerous guns on the property. When Villegas arrived, Deputies Lopez and Lakosky were already at the gate of the Cactus Rose compound.

Villegas later reported,

> *As we entered the fenced residential yard, we could see a red golf cart parked in the front with "VIC" in white paint in large 10-inch letters across the front Plexiglas. We observed a single wide trailer (length is north-south direction) with a sliding glass door (east facing). We proceeded to the front*

door—looked in—I could see an elderly male, subject, seated at the kitchen table and a ledger out on the table. He was speaking to a woman.

Villegas slid the door open. "Are you Victor Houston?"

"Come on, of course I am. You know me. We've worked together."

Villegas said sternly, "Vic, this is not a social call. I have to do this right. Are you Victor Houston?"

Vic replied, "Yes. Just hold your horses." Holding up a contract, he explained, "I have to finish notarizing this and make my logbook entry."

Slowly, Vic finished up the paperwork. After the previous day's warnings, he knew what was coming.

Villegas said, "Vic, stand up please." Deputy Lakosky patted him down. He found a .25 semiautomatic in his right front coat pocket with a round in the chamber.

Villegas instructed Houston to lift his shirt. Vic knew the drill. Although the ink had deteriorated over the years, faint outlines of his tattoos were still visible across his stomach, chest and shoulders. They matched the description Gordon provided.

Later, Villegas recounted, "I could see that across every one of his fingers were stars tattooed across the front, as the PI reported to Gordon. It appears the stars were an attempt to conceal the letters L-O-V-E."

Comparing the tattoos erased all doubt. Villegas's policing instincts told him that Houston was indeed the fugitive Montana wanted. He advised the subject that he had sufficient probable cause to arrest him.

Victor Houston was licensed and bonded as an Arizona notary public. *Author's collection.*

Vic said, "A few days ago, a PI was here asking the same questions. I told him like I'm telling you, I never heard of Frank Valentine. Why is everybody looking for him? What did he do?"

Villegas said, "We'll clarify your identity by checking your fingerprints at the station."

On the drive to the Casa Grande Border Patrol Station, from the back seat of the patrol car, the deacon called his neighbors, Jack and Pat Lindholme.

"Pat, I've been arrested. I'm on my way to Casa Grande."

Pat asked, "What is this about?"

"Not too sure. Could be that Ram Charger Brian [Vic's stepdaughter Wendy's husband] dropped off. I think he might be hiding it from the repo man. It's nothing."

"Vic, they didn't pick you up for nothing!"

Vic came clean. "I've been picked up for a thirty-year-old charge out of Montana. Go get my guns out of the trailer."

"Vic, why would I do that?" Pat asked.

"If Wendy and Cathie get ahold of them, they'll shoot each other! Will you do what I want?" Vic asked.

"OK," Pat said. "I'll send Jack over right now."

Overhearing that, Villegas thought, *Wait a minute. I haven't mentioned a warrant out of Montana.*

He escorted the elderly White male, who was wearing a denim jacket, denim jeans and a "Navy Veteran" baseball hat, into the station. Villegas sat Vic on a chair in the hallway outside Detective Pacheco's office.

Through the hall window, Vic could see Villegas gesturing as he described the tattoos on Vic's fingers to Pacheco. Pacheco observed Vic awkwardly shifting and pretending not to be looking directly at the officers as he strained to hear.

Seated at his desk, Pacheco waved the subject in. "Frank, come on in." Victor Houston shuffled in and sat down. Pacheco asked, "Why did you come in when I called you 'Frank'?"

"I didn't hear you. I know why I'm here. The deputies told me about the warrant out of Montana."

Pacheco said, "Sergeant Villegas tells me he never mentioned Montana."

Pacheco mirandized Frank and then said, "So there wouldn't be any confusion later, I'm taping this interview. Do you want to talk about the warrant?"

"Not really."

"I want to verify if you are the person named in the warrant."

Frank said, "I will talk to you until I don't want to talk anymore. I don't want to incriminate myself."

"We have information from the Montana Interstate Compact Unit that describes the tattoos of a parole absconder, Frank Dryman, a.k.a. Valentine. Sergeant Villegas tells me they match yours. Why would that be?"

"I've never been in Montana. I was born in Napa, California, and raised in Nevada. I was an altar boy for the Catholic church—that was before priests were fags."

In Bellevue, at 1:46 p.m., I received an email that Kathy Gordon had written to Emily and cc'd me on.

> *They have him picked up and are questioning him. They are checking fingerprints—possible problem is if they are on file, since this was from 1955. The tats are faded and ones on his hands covered. He's not talking yet. They are going to talk to the PI and are trying to prove it is him. Good thing is—they have him currently.*

Ten minutes later, Gordon emailed me: "I am looking for other identifiers; he has faded tats, and we are trying to find his fingerprints and trying to pull medical records from our prison records. What do you have?"

Moments later, I got a phone call from Gordon. "Do you have any additional identifying information besides the tattoos?" she asked.

"No, I've sent all that I have."

"We can't find his fingerprints. They must have lost them when the records were moved from the old prison to the new prison. Do you have them?"

I couldn't believe my ears. "No!" I answered. "I've sent you all that I have. Try his brother Jim." I thought, *I can't believe they're going to lose him again.*

At 2:40 p.m., Gordon emailed me, saying, "I had his prints on file. They are interviewing him and will check the prints to see if there is a match. They will email me a new pic. I will send on whatever I can get."

Gordon faxed me a picture of Vic Houston's Arizona driver's license. I didn't recognize him.

At that same time, in Arizona, Pacheco was reading from Gordon's fax: "Fingerprints and more tattoos—Montana. There should be a tattoo of a semi-automatic .45 handgun on subject's back."

"Frank," Pacheco instructed, "get up and remove your shirt."

"Are you looking for the .45?"

"Yes."

"You don't have to look—it's there."

"Why were you in Montana?" Pacheco asked.

"I was hitchhiking. I was picked up by a queer who began to rub my leg while he was driving, so I shot him....I was a mixed-up teenager straight out of the navy. Since I left Montana, I have led a straight life."

Pacheco just looked at Dryman. He'd been hearing similar self-serving stories from perps his entire career. *You'd think after all these decades on the lam, you could come up with a better story,* he thought.

The detective said, "Well, Frank R. Valentine, or Dryman, looks like that's about it. Sergeant Villegas, book 'um."

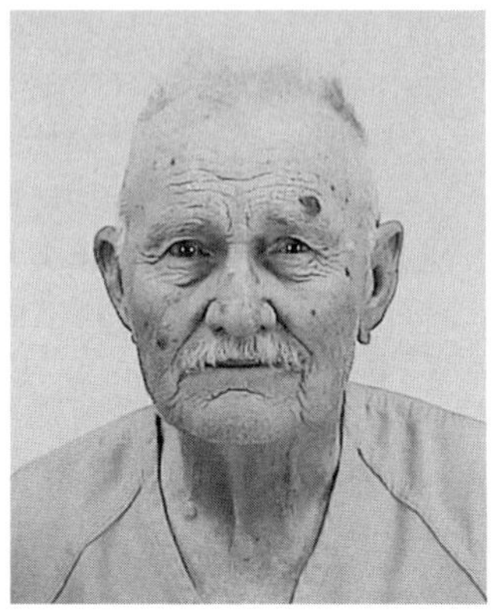

Frank Dryman's mug shot, March 23, 2010. *Courtesy of Pinal County Sheriff.*

As Villegas cuffed him, Dryman said, "I want my one phone call to Pat and Jack Lindholme. I have animals to care for."

At my desk in Bellevue, at 2:49 p.m., I tapped my computer keyboard, and it sprang to life.

> *THEY GOT HIM TO CONFESS—THEY ARE BOOKING HIM RIGHT NOW! YOU GOT HIM—GREAT JOB!*
>
> *He will be coming back, and we will be doing a huge news release. I will be giving your info to our public information officer. Thanks for the work!*

Not believing my eyes, I read it again. My mind flashed back to the moment I found those newspaper clippings, the search, the roadblocks, the revelations, my cancer—the murder. From the start, I had assumed that if I found anything, it would be his headstone. Tracking him down was a pipe dream. I wasn't excited, happy or even pleased. Instead, I felt a strange melancholy.

I called Cynde. "We got him. He confessed."

"I can't believe it! I didn't think this could happen! Come home as soon as you can!"

At 3:45 p.m. in Arizona, Detective Pacheco drove to the Lindholms' home on West Pinevetta in Arizona City and dropped off the keys to Vic Houston's trailer and Frank Valentine's P.O. box. He advised Pat and Jack, "If anyone asks, do not mention the guns—it wouldn't be helpful to Vic."

Pat called the jail to check up on Vic Houston. The jailer said, "There's nobody here by that name." She had no way of knowing he'd been booked as Frank Dryman/Valentine.

PHOTOS PROVIDED BY MONTANA DEPARTMENT OF CORRECTIONS

Dryman, who killed a Montana man in 1951, had been on the lam for 38 years. At left he is shown in his 1955 booking photo. In the center he is shown in a photo taken while he served time in Deer Lodge. The photo at right was taken when he was arrested in March.

Dryman's mug shots over the years. *From the* Great Falls Tribune, *April 4, 2010. © USA TODAY NETWORK.*

At 4:13 PDT, Cynde and I went to one of our favorite haunts, the 520 Bar and Grill. Struggling to get a handle on the events of the day, I spoke first.

"Wow! This is the most amazing thing. How did this happen? I was so sure he was dead; I was just filling in my family's story."

"I've never understood why you've never contacted your family," Cynde said.

"I can't explain it, but it feels wrong. Besides, I started this just a year ago; they've known about it their whole lives. Why didn't they track him down? Montana is going to send out a big press release in the morning. I think this is going to be big. How many times do you track down a murderer after forty years? This is going to hit the news!"

Cynde waved me off. "This will not be big news. Some people in Montana might care, maybe a few in Arizona, but that will be the extent of it."

Bob Arnez, communications director at the Montana Department of Corrections (MT DOC), called me that evening. "Good job," he said. "Do you realize you've captured the longest missing fugitive absconder in Montana history? We're going to send out a big press release tomorrow. Get ready."

"Get ready"—what does that mean? I wondered.

True to his word, Arnez sent out a press release from the MT DOC announcing the capture of the longest fugitive absconder in Montana history at 6:47 a.m. the next day.

> *PRESS RELEASE, MONTANA BOARD OF PAROLE AND PARDONS*
> *Frank R. Dryman, apprehended in Arizona.*
> *Montana corrections officials supplied Dr. Pellett with copies of Dryman's files to aid him in his search and maintained frequent contact with him during this past year. Pellett tracked him to Glendale, Arizona; that is where the trail went cold. He hired a PI, and the search led them to Arizona City and the Cactus Rose Wedding Chapel.*

I chuckled, thinking of the tug-of-war Emily had with "Montana corrections officials," trying to pry Dryman's files out of their hands.

Not to be outdone, Tamatha Villar, Pinal County's public information officer, soon sent out her own press release.

> *On Tuesday* [March 23], *38 years after he absconded, Dryman (78) was arrested after deputies were contacted by the Montana DOC who informed them a private investigator, former Florence Chief of Police Patrick Cote, had been hired by Pellett's grandson (victim) and believed he had located Dryman.*

Sheriff Paul Babeu:

> *This felony warrant suspect and convicted murderer has been hiding out in Pinal County for years. In fact, he carefully cultivated personal friendships with past elected county sheriffs.*
> *I'm proud of Sgt. Jason Villegas, Detective Pacheco and Deputies Lopez and Lakosky for their fine work in apprehending this fugitive. Our arrest was only possible due to the great investigative work of retired Florence Police Chief and PI Patrick Cote, who identified this man as the likely subject of the felony warrant. THEY CAN RUN FROM THE LAW, BUT WITH PERSEVERANCE AND GOOD INVESTIGATIVE WORK, WE ALMOST ALWAYS FIND THEM IN THE END.*

No mention of the other PIs or my research. I guess it's true: success has many fathers.

The press releases launched a media frenzy. No sooner had I hit the back door of my office than CNN, ABC and FOX all wanted interviews. I was beginning to understand what Arnez meant by "get ready."

Before seeing a patient, I did my first interview over the phone with CNN. "I was just putting together an old family story, and then all these serendipitous events lined up and we accidentally caught him."

As I was telling my story, the reporter, Amanda O'Donnell, interrupted, "Geez, this is going to be a book or a movie!"

"I don't know about that."

"What now?" she asked. "What do you think should happen?"

"Whatever the justice system decides, I'm happy with."

Over the course of that crazy day, the media incursion intensified. The Seattle TV stations arranged to come to my office that afternoon. The story was the lead on that evening's broadcasts.

Cathie Houston called, weeping and distraught. "I didn't know anything about this. You're not going to sue me or take away our land, are you?"

Hearing her sobbing, I reassured her, "Of course not. This isn't your fault. There has been too much pain for too many years; it has to stop here."

After that call, Cynde said, "That was a bunch of bullshit. She was checking to see what you know."

On Thursday, at 4:30 a.m., I was at my gym when I happened to look up at the bank of TVs. There on one of the screens was a mug shot of Dryman. On Fox News, Gretchen Carlson commented, "The grandson tracked down the murderer? Why didn't the law get him? Why did it take the grandson to track him down?"

I thought, *That's not what this is about. Law enforcement have their hands full; they don't have the time to be looking into a six-decade-old murder. Thank goodness for PIs.*

As days turned into weeks, the media onslaught didn't let up. My front desk folks had their hands full with calls. I did print, TV and radio interviews with outlets from coast to coast: Cape Cod, New York City, Washington, D.C., Indianapolis, Dallas, Phoenix and Los Angeles.

There were calls of congratulations and calls from law enforcement officers thanking me for sending the message that parole is a privilege, not a pardon.

Said one officer, "You do realize you could file charges against Dryman's family for harboring a fugitive?"

I told him, "There's already been enough pain."

Other calls were from couples whom Deacon Houston had married. "Is our marriage legal?"

WINNING PHOTOS

GREAT FALLS TRIBUNE

Happy Easter! Fun continues today /1M

The capture of Frank Dryman

Long life on the lam

TRIBUNE PHOTO BY JOHN S. ADAMS; SHELBY PROMOTER EXTRA COURTESY OF ACE EHELER

ABOVE: Frank Dryman had been living in Arizona City since the early 1970s under the name Victor Houston. He absconded from parole in California after serving 14 years for a murder he committed in Montana in 1951. Dryman was arrested at his home in Arizona City on March 23 after being tracked down by a private investigator. **TOP**: Great Falls Tribune and Shelby Promoter front pages from the 1950s report on the killing of Clarence Pellett and the search for Dryman.

Killer led a life that belied the crime

By JOHN S. ADAMS
Tribune Capitol Bureau

ARIZONA CITY, Ariz. — "It all began when a young boy was hitchhiking to Canada to see his girlfriend ..."

Frank Dryman wrote those words on May 1, 1960, in an appeal to the Montana Board of Pardons and Parole, seeking commutation of his life sentence for murder.

The commutation was eventually granted, but how Dryman's story ends remains to be written.

Arizona sheriff's deputies arrested Dryman, a.k.a. Victor Houston, on March 23 — 38 years after he jumped parole in California, disappearing into the desert and leaving a wife and five stepchildren behind.

Montana's longest-running fugitive, he was returned to the Montana State Prison in Deer Lodge late Friday afternoon.

Dryman spent 14 years in Deer Lodge for murdering Clarence Pellett 59 years ago today along a muddy road abut 18 miles north of Shelby.

Dryman was paroled in 1969, and, according to prison records, spent the next two years, nine months and 11 days living a productive and lawful life in Southern California. Dryman married, started a sign-painting business and followed the rules of his lifetime parole.

Then, on Aug. 30, 1971, he disappeared without a trace.

Were it not for the nagging curiosity of the victim's grandson, a Bellevue, Wash., oral surgeon, the story might have

See DRYMAN, 6A

PHOTOS PROVIDED BY MONTANA DEPARTMENT OF CORRECTIONS

Dryman, who killed a Montana man in 1951, had been on the lam for 38 years. At left he is shown in his 1955 booking photo. In the center he is shown in a photo taken while he served time in Deer Lodge. The photo at right was taken when he was arrested in March.

Remembering the victim

Clarence Pellett was a family man and a small-town café owner /7A

Left: From the *Great Falls Tribune*, April 4, 2010. © *USA TODAY NETWORK*.

Opposite: From the *Great Falls Tribune*, October 5, 2014. © *USA TODAY NETWORK*.

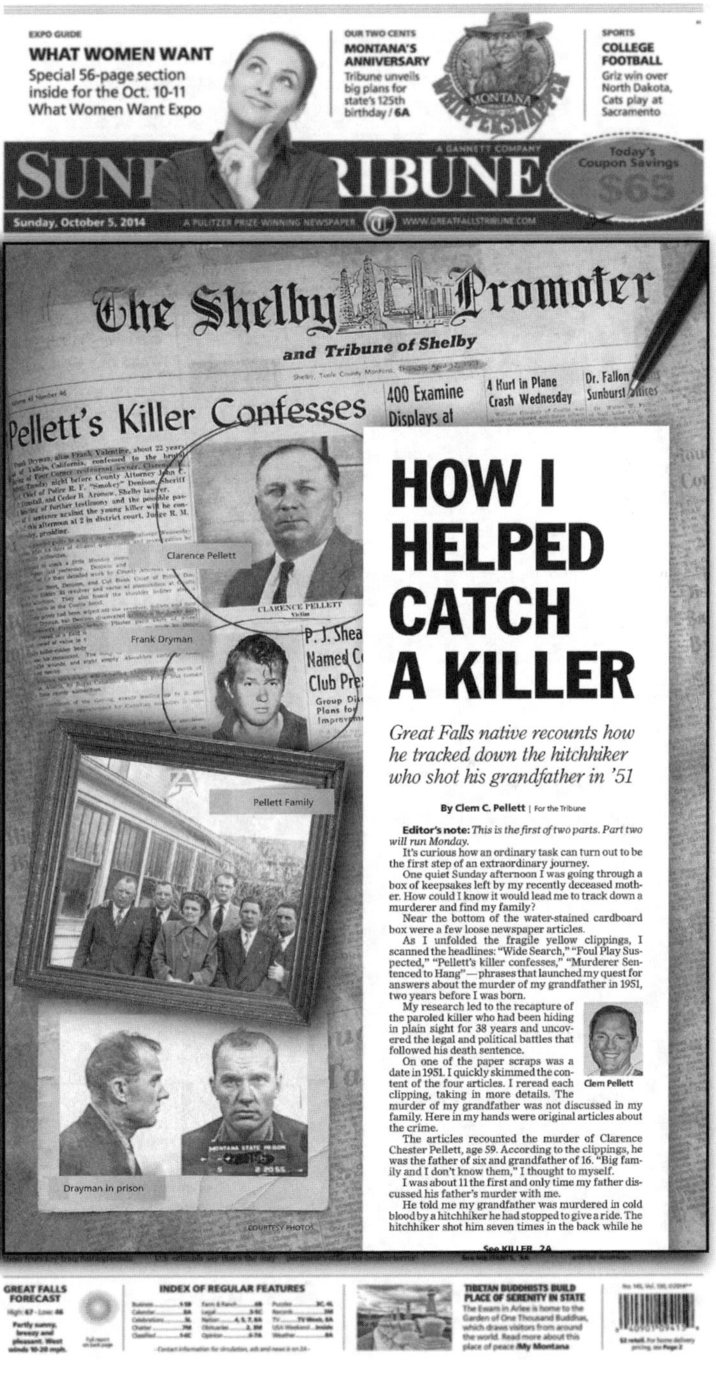

EXPO GUIDE
WHAT WOMEN WANT
Special 56-page section inside for the Oct. 10-11 What Women Want Expo

OUR TWO CENTS
MONTANA'S ANNIVERSARY
Tribune unveils big plans for state's 125th birthday / **6A**

SPORTS
COLLEGE FOOTBALL
Griz win over North Dakota, Cats play at Sacramento

SUNDAY TRIBUNE
A GANNETT COMPANY
Today's Coupon Savings $65
Sunday, October 5, 2014 · A PULITZER PRIZE-WINNING NEWSPAPER · WWW.GREATFALLSTRIBUNE.COM

The Shelby Promoter
and Tribune of Shelby

Pellett's Killer Confesses

400 Examine Displays at

4 Hurt in Plane Crash Wednesday

Dr. Fallon Sunburst Offices

P. J. Shea Named Club Pres

Clarence Pellett

CLARENCE PELLETT Victim

Frank Dryman

Pellett Family

Drayman in prison

COURTESY PHOTOS

HOW I HELPED CATCH A KILLER

Great Falls native recounts how he tracked down the hitchhiker who shot his grandfather in '51

By Clem C. Pellett | For the Tribune

Editor's note: *This is the first of two parts. Part two will run Monday.*

It's curious how an ordinary task can turn out to be the first step of an extraordinary journey.

One quiet Sunday afternoon I was going through a box of keepsakes left by my recently deceased mother. How could I know it would lead me to track down a murderer and find my family?

Near the bottom of the water-stained cardboard box were a few loose newspaper articles.

As I unfolded the fragile yellow clippings, I scanned the headlines: "Wide Search," "Foul Play Suspected," "Pellett's killer confesses," "Murderer Sentenced to Hang"—phrases that launched my quest for answers about the murder of my grandfather in 1951, two years before I was born.

My research led to the recapture of the paroled killer who had been hiding in plain sight for 38 years and uncovered the legal and political battles that followed his death sentence.

Clem Pellett

On one of the paper scraps was a date in 1951. I quickly skimmed the content of the four articles. I reread each clipping, taking in more details. The murder of my grandfather was not discussed in my family. Here in my hands were original articles about the crime.

The articles recounted the murder of Clarence Chester Pellett, age 59. According to the clippings, he was the father of six and grandfather of 16. "Big family and I don't know them," I thought to myself.

I was about 11 the first and only time my father discussed his father's murder with me.

He told me my grandfather was murdered in cold blood by a hitchhiker he had stopped to give a ride. The hitchhiker shot him seven times in the back while he

See KILLER, 2A

GREAT FALLS FORECAST

INDEX OF REGULAR FEATURES

TIBETAN BUDDHISTS BUILD PLACE OF SERENITY IN STATE

SUNDAY, APRIL 4, 2010 GREAT FALLS TRIBUNE WWW.GREATFALLSTRIBUNE.COM PAGE 7, SECTION A

Convicted killer was a man of many names

FROM PREVIOUS PAGE

on Jan. 16, 1969.

In August of that year, Valentine married Bryle Cahill, a divorcée with five children.

The couple moved to Rialto, Calif., where the Valentines continued to operate a sign shop. Business was good, and by the summer of 1970 they were bringing in about $1,000 a month.

"This man continues to make a satisfactory adjustment," Allen wrote in his Aug. 25, 1970, report.

But soon thereafter trouble began to surface. According to parole records, Valentine and his wife began having marital problems. His wife complained that Valentine was working too much and not paying enough attention to her and her children. Valentine, meanwhile, was having difficulties adjusting to life on the outside after spending the better part of 18 years in prison.

The couple split up and his wife moved into an apartment with the children. They reunited months later, and for a while things seemed to be OK. But when the parole officer checked on Valentine in December, Beryl said Frank had disappeared five weeks earlier. The last time she saw him was on Oct. 27, 1971, she told the parole officer. According to his wife, Valentine gave no reason for leaving.

Disappearing act

Dryman's only biological daughter, 28-year-old Cathie Houston of Portales, N.M., said in an a recent interview with the Tribune that her father told her he left his life in California because, "he wasn't happy." She said she didn't know of her father's past life until after he was arrested in Arizona last month. She recently visited him several times in the Pinal County Jail, where she learned more.

"He said he was stuck in a bad marriage with a bunch of kids that weren't his," Houston said. "He just wanted to get away from it all. He didn't care about his parole. He was miserable, and he just wanted to start his life over."

After his disappearance, Valentine's parole officer contacted members of his family but none heard from him until long after authorities gave up looking for Valentine. His ailing mother, Gladys Foster, once wrote a letter to prison officials begging them to help her find her missing son.

"In fact, I hope you people have caught him. At least I would know where he is," Foster wrote in 1976.

Before disappearing, Valentine stocked up on camping equipment and clothes. His wife told authorities he might be living in the desert.

Valentine grew up outside Las Vegas. His father, Frank Valentine Sr., was a construction worker on the Hoover Dam and the family lived near there until Frank was 6.

When Valentine failed to resurface after several months, his wife initiated divorce proceedings. Montana authorities put out a warrant for his arrest on March 27, 1972. His parole revoked, Frank Dryman, a.k.a Frank Valentine, was once again a wanted man.

A new life

It's unclear when, exactly, Frank Valentine arrived in Arizona City, Ariz., and became Victor Houston. Some residents of the small, dusty, desert town about 60 miles south of Phoenix think he rolled into town in the mid-1970s.

Dryman, or Victor Houston as he is known to the 4,000 or so residents there, declined to be interviewed in jail in Arizona.

Dryman may have lived in Nevada for a period of time. A California private investigator contacted Montana prison officials in December 1972, and informed them that Dryman was living in Las Vegas. Authorities issued a warrant for his arrest there, but after years of searching they turned up nothing.

"He told me he spent some time in Nevada once," said Jack Lindholme, an Arizona City man who, along with his wife Patricia, helped care for Houston when his health began to decline in recent years. "I was teasing him about getting his deacon's license out of the back of a magazine, and he told me he had actually gone to seminary in Nevada."

Houston, who ran the Cactus Rose Wedding Chapel from his home in Arizona City, at some point began living with a woman named Debbie, and her daughter Wendy. It's unclear if Houston and Debbie were ever legally married, but they had a child, Cathie, when Houston was 50.

"He never thought he could have kids," Cathie said. "I was a surprise."

The couple split when Cathie was a child, but they remained friendly for years. They even lived on the property for a few years so Cathie would have both of her parents nearby.

Houston was a fan of old Western movie heroes. Posters and autographed photos of John Wayne, Clint Eastwood and Charles Bronson adorn the walls of his humble trailer, alongside dozens of family photos chronicling seven decades of family life.

A plaque above a shelf in his living room showcases several badges he wore over the years as a volunteer for the local sheriff's posse and for a security company he started.

Friends and neighbors say Houston is a gruff and not particularly friendly man, but he is known locally as a hard worker and is generally well-respected in the community.

"Here he was a community activist," Patricia Lindholme said. "He was on the board of directors for the Moose Club. When AARP had a charter here, he was active in that. Everything he did here was diametrically opposed to Frank Dryman."

Lindholme said Houston once told her that he killed a man.

"He said it was a bar fight and that he served his time," Lindholme said. "I just left it at that."

Wedding chapel

In Arizona City, Houston built a very public life.

"Rattlesnake Vic" or "Pink Panther," as he was known to some, bought two acres on the south end of town, which he nicknamed "Jackass Flats" and opened a sign-painting shop and wedding chapel there. He officiated over hundreds of weddings over the years, Cathie said, and his sign-painting truck was a familiar sight throughout the region.

"He was a wonderful artist," his daughter said.

He painted signs on fire trucks and police cars. His services were sought after by shop owners, real estate agents and even the town itself.

"Up until a few years ago, the sign welcoming you to Arizona City was painted by my dad," Cathie said.

He took cash for jobs ranging from hunting rattlesnakes to officiating over weddings to notarizing public documents. He also sold cactuses and desert knickknacks from a small booth inside his fenced cactus garden.

He was the town's official weather reporter for the National Weather Service. He volunteered for the local sheriff's posse and search and rescue team. In 2002, he completed the Pinal County Volunteer Sheriff's Academy, a process that required him to submit to fingerprinting and a background check.

People in town were shocked to learn that the well-known Vic Houston was the same man who murdered a café owner in Montana nearly six decades earlier.

"It's a good thing I was sitting down. It was like somebody had hit me between the eyes with a ball bat," said Gary, a brusque, cowboy of a man who said he was one of Houston's closest friends. Gary did not want his last name used in this story.

"Vic is well-known in this country. Anybody who needed something or needed help, any civic thing, election committee, census. You name it, and Vic helped out," Gary said.

A card hanging on Houston's refrigerator bears a quote from Ethel Percy Andrus, California's first female high school principal, which sums up Houston's life in Arizona: "Do what you can, with what you have, where you are today."

"That's how my dad lived his life," Cathie said. "He wasn't perfect, but he was a good man who tried to do good by others."

Dryman's future

Clem Pellett, the man who led authorities to his grandfather's killer, said he never expected to find Frank Dryman, and he definitely didn't expect to find Dryman alive.

"That was a total shock," said Pellett, who grew up in Great Falls. His father was longtime local dentist Marion Pellett.

Now that Dryman is back behind bars in Montana, Pellett said he's satisfied with whatever the state parole board decides to do with him.

"This isn't about revenge," Pellett said. "I'd happy with whatever their decision is."

It's not entirely clear at this point what the future holds for Frank Dryman. He's in poor health, and his daughter suspects that the cancer he beat years ago has returned. He's nearly blind, mostly deaf and suffers from an ailing liver.

An official for the Board of Pardons and Parole did not immediately respond to an e-mail inquiry about Dryman, but a parole revocation hearing is expected to take place sometime within the next few months. At that point, Dryman could be re-paroled, or he could be sent back to prison to serve out his life sentence. He also could seek a pardon from the governor.

In the meantime, prison doctors are evaluating his health.

Cathie said she just wants her father to be able to return to his trailer and live out his remaining days in the desert.

"I don't know why Montana would even want him back," said Cathie. "He's just a sick, scared old man."

Reach Tribune Capitol Bureau Chief Adams at 442-9493.

Dryman, 78, looks at an extradition waiver with the assistance of Baliff Brett Day, left, during an extradition hearing in the Pinal County Superior Court in Arizona on March 25.

ABOVE: Dryman shows off his certificate at the sheriff's academy in Arizona City. RIGHT: Dryman wears his badge.

COURTESY PHOTOS

RIGHT: Dryman's Cactus Rose Chapel in Arizona City, Ariz. BELOW: Dryman marries a couple. He was also Notary Public.

COURTESY PHOTO

There was much more to Pellet's life than being a victim

By TRAVIS COLEMAN
Tribune Staff Writer

For many, Clarence Pellett's story begins and ends with his murder at the hands of Frank Dryman on an isolated road north of Shelby 59 years ago today.

But there was much more to Pellett's life than being the victim of a high-profile crime, according to a grandson in Cut Bank.

Clem Pellett

Bob Pellett, now 76, lived next to his grandfather in a row of homes on an oil field camp for years. They lived in the camp because Clarence Pellett and his son worked for the Texas Pacific Coal and Oil Company.

It was during this time that Bob Pellett spent a lot of time getting to know his grandfather, a stout junk collector who loved to play cards and who was nicknamed "Shorty."

"Well, he was a short little dude, like me," Bob Pellett said, explaining the nickname.

Bob Pellett's memory is a little cloudy, but he believes his grandfather was born in 1892 and was raised in North Dakota. He married as a teen, but his wife died of the flu around 1917.

His family was starving in North Dakota, so Clarence and his five children moved to Montana in the late 1920s, eventually landing a job with the oil company, Bob Pellett said.

Bob Pellett remembers his dad and grandfather working 12-hour shifts seven days a week for the oil company. They were on call for the remaining 12 hours of the day. It was a tough way to make a living, he said.

His grandfather also was a farmer and kept a few hogs, cows and chickens that helped feed the family, which had grown to six with the birth of Marion Pellett from his new wife.

"That's what it was through the war. That's how we survived," Bob Pellett said.

Marion Pellett went on to become a dentist in Great Falls and is the father of Clem Pellett, who tracked down Frank Dryman in March with the help of a private investigator.

Clarence Pellett's personality came out during road trips to "make some pennies and dimes" hunting for junk. His grandfather would find and try to trade rope, bones and hides, sometimes to Pacific Hide and Fur in Great Falls.

Bob Pellett remembers that his grandfather cut out the back of his car, converting it into a pick-up-type vehicle so he could haul more stuff. Bob Pellett also would often wind up at his grandfather's home playing pinochle for nickels and pennies.

"He was a pretty good card player but not that good," Bob Pellett said.

Around 1947, Bob Pellett's parents and grandparents partnered

COURTESY PHOTO

Clarence Pellett.

to start a restaurant at Four Corners west of Oilmont. Pellett's Café catered to a lot of the people working and living on the oil-fields, serving up home-cooked breakfast, lunch and dinner.

Clarence Pellett wasn't a cook or a waiter, Bob Pellett said. His grandfather was much better at just eating the food. Rather, Clarence Pellett did a lot of a miscellaneous work that needed to be done, such as chasing after supplies.

Bob Pellett doesn't remember much about the day his grandfather was killed — April 4, 1951 — but believes Clarence Pellett, 59 at the time, was probably returning from Shelby on a supply run.

He didn't come home that night though, spurring a frantic search for him. Clarence Pellett's vehicle was found at Sweet Grass. His coat and watch were found in the back seat, and his empty wallet was found in the front seat, according to newspaper accounts.

It was later discovered that Clarence Pellett had picked up 19-year-old hitchhiker Frank Dryman north of Shelby in a cold blizzard. Dryman later confessed that he pulled out a gun, threatened to kill Clarence Pellett and later shot him as he tried to run away. Dryman eventually unloaded seven bullets in Pellett's back. Dryman was arrested the next day by Canadian police.

The memories still sting for some in the Shelby area, not just because of the crime itself, but for the man who was killed.

"I never forgot that. You never forget that," Bob Pellett said. "I can remember my whole family. They were pushing for that death penalty."

Dryman twice escaped hanging before appeals garnered him a second trial in which the judge gave him a life sentence. He was paroled in 1969. With Dryman captured on parole violations, Bob Pellett said he hopes Dryman never again sees the light of day.

Pellett's Café burned down a few years after the murder, and the family broke up. But with this recent resolution, Bob Pellett hopes the family can recall less about Clarence Pellett's death and more about his life.

"You're pretty much struck by total devastation," he said.

Reach Tribune Staff Writer Travis Coleman at 791-1462 or tcoleman@greatfallstribune.com.

From the *Great Falls Tribune*, April 4, 2010.

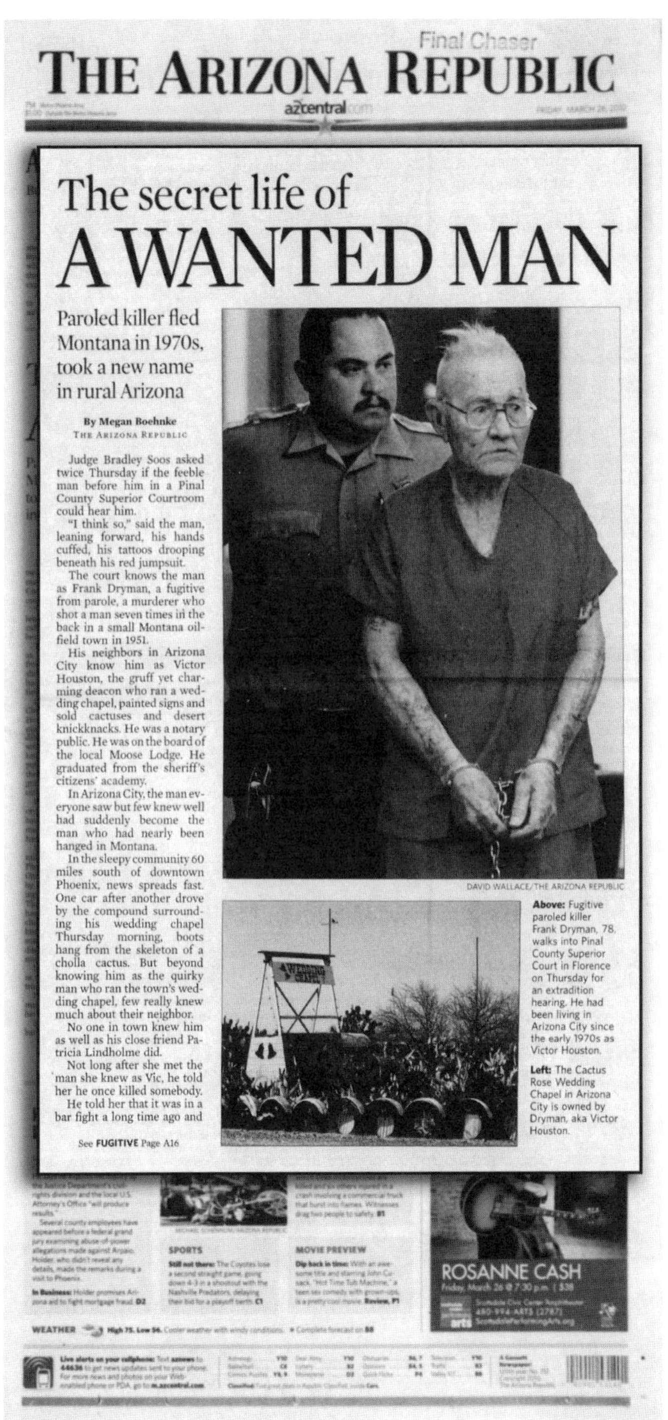

Final Chaser

THE ARIZONA REPUBLIC

azcentral.com

The secret life of A WANTED MAN

Paroled killer fled Montana in 1970s, took a new name in rural Arizona

By Megan Boehnke
The Arizona Republic

Judge Bradley Soos asked twice Thursday if the feeble man before him in a Pinal County Superior Courtroom could hear him.

"I think so," said the man, leaning forward, his hands cuffed, his tattoos drooping beneath his red jumpsuit.

The court knows the man as Frank Dryman, a fugitive from parole, a murderer who shot a man seven times in the back in a small Montana oil-field town in 1951.

His neighbors in Arizona City know him as Victor Houston, the gruff yet charming deacon who ran a wedding chapel, painted signs and sold cactuses and desert knickknacks. He was a notary public. He was on the board of the local Moose Lodge. He graduated from the sheriff's citizens' academy.

In Arizona City, the man everyone saw but few knew well had suddenly become the man who had nearly been hanged in Montana.

In the sleepy community 60 miles south of downtown Phoenix, news spreads fast. One car after another drove by the compound surrounding his wedding chapel Thursday morning, boots hang from the skeleton of a cholla cactus. But beyond knowing him as the quirky man who ran the town's wedding chapel, few really knew much about their neighbor.

No one in town knew him as well as his close friend Patricia Lindholme did.

Not long after she met the man she knew as Vic, he told her he once killed somebody.

He told her that it was in a bar fight a long time ago and

See FUGITIVE Page A16

DAVID WALLACE/THE ARIZONA REPUBLIC

Above: Fugitive paroled killer Frank Dryman, 78, walks into Pinal County Superior Court in Florence on Thursday for an extradition hearing. He had been living in Arizona City since the early 1970s as Victor Houston.

Left: The Cactus Rose Wedding Chapel in Arizona City is owned by Dryman, aka Victor Houston.

SPORTS

MOVIE PREVIEW

WEATHER

From the *Arizona Republic*, March 26, 2010. © *USA TODAY NETWORK.*

One came from the Arizona Association of Notary Public. "We would like your permission to use your grandfather's name on a bill to stiffen the requirements to become a notary in Arizona."

There were also just plain nutty calls. "Dryman is the zodiac killer." "Dryman was the high priest of the prison; he walked around in long robes saying you have to kill to make room for more souls to come to earth."

But there were also threats. "You should be shot in the back just like your grandfather." "Be careful. You never know who might be following you."

After that, I established a policy that no staff member could leave the office alone.

On the Internet, I was admonished. "The grandson needs to learn forgiveness. He's just a harmless old man."

In a letter, an Arizona lawyer connected with MoveOn.org told me, "You should be ashamed of yourself for setting in motion events that are bringing so much pain to the Houston family."

An elderly woman called identifying herself as Dorothy Holeman, the driver of the car who picked up the hitchhiking Dryman on the day of the murder. Wary of another crank call, I asked a question only the real driver would know the answer to. "Where did you drop him off in Shelby?"

She didn't hesitate. "By the Snack Shack." She was genuine.

"I've felt bad about this my whole life," she went on. "If we just hadn't given him a ride from Great Falls that day, your grandfather wouldn't have been murdered."

After a few weeks, the call came that changed my life. My receptionist walked into my office and told me, "There's a woman on the line; she wants to talk to you about your grandfather." After weeks of fielding crank calls, I was skeptical, but my receptionist added, "This one says she's your cousin."

After all these years, what would she have to say? Was she upset that I stirred up bad memories? I picked up the phone and said, "Hello, this is Clem."

A voice on the other end said, "I'm Dorothy. I'm your first cousin. We've never met. This thing between us has got to end."

Unknown emotions from deep within me surfaced, and tears streamed down my cheeks. I didn't know what to say. Dorothy thanked me for finding Dryman.

"We all thought he was dead by now. We have lived in fear of him for so long."

Before we hung up, we made a date to meet at the Pellett house in Shelby, Montana.

On May 1, 2010, Cynde, Reed and I flew to Great Falls and then drove up to Shelby. We pulled up to the Pellett house unsure of what was about to happen. At the door, we were met by a group of unfamiliar faces. From all corners of the country, my relatives were queued up, waiting their turn to welcome the three of us into the Pellett family.

Standing at the front of the line was a gray-haired woman. There was no need for an introduction—it was Dorothy. We embraced, sobbing. In an instant, a lifetime of separation melted away. In that moment, I went from being an only child with no extended family to having scores of cousins, aunts, uncles, nieces and nephews spread out from coast to coast.

Over that two-day visit, I learned firsthand the pain the Pelletts had managed to push away for sixty years. Said Dorothy, "I remember my dad, Curly, crying and crying over the murder of Grandpa Clarence. Dad died of a heart attack in 1954 during Dryman's appeals. I'm sure that it was the stress of all that legal stuff that killed him. I think if Grandpa Clarence had been rich or prominent, Dryman would have never got away with it. For us, the murder will never be forgotten, even a little bit. Dryman got fifteen years; we got life."

There was one eerie moment: I was in the passenger seat of my eldest cousin Bill's car. "Open the glove box," he blurted out. There I saw a .45 pistol. Bill said, "Dryman used this to murder our grandfather." I just stared. Bill gestured for me to hold it. "No thanks," I said as I closed the glove box.

In the course of catching up on a lifetime of estrangement, my family told me that my father was the only member of the Pellett family to attend each of Dryman's parole hearings. This was the first time I'd heard that.

When I told them Dryman was scheduled to appear before the parole board in three weeks, Dorothy piped up: "We're not going to let you go by yourself, not like your father. This time, we will go as a family."

The following weekend, at the invitation of private investigator Pat Shaughnessy, I flew down to Phoenix to address an Arizona private investigators' meeting. It was the first time I had met all three of the investigators—Sheila Klopper, Pat Shaughnessy and Patrick Cote—in person. After my brief presentation reviewing the steps of our investigation, we posed for a picture. We nicknamed ourselves Team Hiding in Plain Sight.

The team offered to take me to Arizona City to see where Vic Houston had been doing just that. Within an hour, we arrived at the front gate of the Cactus Rose Wedding Chapel. As we exited the car, from inside the compound, a young woman in her thirties approached the gate. She was heavyset and disheveled. Her shoulder-length brown hair was uncombed.

IN THE DISTRICT COURT OF THE NINTH JUDICIAL DISTRICT OF THE STATE OF MONTANA, IN AND FOR THE COUNTY OF TOOLE

* * * * * * * * * * * * *

STATE OF MONTANA, Plaintiff, vs. FRANK R. DRYMAN, aka FRANK R. VALENTINE, Defendant.	)	Criminal No. 528 PETITION and ORDER

* * * * * * * * * * * * *

Comes now THERON PELLETT and petitions the Court to withdraw a Colt 45 caliber model of 1911, U. S. Army Serial No. 250666 automatic pistol introduced into evidence at the time of trial of the above captioned matter as State's Exhibit No. H. Petitioner states that he will retain the said weapon in his possession, custody and control and does not wish to gain possession of said weapon for purposes of sale, gift, or otherwise disposing of said weapon, but represents to the Court that petitioner is the son of CLARENCE PELLETT, the person who was killed by use of said weapon, by the defendant, and the petitioner wishes to have said weapon to keep and retain as his own for personal reasons difficult to explain.

WHEREFORE, Petitioner prays for an order of Court authorizing the Clerk of the above entitled Court to release said weapon to him.

DATED this 6th day of June, 1967.

Theron Pellett
THERON PELLETT

(1)

Opposite: Theron Pellett petitioned the court to acquire the murder weapon on June 6, 1967. The gun has been in the Pellett family's possession ever since. *Courtesy of Toole County Clerk of Court.*

Above: Two months after tracking down the longest absconder fugitive in Montana history, Cynde, Reed and I met my first cousins in May 2010. *Back row, left to right*: Jim, Bob, Bill, Clem, Frank Rounds, Jesse. *Front row, left to right*: Dorothy, Cheryl, Sharon. *Author's collection*

Cote whispered, "That's Cathie, Dryman's daughter." As we stepped closer to the gate, Klopper gently tugged my arm, motioning me to stay behind. Cote took the lead and introduced himself.

Cathie said, "So you're the son of a bitch that put my dad in jail! I bet you're happy with all the new business you're getting."

Unfazed, the team followed Cote up to the gate. I put on my sunglasses, pulled down my baseball hat and stayed a few steps behind. I observed how these professional investigators, using soothing tones, de-escalated a potential confrontation. Cathie opened the gate and invited us in.

Still trailing, I witnessed how they teamed up, working Cathie, gaining her trust. Shaughnessy said, "Cathie, it must be so hard on you to have your father arrested."

Klopper told her, "This isn't your fault."

In no time, Cathie was eating out of their hands. Tearing up, she said, "Yeah, I didn't know anything about this. My dad is a good man. He's so

"Team Hiding in Plain Sight." *Left to right*: private investigators Patricia Shaughnessy and Patrick Cote, Clem Pellett, private investigator Sheila Klopper. *Author's collection.*

sick, dying of cancer. He can't go to prison. That guy put his hand on my dad's knee—he had to shoot him." I couldn't believe my ears.

As they continued to pacify Cathie, I broke away from the group and pulled out my cell phone to take pictures of this junkyard masquerading as a wedding chapel. As I raised my phone, Cathie yelled, "Hey, you over there, no pictures! Who are you, anyway?"

Instantly, Klopper stepped in to run interference. "Oh, he's with us."

Satisfied, Cathie turned back to the investigators. She was enjoying the attention.

We thanked her for giving us a tour, exited the compound and drove to lunch. At Duffers Bar, Klopper said, "What a drama queen. She loves attention."

Shaughnessy said, "Clem, don't worry about what she said. Criminals say anything to rationalize their actions."

That afternoon, I visited my mother at her Chandler nursing home. "We found Dryman!" I told her.

"It's about time we told you about that, the murder. Did your father help you?"

In her mind, he was still alive. I answered, "Yes, Dad helped me." It wasn't a total lie. I'd like to think that in spirit, he was beside me in my quest for justice. My mother passed away two months later.

Back in Bellevue, I phoned prosecutor Luke McKeon. I told him that Dryman was going to appear before the parole board in a couple of weeks.

"Will you be there?" I asked.

"No, I'm not up to that. Dryman has served his time."

Surprised, I said, "But you put him behind bars back in 1955. I don't understand."

"I was doing my job, but I don't believe in the death penalty. He has paid his debt to society; they should let him go. I'd like to write a letter to the parole board. When is it again?"

"In a couple of weeks, May 28," I said.

A few days later, he sent me a draft of the letter. He was eighty-five, and his memory wasn't perfect. I edited his draft. He asked, "Will you sign this with me?"

"I'm happy to help you, but I can't sign."

A week before the hearing, I called Dryman's brothers, Hank and Jim. I called Hank Dryman first.

"I'm calling to tell you about the parole hearing in a couple of weeks."

"Why did you do this? He's served his time. Leave him alone!"

Next, I phoned Jim Valentine, who parroted Hank. "Why did you do this? He's served his time. We took him in when he was paroled to California in 1969. We did everything for him: we got him a job, fed and clothed him. All he had to do was report to his PO. We were very angry when he just up and left."

To Jim's credit, he did offer me his condolences. "It must have been hard growing up without a grandfather."

I thanked him and then asked, "Do you think he is mentally ill?"

"No, of course not!" Jim replied. "He's always exaggerated how awful our childhood was; it wasn't that bad. Please leave my family out of this."

"Yes, I intend to, but I know Cathie is going to testify. She's made some ugly accusations about my grandfather," I said. We both knew what I was talking about.

"Yes, I know," Jim said. "Your family doesn't deserve that. She's crazy, always has been."

"If she testifies saying that, I will have no choice but to bring your family into it—after all, you did harbor a fugitive."

Sheepishly, he answered, "I understand."

Before the hearing, I wrote to Dryman, asking to meet with him. The warden agreed, and I prepared a list of questions. But it was not to be. Forty-eight hours before the hearing, he canceled our meeting. It was just like the Billings brothers—first he agreed to cooperate, and then he reneged.

Cowards all, I thought.

On May 28, Cynde and I, Emily and her mother, Debra, traveled to the Montana State Prison in Deer Lodge, Montana, for the parole hearing. I was not the only Pellett family member at this hearing. We met Dorothy and other "new" cousins at a diner. Before we left for the prison, I held an impromptu family huddle.

"I need to tell you about my visit to Arizona. I saw where Dryman has been hiding out. His daughter Cathie was there. She is very dramatic, so don't be surprised if she acts out at the hearing." I gathered myself before I uttered the next sentence. "She claims that Clarence came on to her dad in the car, that he put his hand on Dryman's knee." I was half expecting that I had just aired an ugly family secret, but to my relief, I got nothing—just blank stares.

Once the twelve of us cleared prison security, we were escorted to the warden's conference room. The warden entered and welcomed us to Deer

Clem in front of the parole board. *Photo by David Murray,* Great Falls Tribune.

Lodge State Penitentiary. After giving us a rundown on the dos and don'ts of a prison visit, he left us alone.

Dorothy piped up, "Who wants to speak at the hearing?" Half a dozen hands were raised. "Who is going to be the family spokesperson?" All eyes turned to me. Although I had met the Pellett family just a few weeks before, I was "elected" spokesman.

We were ushered to an all-purpose room. At the front was a rectangular table with three folding chairs behind it. Facing it were five rows of neatly arranged folding chairs. Crowded at the back of the small room were news crews.

Fifty-nine years to the day since Jerry O'Connell made his first appearance in the Toole County Courthouse, the hearing was called to order. With an armed guard on either side, Dryman was guided to a folding chair facing the three-member board, his back to the crowd. I was seated in the front row, immediately behind the killer. I thought, *How could a man so small, so old, so insignificant have inflicted so much pain, so much sorrow?*

As spokesman, I was the first to speak. When I rose to address the board, I towered over Dryman. I could have reached out and tapped the top of his head.

My hands shook as I recounted how I had recently learned that my father was the only Pellett family member who attended all Dryman's parole hearings and that at the parole hearing in November 1968, ten months after my father's death, with no members of the Pellett family there to object, Dryman was granted parole.

"When I stumbled across those old news clippings and started my quest, I unknowingly picked up my father's mantle." I pointed at Dryman's head. "To keep this man in prison to serve his sentence. Your decision today will either send a message to all would-be absconders that if you are a skilled fugitive, stay on the lam long enough or are old enough and sick enough, you will be forgiven your sentence—or you can send the message that a parole is not a pardon. As for me, I have no stake in your decision, no vengeance. Whatever is decided today is fine with me." Thinking of my dad, I added, "However, on behalf of those who no longer have a voice, I object to granting him parole."

Finally, after six decades, the Pelletts had the opportunity to give their victim impact statements. They told the board that the pain resonated within them still. One of my elderly first cousins, Bob, said, "This was a particularly heinous crime that tore our family apart. We are serving the life sentence that Dryman should have. He should be back in jail."

Dorothy said, "We grew up as kids in a lot of fear. When I was in nursing school, we went to the prison infirmary. I removed my 'Pellett' name tag from my uniform out of fear Dryman might see it."

Pretending not to hear, Dryman sat still, staring straight ahead, never reacting. Cathie stood and addressed the board.

"Sure, he messed up, but my dad tried to make up for it by being an honor citizen. He is a prominent member of the community; he's on the search and rescue team; he's deputized to help the sheriff with security. He's sick, dying of cancer—he's a good man!" Overwrought, she threw herself to the floor, wailing, "Please don't take my little girl's grandfather away from her!"

The irony hung in the air. We sat in stunned silence.

The proceedings were temporarily suspended as the guards picked Cathie up off the floor and placed her in a wheelchair. As she was wheeled out, she could be heard saying, "I need a sedative for my nerves."

After thirty-eight years on the lam, Frank Dryman was sent back to prison in May 2010. *Photograph by Thomas Lee.*

After a few minutes, the hearing resumed. A board member said to Dryman, "You went missing for thirty-eight years."

"Yes, sir."

"We didn't know where you were."

"Yes, sir."

"You changed addresses without our permission."

"Yes, sir."

"You married without permission."

"Yes, sir." That two word phrase echoed across the decades back to 1951 when he answered Judge Hattersley's questions about murdering my grandfather with: "Yes, sir."

"Why didn't you divorce?"

"I didn't want any more violence."

Puzzled, the chairman asked, "Why didn't you just leave your wife and stay on parole? Why abscond?"

Dryman sat silent.

When it comes to absconders, the Montana Parole Board is not known for leniency, and its members were not impressed with Dryman's subsequent good deeds. The board sent him back to jail until his next parole hearing. Before the hearing ended, one of its members declared, "Mr. Dryman, if I am still on this board for your next hearing in May 2015, I will not hesitate to keep you in prison."

At the post-hearing press conference, my second cousin Penne said of Dryman,

> *He thinks that he is above the law and above exception. I think it would be a tremendous disservice to the community and to Montana to let him be paroled. It was a vicious, vicious murder. People like that, you can't rehabilitate them. They have no empathy. If they don't get what they want, they just take it—whether it's somebody's life or whatever it is. He had the opportunity when he was paroled to follow the rules just like everybody else, and he chose to be above the law—again. Nobody else gets to do that.*

On our drive back to Helena, Emily read an April 21, 2010 letter from the father of Nathan Rose, Cathie's first husband.

> *When my son came home from honeymooning, he was very adamant about getting me alone, so he could talk to me. "Vic is a very threatening person. He told me that if I ever hurt his daughter in any way, he would kill me." I*

> *told my son that most fathers of the bride do in fact say similar things when it comes to their daughters and not to worry. "Dad, you don't understand. He is a killer and has killed before. Everyone in his family tells the same story. Cathie considers this a badge of courage, that her father is secretly a wanted killer.*

I shouted, "Cynde, you were right about that phone call from Cathie—she was fishing to see what I knew!"

Emily agreed. "I just started as a public defender; it's ironic that for my first case, I sent a defendant back to prison."

Waiting for our flight from Helena, I called prosecutor Luke McKeon. "Why didn't you send your letter to the parole board?" I asked.

"What?" he answered. "The hearing has happened?"

"Yes, it was yesterday."

"I thought it was next week. What happened?"

"He's back in prison. The next parole hearing is in five years."

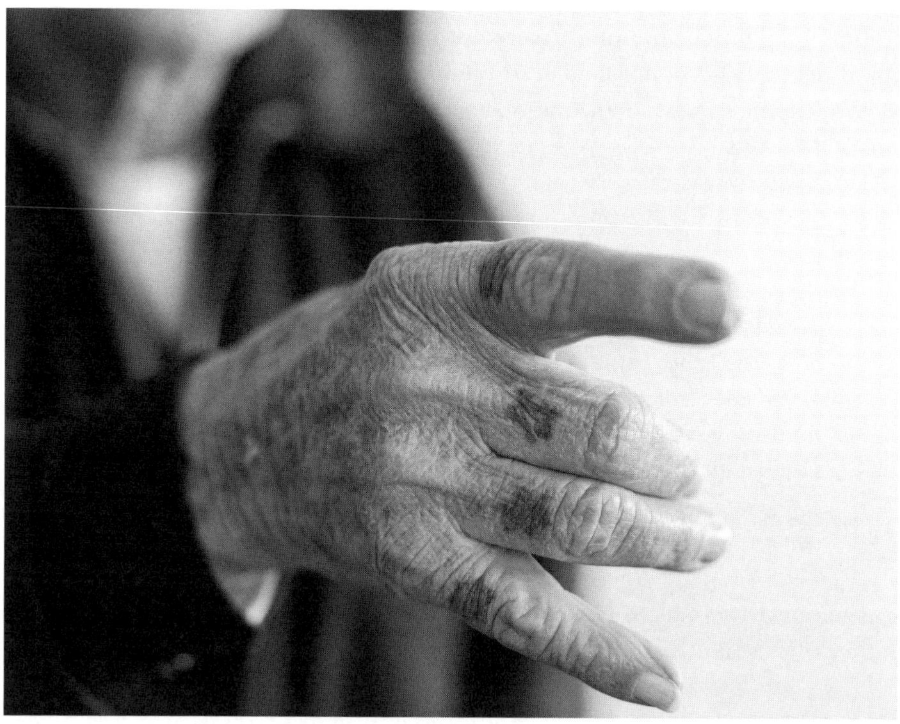

The star tattoos that covered the letters L-O-V-E on Dryman's knuckles. *Photograph by Thomas Lee.*

McKeon exclaimed, "It's not right! I'm going to send it anyway; it needs to be a part of his file."

After his return to prison, Dryman put pen to paper and wrote his own obituary. Included was an ink self-portrait. He dated it April 4, 2011—sixty years to the day since he murdered my grandfather.

The evening before Associated Press reporter Matt Gouras was going to do a prison interview with Dryman in June 2010, he called to ask if I had anything I'd like him to ask Dryman. I told him that a group of PIs, working pro bono, was investigating Dryman's life on the lam and had found evidence that Dryman and Cathie may have killed Nathan Rose. "Ask him about that."

After the interview, Gouras called me. "When I first mentioned Nathan Rose, he denied knowing anyone by that name. I pressed him more, giving him the date of his death: October 25, 2001. He then became very nervous and fidgety, finally saying, 'Oh yeah, my son-in-law… I wasn't in the area during that time.' Clem, I think there's something there."

Gouras's article, "Fugitive Hid Forty Years in Plain Sight," was published on June 15, 2010. He wrote,

> *Dryman didn't deny the murder. "That kid, Frank Valentine, he just exploded," Dryman says of his crime. "I didn't shoot that man in the back. That wild kid did. That's not me."*
>
> *"I never thought I was a parole violator. I was Victor Houston. I never looked over my shoulder. I just forgot about it." Frank Dryman had hidden in plain sight for so long that he forgot he was a wanted man. "I have lived longer as Victor Houston than any of my other names. They just forgot about me."*
>
> *On his birthday he used to get two cards from his brother: one for Houston and one for Valentine. "I thought it was cute. I had no fear," said Dryman….*
>
> *He is not kindly disposed to the victim's grandson. "I can't blame him for what he did, but I think it was so wrong he spent so much money getting me here. I feel it is unfair….He should be happy. I think they got their pound of flesh, and I accept it."*

The article launched another media frenzy. Sky News, Der Spiegel, *20/20*, *Dateline* and *48 Hours* picked up the story. It was the No. 1 news item on Yahoo News and the Huffington Post. It was even published in the *Globe* supermarket tabloid.

I Frank R. Dryman AO18717 is hereby making it known that I do not wish to speak with Clem Pellet now or in the future for any type of interview.

Frank R. Dryman AO18717

Dryman's message to the author, April 2015. *Author's collection.*

Over the ensuing five years, I was persistent in attempting to get Dryman to meet with me. More than a dozen times, he steadfastly refused. Finally, on April 15, 2015, he sent me a note:

> *I Frank R. Dryman A018717 is hereby making it known that I do not wish to speak with Clem Pellet* [sic] *now or in the future for any type of interview. Signed Frank R. Dryman AO18717*

On May 19, 2015, the Pellett family attended the parole hearing at the Montana Women's Prison in Billings. Dryman appeared via TV monitor.

I spoke first. "Frank Dryman, I forgive you. Not that you deserve it, because you haven't shown one, even a minuscule, morsel of remorse. But in forgiving you, I can separate myself from you and move on to enjoy my new family."

Dorothy was next.

> *The murder shook Shelby and the Hi-Line to its core for years. We grew up as kids with a lot of fear. We were afraid Dryman would carry through with his threats he made from prison to retaliate against us. This murder still is impacting our family. It was a huge thing that changed our entire family, forever. He needs to stay where he's at.*

Dryman stared stone-faced into the camera. When it came his turn to speak, he expressed no regret for his decisions, no remorse. Instead, he claimed to be the victim.

"Let's face it," said Dryman. "Montana State Prison in 1969 found that I was eligible for parole. Yes, I was gone forty years. I am very sorry about it, yes. What the heck. Why am I even here? You people have already made up your minds. I'm eighty-four years old, and I don't give a damn. Mr. Pellett, the man who started this, is not from this state, and he wrote all the scripts that the people just read."

The board denied Dryman's request to be released. After administrative review, his next hearing was scheduled for the following year.

I met Dorothy and her brothers, Jim and Jess, outside the Montana Women's Prison on Thursday, May 19, 2016. We were patted down and escorted into the activities room of the prison. Dryman appeared via phone from the assisted living infirmary for elderly prisoners in Lewistown, Montana.

Dryman's case worker stated, "Mr. Dryman requests to be released to an assisted living facility for U.S. veterans. Mr. Dryman is on oxygen and has numerous health conditions. I have confirmed there is an open VA bed available."

I rose to object. "Even a cursory review of his navy record shows that Mr. Dryman does not deserve to live among our nation's veterans who served honorably. He did not serve honorably. In fact, he received government checks that helped fund his thirty-eight years on the lam. He should stay among those who are justice-involved. It was the Social Security number Dryman used to claim those benefits that led to his location in Arizona."

The board asked, "Mr. Dryman, are you remorseful?"

Defiantly, Dryman said, "I'm sorry for my violent actions, for decades."

"Have you reached out to the Pellett family?"

Silence.

"In fact, you sent a note, signed by you, to Dr. Pellett stating that you wish not to ever have any contact with him or any family member."

Silence.

The board denied Dryman's request for release. "You already were granted parole, and not content with that good fortune, you skipped out and evaded authorities for four decades. Coupled with your repeated refusal to have contact with the victim's family to atone for your crime and your delayed expression of remorse that rings hollow, we do not feel you deserve another chance."

The next hearing was scheduled for 2018.

On November 7, 2017, the day that would have been my mother's ninety-first birthday, Frank Dryman, inmate 18717, died. Asked by a reporter, "Did he ever regret what he did?" I responded emphatically, "A resounding *no*! His statement 'Only since I have been back here [in prison] did I start to think about it [the murder]—to be honest, I didn't even remember the victim's name,' reveals his true lack of remorse."

Of Dryman's death, I said, "It closes a painful chapter in the Pellett family story. I have faith that he has passed on to reap the rewards he earned in this life. In a sense, the saga continues."

When I tracked down my grandfather's murderer, I uncovered several conflicting agendas: closure for a blue-collar family, justice for a community, a vehicle to jump-start O'Connell's flailing legal career and a platform for opposing capital punishment and thwarting Montana law. Upended among these intersecting priorities, the Pellett family was forced to endure the nagging sense that a blackhearted murderer had beaten the rap by faking insanity. They accepted their impotence against the politically connected and endured the torment for almost six decades.

As I reflect on it, I understand why my father didn't encourage me to contact my extended family. Much as he was protecting me physically with his emphatic "Never pick up a hitchhiker," his no-contact message was not delivered out of spite. Had he lived beyond the age of forty-two, perhaps he would have confided more details of the saga.

Hearing firsthand about the pain the Pelletts had been harboring, it dawned on me why my dad simplified the story to "He got away with it because they couldn't find the gallows" and why he discouraged me from reaching out to the Pelletts. He wasn't simply being bullheaded over his mother's betrayal; it was his way of sheltering me from not only the pain of the loss but also a lifetime of shouldering the injustice of the fact that Dryman actually did beat the rap.

Whether this was a case of denial of justice for the slain patriarch of a blue-collar family or of sparing the Treasure State the shame of a lynching, after seventy years, the contrails of Clarence C. Pellett's murder linger still across Montana's Big Sky.

BIBLIOGRAPHY

Allen, J. "Parole and Probation Form 4." January 16, 1969; February 3, 1970.

Andrews, Emily. Personal communications with the author: Cathy Gordon, December 1, 3 and 4, 2009, and March 22, 2010.

Associated Press. "Inmate's Death Closes Chapter for Family of Murdered Man." November 8, 2017.

Bach, L.A. "Bonner Refuses to Interfere in Dryman Case." *Independent Record* (Helena, MT), May 25, 1951.

———. "Differences in Diagnosis of Dryman's Mental State Form Testimony in Phase of Trial." *Havre (MT) Daily News*, February 18, 1955.

———. "Dryman Is Found Guilty; Is Given Life Sentence." *Havre (MT) Daily News*, February 19, 1955.

———. "Dryman Testifies That He Did Not Remember Shooting Pellett." *Havre (MT) Daily News*, February 17, 1955.

———. "Former Toole County Atty. John Hoyt Testifies as to Dryman's Confession in Pellett Slaying." *Havre (MT) Daily News*, February 16, 1955.

Billings, Gretchen G. Communications: Cedor B. Aronow, April 18 and 24, 1951; Frank R. Dryman, August 14, 1962; W.P. Pilgeram, January 23, 1952; M.A. Ruona, January 12, 1953; Myron Tripp, April 17, 1951.

———. Handwritten notes on Frank R. Dryman Case. Montana Historical Society Archives, circa May 26, 1951.

———. "High Court Hears Dryman Appeal for New Trial." *The People's Voice* (Helena, MT), January 1951.

———. "The Quality of Mercy." *The People's Voice* (Helena, MT), May 11, 1951.

———. "Should Frank Dryman Be 'Represented' in Court?" *The People's Voice* (Helena, MT), May 18, 1951.

———. "Swift Vigilante-like Justice?" *The People's Voice* (Helena, MT), April 27, 1951.

———. "United States Navy Says Dryman Discharged Because of 'Mental Disability.'" *The People's Voice* (Helena, MT), May 25, 1951.

———. "'Vigilante Justice' Is Not for Montana, Says State Supreme Court." *The People's Voice* (Helena, MT), February 22, 1952.

Billings, Harry. Communication: W.M. Black, circa June 1, 1951.

Black, W.M. Communications: Gretchen and Harry Billings, May 22, 1951; Harry Billings, May 30, 1951.

Bollinger, Lari. Communication: Montana State Parole Board, April 21, 2010.

Brandt, Angela. "Cold Case Collaborators." *Independent Record* (Helena, MT), April 11, 2010.

Bruce, H.S. Communication: Gretchen and Harry Billings, summer 1951.

Clark County, State of Nevada. Marriage Certificate for Victor H. Houston and Debbie Kay Jones. June 23, 1981.

Coleman, Travis. "Fugitive Found Running Chapel After 38 Years on the Lam." *Great Falls (MT) Tribune*, March 25, 2010.

Cote, Patrick. Communications: Sheila J. Klopper, March 20 and May 6, 2010.

Crime Stories. "The Kid with the Hollywood Haircut." Season 8, episode 6, aired December 16, 2010.

Cuff, George M. Communication: Rae V. Kalbfleisch, December 6, 1977.

Cut Bank (MT) Pioneer Press. "County Attorney Writes Ominous Argument on Dryman Murder Case." March 27, 1952.

———. "Dryman Appeal Brings Stay of Execution." June 1, 1951.

———. "Dryman Hangs." May 25, 1951.

———. "For the Murder of This Man—Swift Justice." April 13, 1951.

———. "Hattersley Again Sentences Dryman to Hang [Friday] Feb. 13." January 15, 1953.

———. "More Time Given on Dryman Case." March 20, 1952.

———. "Murder Victim Left in Field." April 6, 1951.

———. "Neighbors of Two Counties Join Search for Riddled Body." April 13, 1951.

———. "Wide Interest in Dryman Murder Case in Shelby." January 8, 1953.

Davis, Eugene D. Communication: State of Montana Board of Paroles, November 12, 1968.

Dryman, Frank R. "Application for Commutation of Sentence to Montana Board of Pardons." May 1, 1960, and July 1, 1961.

———. Arrest/booking record. Casa Grande, Arizona. March 23, 2010.

———. Communications: Gretchen Billings, July 16 and August 17, 1962; "Mother and Dad," April 12, 1951.

Dunstall, C.O. Invitation to Witness the Execution of Frank R. Dryman in Shelby, Montana. June 1, 1951.

———. Request to Montana State Board of Prison Commissioners to Remove Frank R. Dryman from the Toole County Jail to the State Penitentiary at Deer Lodge. June 5, 1951.

Federal Bureau of Investigation. Freedom of Information/Privacy Acts Release. FOIPA No. 0958848-00. Subject: O'Connell, Jeremiah Joseph.

Fisher, Andrea. "Runaway Killer Is Again Denied Release." *Great Falls (MT) Tribune*. May 19, 2016.

Goare, Aja. "Parole Denied at Hearing in Billings for Shelby Murdered Who Vanished for 40 Years." MTN News, KTVQ.com, May 19, 2016.

Gordon, Cathy. Communications: Emily Andrews, December 9, 2009, and March 23, 2010.

Gouras, Matt. "AP Interview: Fugitive Hid 40 Years in Plain Sight." Associated Press, June 15, 2010.

———. "Dryman Waives Extradition." *Great Falls (MT) Tribune*. March 26, 2010.

Great Falls (MT) Tribune. "Dryman, Hitchhiker, Admits Killing Pellett Near Shelby; Judge to Sentence Him Today." April 10, 1951.

———."Dryman Tells Life Story During Trial for Murder." February 18, 1955.

———."Dryman to Die on Scaffold from Missoula." April 14, 1951.

———."Dryman to Receive Trial…State Supreme Court Gives Slayer New Chance at Life." February 16, 1951.

———."Jerry O'Connell, 46, State Lawyer and Former Congressman, Dies Here." January 17, 1956.

———."Jury Convicts Dryman in Hitchhike Slaying, Sentenced to Life Term." February 20, 1955.

———."Jury Finds Dryman Guilty of First Degree Murder." January 12, 1953.
———."Many Attend Shelby Court Murder Trial." January 8, 1953.
———."Mounties Catch Suspect." April 6, 1951.
———."O'Connell Linked with Red Party." December 12, 1950.
———."Officers Fear Foul Play in Disappearance." April 5, 1951.
———."Shelby Trial Delayed as Lawyer Ill." January 9, 1953.
———."Son of Slain Man Witness in Dryman Murder Trial." February 16, 1955.
———."State Asks for Death Sentence…Dryman Trial for Murder Will Go to Jurors Today." February 19, 1955.
———."State High Court Orders New Trial for Frank Dryman on Murder Charge." April 30, 1954.
———."Suspect Lead Officers to Pistol Cache." April 10, 1951.
———."Three Medics Deny Dryman Can Be Called Schizophrenic." January 11, 1953.
———."Youth Clings to Denial of Shelby Death." April 7, 1951.
Hanlon, M.D. "Parole and Probation Form 4." May 21, August 25 and November 18, 1970; February 11, May 6 and August 10, 1971.
Haugen, Mrs. Oscar. "Dryman Responsibility of the Navy, Says Reader." Letter to the editor. *The People's Voice* (Helena, MT), October 12, 1951.
Helena (MT) Independent. "Who Sent Jerry to Spain?" November 15, 1937.
Holmes, Krys. "3-7-77." *Montana: Stories of the Land*. Helena, MT: Montana Historical Society Press, 2008.
Houston, Cathie. Interview with Todd Moore, May 23, 2005.
Hoyt, John C. Communication: Arnold H. Olson, December 18, 1951.
Hungry Horse News (Columbia Falls, MT). "Dryman Case a Problem." June 1951.
Independent Record (Helena, MT). "Committee Will Try to Save Life of Slayer." May 17, 1951.
———."Counsel for Dryman Says Navy Should Be 'In Penitentiary.'" January 16, 1952.
———."Dryman Attorney to Ask New Order on Venue." July 1952
———."Dryman Convicted, Given Life Term." February 20, 1955.
———."Dryman Gets Death Sentence Today for Second Time." January 13, 1953.
———."Dryman Hearing Is Set for Jan. 5 by Court." December 19, 1953.
———."Dryman Is Examined by Psychiatrists; Results Under Study." May 3, 1951.
———."Dryman Is Given Temporary Lease on Life." February 10, 1953.
———."Dryman Permitted to Change His Pleas to Innocent." February 16, 1952.
———."Dryman Retrial Started at Shelby Today." January 5, 1953.
———."Dryman's Third Murder Trial Is Set Feb. 14." January 20, 1955.
———."Dryman, Under Noose Shadow Since 1951, Given New Reprieve." September 22, 1954.
———."Dryman Will Be Placed in Safe Keeping." June 7, 1951.
———."Five Are Admitted to Practice Law in Montana." June 23, 1950.
———."Frank R. Dryman Is Granted New Trial and Change of Venue in Supreme Court Split Decision." April 30, 1954.
———."Governor Will Not Interfere in Dryman Execution." May 8, 1951.
———."Hard-Fought Dryman Case May End on Friday the 13th." January 14, 1953.
———."Mental Experts Disagree on Dryman Sanity." February 18, 1955.
———."Montana Supreme Court Sets Aside Toole County District Order Moving Site of Dryman Trial." November 22, 1954.
———."New Trial Is Sought by Man Condemned After Shelby Trial." September 16, 1951.
———."Portable Gallows Returned When Need Is Averted." April 22, 1955.
———."Supreme Court Gets Second Appeal from Frank Dryman." July 22, 1953.
———."Supreme Court Says Dryman Gets New Trial." March 27, 1952.

———."Third Murder Trial for Dryman Is to Be Opened Aug. 30." June 13, 1954.
———."Youthful Confessed Murder Gets Death Sentence for Killing Café Owner in Northern Montana." April 13, 1951.
Kalbfleisch, Rae V. Communications: George M. Cuff, November 21, 1977; Montana State Board of Pardons, April 6, 1966.
Kesselheim, Alan. "Lose-Lose: Searching for Justice in the Strange, Remarkable Case of Frank Dryman." *Montana Quarterly* (Spring 2011): 15–19.
Klopper, Sheila J. Communication: Emily Andrews, March 19 and 20, 2010; Patricia Shaughnessy, March 20, 2010.
Kruckenberg, Molly. Communication: Bill Hess, May 17 and 19, 2010.
Lethbridge Herald (Alberta, Canada). "Dryman Gets Life Sentence for Murder." February 22, 1955.
———. "Hitch-Hiker Charged with Murder at Shelby." April 7, 1951.
———. "Murder Charge in Border Slaying." April 6, 1951.
———. "Swift Justice Meted Out at Shelby to Border Slayer." April 13, 1951.
———. "Won't Admit Killing, Leads Police to Spot Gun Hidden." April 10, 1951.
———. "Young Transient Receives New Lease on Life." May 30, 1951.
———. "Youth Said to Be Sane So Will Hang." May 8, 1951.
Lindholme, Pat. Interview: Pat Shaughnessy, May 4 and 6, 2010.
McDonald, Verlaine Stoner. *The Red Corner: The Rise and Fall of Communism in Northeastern Montana*. Montana Historical Society Press, 2014.
McLemore, Lucy T. Communication: Gretchen Billings, January 9, 1953.
McPhillips, R.D. Communications: Montana State Board of Pardons, April 8, 1966, and January 13, 1969.
Montana State Board of Prison Commissioners. "Resolution Passed Remanding Frank R. Dryman from Toole County Jail to Deer Lodge Penitentiary for Safekeeping." June 6, 1951.
Murray, David. "The Clarence Pellett Murder: Dryman Denied Parole in 64-Year-Old Killing." *Great Falls (MT) Tribune*. May 20, 2015.
Nicolls, Don. Interview with Leon G. Billings, November 29, 2001.
"O'Connell, Jerry J. United States Congress (1937–1938)." In *Official Congressional Directory*. U.S. Government Printing Office, December 20, 1936.
O'Donnell, Amanda. "Grandson Finds Grandfather's Killer After More Than 40 Years." CNN, March 30, 2010.
Oldenburg, Mildred. "Navy, Not Hangman, Should Take Charge of Dryman." Letter to the editor. *The People's Voice* (Helena, MT), November 1951.
Pellett, Clem C. "Catching a Montana Killer." *Great Falls (MT) Tribune*, October 4, 2014.
———. Communications: Emily Andrews, November 15 and 21, 2009; December 9, 2009; Bob Anez, March 24, 2010; Debbie K. Barker, November 13 and 23, 2016; Mike Billings, September 15, 2009; Patrick Cote, April 19, 2010; Frank R. Dryman, May 25, 2010; Lois Fenske, February 6, 2011; Jane Freydenlund, March 25, 2010; Edwin Gallaway, April 5, 2010; Cathy Gordon, February 15, March 22, March 23 (5), March 24 (6), March 25, April 2, and April 5 (8), 2010; Dorothy Holeman, March 31 and April 11, 2010; Cathie Houston, April 9, 2010; Dick Irwin, May 2010; Jane Johanson, May 3, 2010; Shannon Johanson, May 3, 2010; W. Bjarne Johnson, November 9, 2009; Sheila J. Klopper, April 19 (2) and 27 (3), 2010; Molly Kruckenburg, spring 2009; Jack and Pat Lindholme, July 10, 2010; Bill May, May 7, 2010; John "Luke" McKeon, October 6, 2009, and April 6, 2010; Tina Rodriguez, June 16, 2010; Kermit Sanfield, April 23, 2014; Patricia Shaughnessy, April 13, May 13 and September 11, 2010; Tom Sparks; February 18, 2017; Jim Valentine, May 19, 2010; Jason Villegas, March 24, 2010;

Montana State Board of Pardons and Paroles, June 26, 2011; Pat Shaughnessy, April 21 and September 13, 2010.
———. "Was Justice Served or Was It Manipulated?" *Great Falls (MT) Tribune*, October 5, 2014.
Pellett, Lyle. Communication: Montana State Board of Pardons, January 12, 1969.
Pellett, Theron. Communication: Montana State Board of Pardons, April 6, 1966.
The People's Voice (Helena, MT). "Dryman Appeal Stressed Records of Naval Medical Inquiry Board." November 23, 1951.
———. "Navy Discharged Frank Dryman Because Youth Was 'Insane'!" June 1, 1951.
———. "Second Reversal of Lower Court Sought by Dryman Attorney." January 1, 1954.
Pierson, Edwin. Communication: Montana State Board of Pardons, April 5, 1966.
Pilgeram, W.P. Communication: Gretchen Billings, January 22, 1952.
Pinal County Sheriff's Office. "Deputies Capture Murderer on the Run for 38 Years." March 24, 2010.
Prentice, Robert H. Communication: Fellow Ministers of Montana Council of Churches, May 15, 1951.
Sharpe, Franklin. "'A Guy Never Thinks of Everything." *Official Detective Stories*, January 1953.
Shaughnessy, Patricia. Communication: Cleaver Tripp, June 16, 2010.
———. "In Re: Frank Dryman from Nancy Goodrich, Goodrich Investigations." May 5, 2010.
Shelby Promoter and Tribune of Shelby (MT). "Dryman Sane at Time of Killing; Denied Clemency." May 10, 1951.
———. "Dryman's Counsel Hurls Misconduct Charges Against County Attorney." November 22, 1951.
———. "Extra: Frank Dryman to Hang." April 12, 1951.
———. "Hanging of Frank R. Valentine Delayed; Valentine Denied Motion for New Trial; Petition for Plea of Not Guilty." May 31, 1951.
———. "Local Man Object of Wide Search." April 5, 1951.
———. "Pellett's Killer Confesses." April 12, 1951.
———. "Seek to Use Civic Center for Frank Dryman Hanging." April 19, 1951.
State of Montana Board of Pardons. Notification of Granting of Parole to Frank R. Dryman. November 22, 1968.
———. Notifications of Denial of Commutation to Frank R. Dryman. July 6, 1961; March 26, 1962; February 24, October 9 and October 26, 1964; June 29, 1965.
State of Montana Department of Corrections. Communication: Pinal County Police Department Re: Warrant for Frank Dryman's Arrest, March 22, 2010.
State of Montana Department of Corrections, Community Corrections Division. Warrant to Arrest & Hold Parolee Frank Dryman, No Bond. March 27, 1972; February 21 and September 9, 1983.
———. Parole Violator at Large. July 1998; March 23, 2010.
State v. Dryman. 269 P2d 796 (1954).
———. No. 9123. Supreme Court of Montana. Submitted January 29, 1952. Decided February 15, 1952.
———. No. 9325. Supreme Court of Montana. Submitted January 5, 1954. Decided April 29, 1954.
Tucker, Edward M. Communication: Gretchen Billings, June 26, 1951.
U.S. Department of the Navy. Medical File of Frank Robert Valentine. May 16, 1951.
Valentine, Jim. Communication: State of Montana Board of Paroles, November 3, 1968.
White, Fred, Jr. Communication: R.D. McPhillips, January 22, 1969.
Wikipedia. "Willie McGee (Convict)." https://www.wikipedia.org.

ABOUT THE AUTHOR

Photograph by Kelly Gorham, Montana State University.

Dr. Clem C. Pellett, a Montana native, received his undergraduate degree from Montana State University in Bozeman, Montana; earned a doctor of dental surgery degree from Creighton University in Omaha, Nebraska; and completed his residency in oral and maxillofacial surgery at the Mayo Clinic's Graduate School of Medicine in Rochester, Minnesota.

While practicing in Bellevue, Washington, he earned numerous awards—including a citation for meritorious service from the people of Zimbabwe. After practicing for nearly three decades, Dr. Pellett changed careers. Inspired by his successful quest to track down the murderer of his grandfather, he earned a certificate of private investigation from Boston University. As a freelance writer, he has published in the *Great Falls Tribune*. Accounts of his extraordinary story have been publicized in print and broadcast media both nationally and internationally.

Dr. Pellett travels extensively across the United States sharing his experiences with a wide variety of audiences: law enforcement, legal investigators, university students, healthcare providers, forensic scientists, historical societies and lawmakers in Washington, D.C. He also has delivered keynote addresses to the California Association of Legal Investigators and the World Association of Detectives.

Currently, Dr. Pellett is part of the production team for the movie *Pellett*. Based on his true story, this feature film will be released in 2025.